Balkan Yearbook of European and International Law

Volume 2023

The Balkan Yearbook of European and International Law publishes peer-reviewed scholarly articles, notes, comments and book reviews on private and public European and International Law. The yearbook contains summaries and analyses of recent decisions by national and international courts and arbitral or other tribunals. The yearbook has one section with a special hot topic or focus as well as sections about European and international law in each volume. Moreover, it presents book reviews to recent publications from the region or with a major impact for the region. The yearbook focuses on recent developments of European and International Law and presents a forum for scholarly discourse on European and International Law from the perspective of the region of South-East Europe. However, the publication is not exclusive in that regard: contributions from the perspective of the wider world are also strongly encouraged and welcomed.

Enis Omerović • Ivana Kunda
Zlatan Meškić • Dušan V. Popović
Editors

Balkan Yearbook of European and International Law 2023

Springer

Editors
Enis Omerović
Faculty of Law
University of Zenica
Zenica, Bosnia and Herzegovina

Ivana Kunda
Faculty of Law
University of Rijeka
Rijeka, Croatia

Zlatan Meškić
Prince Sultan University
Riyadh, Saudi Arabia

Dušan V. Popović
University of Belgrade, Faculty of Law
Belgrade, Serbia

ISSN 2524-8715 ISSN 2524-8723 (electronic)
Balkan Yearbook of European and International Law
ISBN 978-3-031-69669-5 ISBN 978-3-031-69670-1 (eBook)
https://doi.org/10.1007/978-3-031-69670-1

This Springer imprint is published by the registered company Springer Nature Switzerland AG
The registered company address is: Gewerbestrasse 11, 6330 Cham, Switzerland

Preface

We are pleased to present the fifth edition of the *Balkan Yearbook of European and International Law* (BYEIL), in which we proudly offer the readers diverse and actual legal topics of international and comparative dimensions and angles.

In addition to the two already standard sections, the third section of BYEIL 2023 focuses on the special topic of *Human Rights at Multiple Levels*. This edition aims to contribute to the extensively researched field characterised by emerging trends, with the authors providing a deeper and more concise understanding of human rights-related issues. Discussions surrounding indivisibility, interdependence, universalism versus cultural relativism inevitably led to exploring human rights at various levels.

Human rights and fundamental freedoms have faced global restrictions in the current decade. The COVID-19 pandemic and its aftermath presented significant challenges for citizens in many countries, including human trafficking, refugee crises, abuses of workers' rights, gender inequality, the rise of nationalism, the spread of misinformation, and, most importantly, the lack of adequate international response to widespread and systematic violations of human rights worldwide. The world has witnessed the resurgence of armed conflicts and internal violence. Human rights crises do not arise spontaneously. While modern technology has genuinely transformed relationships and greatly enhanced the quality and effectiveness of various services, legal protection for individuals in this context has developed differently.

Therefore, it is crucial to understand the state of human rights and freedoms as it serves as the first step in defending rights in every aspect of human life and within all segments of society. The international protection of human rights is a central concern in the contemporary European and global context, particularly regarding the availability of individual complaint mechanisms at the international level. These mechanisms include, among others, the treaty-based human rights committees and the European Court of Human Rights. This particular edition of BYEIL has invited the authors to explore and analyse actual human rights topics including, but not limited to, the study of human rights in crises, gender equality, climate change, the right to a healthy environment, the rights of children, the rights of migrants, refugees and asylum seekers, minority rights, disability rights, the right to privacy, the use of surveillance technology, and the impact of digital technology in general, including artificial intelligence. In this special topic section, three articles found their place, all of them analysing different areas: *Brčko Arbitration: An Analysis of Legal and Peacebuilding Dimensions*, second one with the title *Navigating the Intersection between Islam, European Values, and the Integration of Muslims in Europe*, and the last one exploring *Environmental Security as a New Challenge to International Relations and International Community.*

The two permanent sections on *European Law* and *International Law* are focused on recent developments in these highly dynamic and developing areas. They are intended to serve as a forum for scholarly discourse on these topics from the South-East European perspective. However, BYEIL is not exclusive: contributions from any other perspective have also been welcomed. In the European Law part, we are bringing before you three articles, each of which brings a new approach to multiple and diverse legal concerns, such as *Analysis of New Rule on Form of Power of Attorney in Serbian Law with Reference to Legal Approaches in Selected European Countries*, *New ESG 1 Obligations for Enterprises in Supply and Value Chains through Corporate Sustainability Due Diligence Acts in the European Union and Germany*, and *The Crisis of the Rule of Law: "Chronicle of a Death Foretold"*. In the International Law part, this time, there is only one contribution discussing certain legal issues in the field of investment law under the title: *The Legitimacy Crisis in International Investment Law: Towards an Overcoming?*

We hope the readers of the fifth edition will find the seven articles, which have been selected after a careful double peer-review procedure, exciting and valuable for their research in different scientific areas. Contemporary challenges in public and private law disciplines are brought to the professional and general public with new standpoints.

Zenica, Bosnia and Herzegovina — Enis Omerović
Rijeka, Croatia — Ivana Kunda
Riyadh, Saudi Arabia — Zlatan Meškić
Belgrade, Serbia — Dušan V. Popović

Contents

Contents

Part I
Special Topic on the Human Rights at Multiple Levels

Brčko Arbitration: An Analysis of Legal and Peacebuilding Dimensions

Adisa Avdić Küsmüş

1 Introduction

When the Dayton peace agreement was signed in 1995, it failed to resolve the status of the small Bosnian border town of Brčko; this marked the beginning of one of the most intensive and innovative peacebuilding engagements ever undertaken by international actors. Due to its critical geopolitical position, Brčko was described as the "mother of all difficulties in the Bosnian peace process".[1]

The legal attempts to resolve the status of Brčko started with an unorthodox arbitration process and resulted in revisiting the almost forgotten concept of internationalized territories as a means of resolving territorial disputes. Adding to the oddity of Brčko's case was the decision to place it under direct international supervision, granting nearly unlimited authority to the externally appointed diplomat (the 'Supervisor'). The Final Award declared Brčko a semi- independent condominium which allowed it to exercise nearly full autonomy in relation to the State and the Entities. With its own multi-ethnic government, ministries, police force, multi-ethnic schools and high living standards, the town started to resemble a state in and of itself and gained the nickname of 'Europe's only free city'.[2]

This paper aims at examining the sui generis case of international arbitration for Brčko as a valuable case study that offers insight not only into arbitration as a means of resolving territorial disputes but also as a peacebuilding tool. It will focus on the

[1] Bildt (1998).

[2] Geoghegan (2014).

A. A. Küsmüş (✉)
Department of International Relations, Ankara Yıldırım Beyazıt University, Ankara, Turkey
e-mail: aavdic.kuesmues@aybu.edu.tr

E. Omerović et al. (eds.), *Balkan Yearbook of European and International Law 2023*, Balkan Yearbook of European and International Law 2023,
https://doi.org/10.1007/978-3-031-69670-1_1

peculiarities of the arbitration process and the solutions imposed by the Presiding Arbiter that often defied legal logic and prioritized the security situation on the ground. Furthermore, the paper explores the implications of the Brčko arbitration process for peace-building initiatives in other conflict-ridden regions. It examines how the establishment of a peculiar model of international supervision and civilian administration in Brčko can serve as a precedent for addressing territorial disputes and building sustainable peace in post-conflict environments. While the arbitration's unorthodox approach successfully prevented further escalation of conflict, its impact on peacebuilding remains limited.

Following a decade of direct international supervision of Brčko District, the Supervisor's authorities were suspended in 2012. The years that followed have tested the degree of success and sustainability of this model of conflict resolution. Many of the initial achievements of peacebuilding have since been reversed. Previously multi-ethnic schools have been re-segregated, inter-ethnic disputes led to economic decline, and the overall climate of stability and prosperity was replaced by growing tensions. Despite the peacebuilding success narrative, the city remains essentially divided. Most of the suburbs are inhabited by only one ethnic group, cafes and restaurants are separated, and there is limited communication between different ethnic groups in the private sphere. These developments are clearly contrary to the international claims of building a stable and integrated multi-ethnic society.

2 Arbitrations in Cross-Border Disputes

Territorial conflicts are notoriously difficult to resolve. While international law unequivocally rejects the use of force, it does not provide a clear, prioritized set of norms—established through international conventions or jurisprudence—for determining national sovereignty over disputed territories.[3] Article 33 of the UN Charter refers to the peaceful resolution of international conflicts through diplomatic dialogue, negotiation, mediation, arbitration, or judicial settlement.[4] Member states are expected to seek peaceful solutions, and utilize various mechanisms and forums, such as the International Court of Justice (ICJ) and the Security Council. The use of arbitration in resolving a territorial dispute means adopting a conflict management process based on legal norms and principles. As such, legally binding approaches are rooted in well-established international norms that emphisize the prinicples of sovereignty, self-determination, and respect for territorial integrity.

Arbitration is broadly defined as a non-judicial form of dispute resolution that involves an independent third party ('arbitral tribunal') issuing a legally binding decision ('final award'), which is consequently enforceable through the courts. The

[3] Carter Center Report (2010), p. vi.

[4] UN charter, Chap. 6, Article 33.

tribunal generally consists of several arbiters, appointed by parties to the dispute and the proceedings can be tailored to suit parties' particular needs and timeframes. The tribunal might be created ad hoc, or it could be institutionalized as in the Permanent Court of Arbitration. Arbiters must rely on legal rules in rendering a decision and some influential legal principles include (1) *uti possidetis*, (2) *pacta sunt servanda*, (3) equity, or (4) in the case of maritime claims, the Law of the Sea Treaty.[5] Arbitration produces *legally binding* outcomes and states have an obligation to follow whatever ruling might emerge from the case. Arbitration is an appealing means of dispute resolution because its awards are relatively easy to enforce. The vast majority of disputes referred to arbitration are cases in which one or both parties are states;in such cases domestic court rulings may seem inadequate or potentially biased.

The Brčko case was not unique in using international arbitration to resolve a territorial dispute. The international legal practice had a few documentedcomparable cases prior to the establishment of the Brčko tribunal. A notable example is the 'Rann of Kutch' arbitration (1965) that had the task of deciding whether a portion of territory that stretched along the southwestern joint border was to belong to India or Pakistan. The tribunal's task was relatively simple as the proceedings were factual in nature and based on; analyzing historical maps; evidence of whether the territory had historically been used by inhabitants of either the Indian or Pakistani province; and which province's governments had exercised tax and police authority over the territory.[6]

A penultimate example of a long-standing border dispute that was resolved through arbitration was the Ethiopia-Eritrea border dispute. The conflict emerged in 1998 and two years later, the United Nations established the Eritrea-Ethiopia Boundary Commission (EEBC) in order to reach a peaceful resolution.[7] The commission's primary task was to demarcate the border between the two nations based on colonial-era treaties and applicable international law. In 2002, the EEBC issued its final and binding decision, which delineated the border between Ethiopia and Eritrea. While the arbitration process played a crucial role in setting the foundation for peace and resolving the border dispute, the implementation of the ruling was challenging and both sides refused to comply.

Another example of arbitration dealing with a land dispute was the Abyei Arbitration that addressed the territorial claims of Sudan and South Sudan over the oil-rich Abyei region located along their shared border. The dispute had previously escalated and resulted in widespread violence. To resolve the dispute, an arbitration tribunal was established in 2008 by the Permanent Court of Arbitration (PCA). The tribunal issued its final ruling on July 22, 2009 and assigned the Abyei region a special administrative status.[8] The Award stated that the region would be shared by

[5] Goertz (2016).

[6] ILM (1968); Parish (2010), p. 50.

[7] Duijentkunst and Dawkins (2015), p. 15.

[8] PCA-CPA Final Award (2009).

both states in condominium. This example resembled the solutions adopted in Brčko and the efforts to implement the arbitration ruling were met with similar challenges in terms of security and political tensions. Following the Abyei arbitration, the Abyei town was burn to the ground and more than 100 thousand people were forced to flee from the disputed territory.[9]

The final and most recent example is thr arbitration between Slovenia and Croatia that aimed at resolving a long-standing territorial dispute over the maritime border in the Adriatic Sea and the territorial status of Piran Bay. Unlike the Brčko case, this arbitration was between states and was conducted under the auspices of the Permanent Court of Arbitration in The Hague. The arbitration process began in 2009 and the Final Award was issued in 2017 and ruled that Slovenia should have direct access to international waters in the north Adriatic Sea using a corridor crossing Croatian waters. The arbitration process was marked by a number of contraversies that resulted in Croatia's withdrawal from the arbitrartion and the refusal of the Final Award.

It is clear from the above cited cases that territorial disputes are inherently more likely to occur between two states or one state and one non-state actor. Brčko case is peculiar because it involved a territorial dispute between two non-state entities. Non-state actors have a limited recognition in international dispute resolution and cannot stand before the International Court of Justice. The ICJ Statute categorically rejects any possibility of direct participation of entities other than states in disputes brought before it.'[10]

3 Background to the Brčko Arbitration

Brčko is a small town in northeast Bosnia, located on the immediate border with Croatia and only 40 kilometers away from the Serbian border. It can be described as a narrow corridor between regions of Bosnia and Croatia that have high concentrations of ethnic Serbs. For most of its history, Brčko was richly multiethnic. The last population census prior to the dissolution of Yugoslavia showed that the town's population of over 87,000 inhabitants was 44% Muslim, 21% Serb, 25% Croat and 10% Others.[11] After the war broke out the town became notorious for war crimes, concentration camps and the ethnic cleansing of its non-Serb population. This meant that by the time peace negotiations had started, the formerly diverse population was now 97.5% Serb.[12] Control over the city center and of the areas along the Sava River was vital to the Serb military leadership as this narrow corridor (at

[9] Duijentkunst and Dawkins (2015), p. 157.

[10] Vail (2018), p. 319.

[11] Statistički godišnjak Jugoslavije (1991).

[12] ICG (2003), p. 3.

certain points only 5 km wide) was the only land connection between the two parts of Serb-controlled territories.

The Dayton agreement ended the war in Bosnia and Herzegovina and established a unique political structure that divided the country into two entities: The Federation of Bosnia and Herzegovina (FBiH) and the Republika Srpska (RS). The entities gained a great degree of autonomy, functioning de facto as "states within a state." They were granted a defined territory, a government, a flag and a right to conclude treaties (called "special parallel relationships"). Legally, entities can be aligned with de facto regimes which claim to control a certain territory but have no international recognition. While they may exercise effective control, they lack full legal personality under international law and are exclusively recognized as constituent parts of Bosnia and Herzegovina.

The peace negotiations at Dayton were essentially a process of dividing territory and assigning it to one of the newly established entities. Brčko became the most contentious issue as neither entity was ready to give up their claims over this small but strategically important area.

The Serb side claimed that Brčko was vital to Republika Srpska's integrity as it was the only link connecting its northern and eastern part and that without it, the continuity and survival of the Republika Srpska would be undermined.[13] The Bosniak and Croat side claimed that as the town had a pre-war Muslim and Croatian combined majority, under the principles governing the Dayton agreement, Brčko should be awarded to the Federation.[14] Moreover, they insisted that assigning Brčko to Republika Srpska would be rewarding war crimes and ethnic cleansing and legitimizing them as a means of expanding borders.

Following futile attempts to resolve this issue, the Dayton agreement only stated that the final status of Brčko would be subject to an international arbitration process and that the tribunal's decision would be binding for both entities. Annex 2 (Article 5) of the Dayton agreement refers to postponing the decision about the final status of Brčko:

> The Parties agree to binding arbitration of the disputed portion of the Inter-Entity Boundary Line in the Brčko area indicated on the map attached at the Appendix. No later than six months after the entry into force of this Agreement, the Federation shall appoint one arbitrator, and the Republika Srpska shall appoint one arbitrator. A third arbitrator shall be selected by agreement of the Parties' appointees within thirty days thereafter. If they do not agree, the third arbitrator shall be appointed by the President of the International Court of Justice. The third arbitrator shall serve as presiding officer of the arbitral tribunal [...] The arbitrators shall issue their decision no later than one year from the entry into force of this Agreement. The decision shall be final and binding, and the Parties shall implement it without delay.[15]

The Brčko arbitration decision was unusual, in that it was a public international law arbitration not between states, but between semi-independent entities (Federation of

[13] ICG (2003), p. 2.

[14] Klemenčić and Schofield (1998), p. 69.

[15] Dayton Agreement, Annex 2, article 5.

BiH and Republika Srpska). In this sense, Brčko was an entirely domestic issue since both entities fell under the sovereignty of the independent state of Bosnia and Herzegovina.[16] The case was delegated to international actors because the court system did not exist in Bosnia at the time of the signing of the Dayton agreement and even if they did, their position and impartiality were likely to be compromised in post-conflict circumstances.[17]

4 Arbitration Proceedings

The Brčko Arbitral Tribunal was formed in 1996 and each entity appointed one arbiter (Dr. Vitomir Popović from RS and Prof. Ćazim Sadiković from FBiH). After failing to agree on the presiding arbiter, the International Court of Justice appointed Roberts Owen to this position. Owen was an experienced lawyer and a member of the US negotiating team who took part in the Dayton peace talks. He had significantly contributed to the drafting of the Bosnian Constitution. Moreover, Owen himself drafted the Brčko arbitration agreement.

The tribunal was given the task of deciding about the *'the disputed portion of the Inter-Entity Boundary Line in the Brčko area indicated on the map'*.[18] In fact, there was no map attached marking the disputed area. This made the Tribunal's task rather ambiguous and open to various interpretations. From the legal perspective, the most unusual condition was the fact that the arbitration agreement failed to give any guidance in terms of legal rules the tribunal was expected to apply. It only briefly stated that *'the arbitrators shall apply relevant legal and equitable principles'*,[19] without providing any reference to which legal and equitable principles were considered relevant. Parish (2010) points out that the constitutional law of the former SFRY, or of the SRBiH, could hardly be relevant, as the entire constitutional order of pre-war Yugoslavia had been superseded within the territory of Bosnia and Herzegovina.[20] As entities did not exist before the Dayton agreement, the laws that existed before could hold no relevance to current disputes. At the same time, the application of international public law regulations that regulate relations between states was disputable as parties to the arbitration were entities and not states. In essence, the degree of ambiguity allowed the Tribunal to resolve the case in any way it considered fair and equitable.

Owen soon realized that the entity-appointed arbiters were not open to compromise and that they identified entirely with the positions and interests of the entities that had appointed them. In practice, this meant that awarding Brčko to either side

[16] Ibid, p. 49.

[17] Vail (2018).

[18] Dayton Agreement, Annex 2, article 5.

[19] Ibid.

[20] Parish (2010), p. 52.

had to go along the lines of 'winner takes all' and in such circumstances, the presiding arbiter would be forced to pick a side. The Tribunal was hesitant to issue an award and to risk reigniting armed conflict and to potentially further destabilize the region.[21] In such conditions, the Tribunal's deadline to issue the final decision 'no later than one year' from the signing of the Dayton agreement was unattainable and the final award was consequently postponed.

The Brčko arbitration process unfolded in three stages (1997 First Award, 1998 Supplemental Award, 1999 Final Award) and was directly influenced by political and security developments on the ground. In order to understand the Tribunal's final decision and the unique approach adopted in Brčko, it is necessary to consider the local context and the key obstacles that stood in the way of resolving the dispute.

The arbitration period (1996–1999) was marked by three crucial issues: establishing freedom of movement and refugee returns; the opening of the Office of the High Representative for Brčko; and holding the first democratic elections. These three aspects had a direct impact on the Tribunal's decision as their implementation grew into an intense political struggle thereby escalating tensions and violent occurrences. These factors, combined with Brčko's profound political and symbolic significance, forced the Presiding Arbiter to base his decisions on political pragmatism rather than on legal logic.[22]

4.1 The First Award (1997)

The First Arbitration Award was announced on February 15, 1997, the essence of whichwas to avoid the impossible choice of awarding Brčko to either entity. It stated that:

> 'considering a host of historical, economic and psychological factors that served to mold perceptions on both sides, the tribunal was unable ... to say that either side is 100% right in its position or 100% wrong'.[23]

The First Award cited the ongoing failures to comply with the Dayton agreement by the RS leaders in Brčko (especially in terms of preventing the freedom of movement and the return of refugees) and the high levels of violence as the main reasons to postpone the Final Award. The only conclusion that the Tribunal could reach at this point was that:

> 'any 'simple solution' had to be rejected in favor of an approach that was consistent with law and equity and was designed gradually to relieve the underlying tensions and lead to a stable and harmonious solution'[24]

[21] Dahlman and Tuathail (2006), p. 9.

[22] Parish (2010), p. 62.

[23] Arbitral Tribunal (1997), p. 25.

[24] Ibid.

To help move the process forward, the presiding arbiter Owen, decided to establish a program for the implementation of the Dayton Accords in the area and called on the Office of the High Representative (OHR) to "*(a) supervise Dayton implementation throughout the Brčko area for a period of not less than one year, and (b) to strengthen local democratic institutions in the same area*".[25]

This decision significantly increased the level of international intervention in Brčko and placed it under the strict supervision of the Office of the High Representative in Brčko headed by the 'Brčko Supervisor'. Appointing an international civil servant to supervise the disputed area was an unprecedented move in the practice of international arbitrations. While the standard practice was to rely upon domestic courts to enforce arbitral awards, this time the Tribunal appointed its own officer to oversee the implementation of awards. On top of that, the Supervisor was granted extraordinary powers with extensive unilateral legal and executive authority:

> 'The Supervisor will have authority to promulgate binding regulations and orders in aid of the implementation program and local democratization. Such regulations and orders shall prevail against any conflicting law. All relevant authorities, including courts and police personnel, shall obey and enforce all Supervisory regulations and orders. The parties shall take all actions required to cooperate fully with the Supervisor in the implementation of this provision.'[26]

No explicit limit on the scope of these powers was defined, lacking even the requirement of the Supervisor's orders being in accordance with the Constitution.

4.2 *The Beginnings of International Supervision*

Following the First Award, the Steering Board of the Pace Implementation Council (PIC) met in Vienna in March 1997, and appointed an American diplomat, Robert William Farrand, as the first Brčko Supervisor. He arrived in Brčko in April 1997 and was given a list of priorities that ranged from ensuring the return of refugees and organizing local elections to initiating economic recovery. Describing his first days as the Supervisor, Farrand notes:

> 'You could sense the danger of renewed violence below the outward calm' [...] 'the typical diplomat's duties to represent, observe, analyze, report, and carry out instructions were supplanted by a new set of operating principles: more demanding, forceful, and fraught with consequences. In Brčko, I was given the authority—and responsibility—to exert direct control over the governance of a divided city and its surroundings'[27]

The area which resembled a 'maze of minefields and demolished buildings'[28] was divided into three small mono-ethnic municipalities: Brčko Grad (Serb), Brčko-Ravne (Croat) and Brčko-Rahic (Bosniak).

---

[25] Arbitral Tribunal (1997), p. 40.

[26] Arbitral Tribunal (1997), Article II.

[27] Farrand (2011), p. xii.

[28] Parish (2010), p. 77.

The Supervisor's initial agenda was to start a process for Bosniaks and Croats to return to their pre-war homes and to secure freedom of movement and hence start reintegrating the city. Whereas before the war Brčko's population had been distributed throughout the municipality with very few neighborhoods dominated by one ethnic group, the situation in 1996 was strikingly different. Even in the absence of a formal census, it was clear that the area north of the IEBL was inhabited exclusively by Serbs. Around 80 percent of them were Serbs who moved to Brčko during the war, occupying the houses and apartments owned by Bosniak and Croat pre-war residents.[29]

Any Bosniak attempts to cross the IEBL and visit their homes were met with violence as Serb police established illegal checkpoints and harassed, fined, or even detained members of other ethnic communities.[30] Establishing freedom of movement was a critical condition in moving forward with the peace process. Without the freedom to move freely, the displaced citizens would not be able to return to their homes and the prospect of holding democratic elections would suffer a blow.

A sudden push towards establishing freedom of movement came from US Secretary of State Madeline Albright who paid an unexpected visit to Brčko in late May 1997. The US State Department was aware of Brčko's crucial role in the peace process and therefore made room in Albright's schedule to visit Brčko and express the support and the commitment of the US government to building peace in Brčko. During her short address, standing in front of the war-scarred bridge across Sava, she made a surprise announcement that the bridge would now be open for civilian traffic. This was not discussed before as it was deemed too risky, but this seemingly simple gesture carried significant implications for freedom of movement and consequently for the return of refugees.[31]

4.3 Supplemental Award (1998)

By the end of 1997, the international actors had set the foundations of a nationally mixed executive, legislature and police force in Brčko. The degree of success, however, was limited in terms of economics and refugee returns with 'the fields planted with mines rather than crops' and the town described as 'disaster area with

[29] Farrand (2011), p. 60.

[30] Ibid, p. 61.

[31] The opening of the bridge for civilian traffic was more symbolic than practical in nature. The border authorities on both sides of the bridge had no experience with regulating international border crossings as the Sava river used to be an internal border within Yugoslavia. In order to cross the international border, all passengers would have to have a valid passport, a visa and a green card. As Republika Srpska was not issuing passports, virtually none of the Brčko residents had a valid passport and, in order to obtain one, they would have to travel to Sarajevo. This meant that actually crossing the bridge was a near impossibility.

non-existent utilities and public services'.[32] Having accomplished such limited progress despite international supervision, the Tribunal issued a Supplemental Award in March 1998.

The Award stated that despite significant progress in terms of freedom of movement and return of refugees, evidence presented during the hearings revealed that the RS authorities in Brčko had seriously obstructed all attempts to implement peace in the area. Concerns for safety and the persisting hostility towards the citizens attempting to return to their homes in Brčko, resulted in the Tribunal's decision to postpone the Final Award one more time and scale-up the Supervisor's authority:

> 'The supervisory regime established by the Award shall continue in existence, with the powers and responsibilities therein provided. The Supervisor, being Deputy High Representative for Brčko, shall enjoy in the Brčko area powers equivalent to those conferred upon the High Representative by the Bonn Conference of December 1997, including the power to remove from office any public official considered by the Supervisor to be inadequately cooperative with his efforts to achieve compliance with the Dayton Accords, to strengthen democratic institutions in the area, and to revitalize the local economy.'[33]

The Supplemental Award significantly increased the Supervisor's authority and earned him the nickname of 'American viceroy'.[34] Brčko was consequently described as an 'American colony in Bosnia' and was portrayed as an American project as there was a silent agreement among PIC members that all High Representatives in BiH would be coming from the EU and that all Brčko Supervisors would be American citizens. The Supervisor gained the power to implement laws single-handedly, annul decisions of local councils and remove elected officials from office.

A number of authors have also argued that granting custody of Brčko to a single foreign power proved to be more effective than devolving responsibility to a vaguely defined 'international community'.[35] The advantage of such an approach was having clarity on who was in charge of the process and avoiding the bureaucracy of coordinating actions with multiple international actors. The hope was that with such broad powers and financial incentives, the Supervisor could hasten the peace process and make it easier for the Tribunal to speed up the arbitration and reach the final decision.

4.4 *Final Award (1999)*

After more than three years of the arbitration process and with limited progress achieved on the ground, issuing a definite and binding decision on the final status of Brčko became the only way to further the peace process. The uncertainty regarding

---

[32] ICG (2003), p. 6.

[33] Supplemental Award (1998), Article 24.

[34] Landler (2003).

[35] Parish (2010).

Brčko's status was acting as an obstacle to the implementation of the Dayton agreement throughout the country and the Tribunal faced immense pressure to reach a decision. The Final Award was announced in March 1999 and it summarized the developments in Brčko as obstructing the attainment of Dayton's and the Tribunal's objectives and being particularly at odds with:

> '(a) encouraging and enabling displaced persons and refugees to return to their pre-war homes, (b) helping to develop democratic multi-ethnic institutions, and (c) cooperating with the international supervisory regime.'[36]

At the heart of the Final Award was the unification of the pre-war Brčko municipality in a territory that would be formally recognized as 'The Brčko District of Bosnia and Herzegovina'. The District would nominally be part of both Entities and shared by them in condominium. It would, at the same time, gain a level of de jure (if not de facto) independence from the entity governments:

> '[...] each entity shall be deemed to have delegated all of its powers of governance within the pre-war Brčko Opstina to a new institution, a new multi-ethnic democratic government to be known as "The Brčko District of Bosnia and Herzegovina" under the exclusive sovereignty of Bosnia and Herzegovina. [...] Upon the establishment of the new District, the entire territory, within its boundaries (i.e., the pre-war Brčko Opstina) will thereafter be held in "condominium" by both entities simultaneously [...] Neither entity, however, will exercise any authority within the boundaries of the District, which will administer the area as one unitary government.[37]

This solution meant that the Entities would both 'gain' territory even as they 'lost' administrative authority.[38] The Final Award failed to fulfill the expectations and hopes of either party and the critics pointed out that the Tribunal was merely creating a temporary solution to the problem by keeping the status of Brčko ambiguous and, in essence, still disputed. Historically speaking, condominiums were rare in international practice and were usually conceived as temporary solutions to the territorial claims of sovereign powers. Considering the complexity of ensuring the cooperation between the powers that exercise rights over condominium, it was difficult to imagine it as a long-term solution.

With the Final Award in place, Brčko became almost entirely self-governing, a unit of territory beyond the control of the Entities and under the exclusive sovereignty of Bosnia and Herzegovina.[39] It is important to note, however, that the District's self-government only applied to its relations with the Entities while the powers of the Office of the High Representative (later renamed as"The Office of the

---

36 Final Award (1999), Article 6.

37 Final Award (1999), Paragraph 9–12.

38 ICG (2003), p. 7

39 The Statute of Brčko District defines the competences of the public authorities in the District and areas in which the District government held the supreme authority: District economy, District finances; public property; public services/infrastructure; culture; education; health care; environment; social welfare; judiciary and legal services; police services; housing; urban development and zoning.

Final Award") were scaled up and essentially centralized in the hands of the Supervisor:

> 'All legislative responsibilities within the District shall be vested in the District Assembly. The total membership, composition and modality of selection of the Assembly shall be specified by the *Supervisor* in the Statute for District Government. The initial election of members of the Assembly shall take place when and as directed by the *Supervisor*, and subsequent elections shall take place as provided by the enactment of the Assembly with approval of the *Supervisor*. If he deems it necessary, the *Supervisor* may devise and incorporate into the Statute an "ethnic formula" designed to minimize the incentive for any ethnic group to seek to increase its population in the District in order to achieve exclusive political control'.[40]

The Final Award essentially established a fully fledged, if small-scale, international trusteeship, with the proclaimed goal of teaching the local population both how to govern itself and to live together again in civilized comity.[41] Every politically sensitive decision (such as the education reform and order on privatization) was imposed by the Supervisor, without the consent of the District's Assembly. According to international observers, this approach was the only way achieve progress in a reasonable timeframe. The Supervisor admitted that the international approach was driven by the need for practical, deliverable outcomes, instead of by the philosophical purity of the process. Pragmatism had to supersede idealism.[42]

Brčko District offered an alternative to the idea of creating ethnically homogenous and distinct territories as a means of achieving peace. Unlike the central state governance structures, the District's political system was not based on consociational logic and the Statute did not prescribe any special representation formula in terms of constitutive groups. Nonetheless, an unofficial 'ethnic key' was still applied in all governing institutions,[43] with the distribution of positions in the ratio 2:2:1 (Bosniak: Serb: Croat).[44] Veto rights that were granted to constituent nations on the state level, were not granted to any of the communities in Brčko District. Instead, most decisions required a three-fifths majority (e.g. election of the mayor, budget, laws, and appointment of police chief and their deputies) and therefore relied on inter-ethnic consensus. This was a deliberate attempt to avoid institutionalizing ethnic divisions in hopes of establishing a more effective decision-making process. The long-term goal was to establish a strong multi-ethnic democratic system that would eventually grow out of the need for international involvement.

---

[40] Annex to the Final Award (1999), Paragraph 2.

[41] ICG (2003), p. 9.

[42] Farrand (2011), p. 162.

[43] Oner and Kirbac (2013), p. 14.

[44] This informal rule granted Croats a gross over-representation in District institutions considering that after the war they accounted for only 10 per cent of overall District population.

5 Transfer of Competencies Controversy and the Constitutional Amendment

In the first few years following the arbitration, successful privatization and the increasing flow of foreign investment turned Brčko into the most attractive place to live in all of Bosnia. The overwhelming progress achieved in Brčko was in sharp contrast with slow reforms and lack of development in other regions. The High Representative feared that this growing gap would negatively affect the peacebuilding efforts in the rest of BiH.

The Final Award (1999) had not addressed the relations between the state institutions and the District and left Brčko without any political representation at the state level. The underlying assumption of the Presiding Arbiter that the state and the entities would protect the District proved to be unfounded and Brčko ended up a 'territory in legal limbo'.[45] In May 2002, the High Representative who was appointed to oversee the implementation of the Dayton Agreement at the state level, initiated state-wide reforms to centralize the judiciary administration. The reform proposal was to grant the Entity officials the right to appoint judges and prosecutors in the District. The Brčko Supervisor argued that such law would be a clear violation of the Final Award which stated that the Entities were to have no legal authority within the District.[46] This issue revealed the downside of the Final Award and highlighted the more profound competency issues that would come to be known as 'transfer of competences controversy'.

The High Representative's long term strategy for BiH was to gradually transfer power from entity to state level thus limiting the effects and financial costs of extreme fragmentation of power and competencies. The strengthening of the state institutions at the expense of entities meant persuading the entities to sign the so-called "Inter-Entity transfer agreements" (IETA). While this process was burdened by legal ambiguity and lack of clarity on due process, the most controversial question was whether the consent of the District was also necessary for the transfer of competencies. The Constitution and the Final Award did not address this issue and the High Representative held the view that the transfer of competencies would be binding for the District, even without its consent. The Supervisor fiercely opposed this view and insisted on the necessity of Brčko's consent.

The Final Award failed to define the nature of relations between the District and the state and this lack of clarity created a legal vacuum that made the District's status and competences open to various interpretations. The Supervisor's primary goal was to protect Brčko's sui generis status and shield it from entity ambitions by guarding its relative independence. The High Representative, on the other hand, aimed at transferring power to central state institutions and viewed Brčko's special status as a temporary anomaly. His attitude was that international supervision of the District was no longer needed and that Brčko ought to be placed under direct state

[45] Parish (2010).

[46] Clarke (2005).

control. This view was further justified by claims that the District's ambiguous and unique status within the Bosnian state was incompatible with modern European statehood and presented a potential obstacle to EU membership.

The crisis and concerns that were caused by the transfer of competencies stretched until 2005 and finally had to be addressed by the Arbitral Tribunal when the Presiding Arbiter was invited to clarify his position on the matter. The view he expressed was in accordance with the District's position - powers could not be removed without its consent. However, following the OHR's demand to re-examine his position, Owen called for both parties to present their case before the Tribunal.

These new developments led the Presiding Arbiter to question the sustainability of the District considering that the state-wide crisis was starting to undermine its autonomy. As this was in opposition to the proceedings of the Final Award, Owen issued a rebuke that addressed the status of the District vis-a-vis the entities:

> ‚…the Tribunal feels obliged to express an important caveat as to the legal impact of a two-Entity transfer of power to the State without an equivalent transfer by, or the consent of, the Brčko District. The caveat is as follows: So long as the Entities continue to exist under the BIH Constitution, any purported two-Entity transfer to the State, made without an equivalent transfer by, or the consent of, the Brčko District, would be contrary to and illegal under the Final Award if that transfer had the effect of significantly diminishing the District's ability to function as a single, unitary, multi-ethnic, democratic government for the Brčko Opstina.'[47]

The transfer of competency controversy revealed the urgent need to recognize the District's status in the Constitution, grant it representation in state-level institutions and precisely define the scope of authority that the state and the entities could exercise in the District. The District's position was finally codified in an amendment to the Bosnian constitution in March 2009.

The amendment, however, fell short of resolving the most critical questions, leaving the legal status of the District unresolved and failing to provide the District with representation in state institutions. The amendment essentially only reaffirmed Brčko's status by granting the Constitutional Court the authority to decide legal matters between the central government and the District.[48] The issue of 'transfer of competencies' was once again left unaddressed:

> "The Brčko District of Bosnia and Herzegovina, which exists under the sovereignty of Bosnia and Herzegovina and is subject to the responsibilities of the institutions of Bosnia and Herzegovina as those responsibilities derive from this Constitution, whose territory is held in condominium by the Entities, is a unit of local self-government with its own institutions, laws and regulations, and with powers and status definitively prescribed by the awards of the Arbitral Tribunal for the Dispute over the Inter-Entity Boundary in the Brčko Area. The relationship between the Brčko District of Bosnia and Herzegovina and the institutions of Bosnia and Herzegovina and the Entities may be further regulated by a law adopted by the Parliamentary Assembly. The Constitutional Court of Bosnia and Herzegovina shall have jurisdiction to decide in any dispute relating to protection of the determined status and powers of the Brčko District of Bosnia and Herzegovina that may arise between an Entity

[47] Addendum to the Final Award (2007).

[48] Merdzanovic (2015), p. 175.

> or more Entities and the Brčko District of Bosnia and Herzegovina or between Bosnia and Herzegovina and the Brčko District of Bosnia and Herzegovina under this Constitution and the awards of the Arbitral Tribunal."[49]

Compared to previous cases of free cities and internationalized territories whose status was clearly defined and confirmed through treaties, the Presiding Arbiter failed to predict the hostile attitude of actors outside the District and did not clarify its position vis a vis the State. This led to a profound crisis of authority that was further intensified by the Supervisor's gradual disengagement from the District.

5.1 *The End of International Supervision: Examining the Success Narrative*

The most difficult challenge any international administration faces is finding an exit strategy that will not undermine the achieved progress and that will leave behind an effective system of local governance. Internationalized territories tend to be unpopular among local actors as citizens dislike being subject to an appointed and unaccountable international regime. This makes the supervisory regime inherently unstable and unlikely to outlive the withdrawal of international actors. The suspension of international supervision in Brčko District in 2012 had a similar effect as the local actors gradually relapsed intointer-ethnic disputes and started to mirror the state-wide issues.

In March 2000, the US Secretary of State, Madeline K. Albright, attended the ceremony of inauguration of Brčko Statute. It was her second visit to Brčko in two years, meant to reaffirm the US commitment to the long-term success and sustainability of Brčko District. In her speech, she praised the Brčko model and declared it a success story:

> "The Brčko Final Award and this new District Statute are models for this country and for the entire region not because the specific circumstances here will be found in other places. They will not. But Brčko shows that seemingly irreconcilable problems can be overcome if there is a clear understanding that failure is simply not an option …"[50]

Her speech was perhaps the first indicator of the discourse the international actors were going to put forward in Brčko – the image of success, reconciliation and prosperity. It was, in fact, much too early to claim success in Brčko as the reality on the ground was far from reflecting the optimistic visions of the District's future. The story of Brčko District's success is important to the narrative constructed and reproduced by international actors in BiH.

The Supervisor announced the decision to suspend the supervisory powers in Brčko District in August 2012. In a public address, the Supervisor Roderick Moore

[49] Amendment I to the Constitution of Bosnia and Herzegovina.

[50] Secretary of State Madeleine K. Albright (2000): Remarks At Inauguration of Brcko Statute, full speech available at: https://1997-2001.state.gov/statements/2000/000308b.html

listed the District's achievements and described it as a model for the rest of Bosnia and Herzegovina:

> "Throughout the past decade the District had established multi-ethnic institutions and witnessed high rates of refugee returns. Moreover, it established an integrated multiethnic system and became a role model for the rest of Bosnia and Herzegovina. Because of this extraordinary list of achievements – that was made possible thanks to the strong spirit and hard work of Brčko citizens- it is now time for the local actors to assume full responsibility of governing the District".[51]

The post-supervision period was marked by increasing unemployment, declining wages, and deteriorating living conditions. The widespread corruption and criminal activities have caused the business climate in the District to deteriorate with fleeing investments, empty streets and abandoned shopping malls. The data presented in the 2017 report of the *Union for sustainable return and integration in BiH* illustrate the depth of the problem. The report states that in the past five years more than 150 thousand people had left the country and that Brčko District takes the first place in BiH when it comes to the number of citizens who had chosen to immigrate.[52] The extent of the brain drain in the District reveals the degree of citizens' disillusionment and the extent of pessimism caused by reversed reforms, political deadlock, and economic stagnation.

Probably the most cited example of the District's success is the educational reform that integrated the schools, making Brčko the first city in post-conflict Bosnia to remove physical barriers between the students and place them in mixed multi-ethnic classes. This is what led many external officials and observers to label Brčko a success and a 'job well done'. The Supervisor conceived the education reform in Brčko in terms of reaching an endpoint: a successful and integrated multiethnic education system reflective of the wider success and reconciliation in Brčko District. At the time when the Supervisor's authorities were suspended (2012), the education reform in Brčko was unanimously declared a success and regarded as one the most significant achievements of international peacebuilding efforts. Integrated and multiethnic schools were seen both as a goal to itself and as a tool to achieving reconciliation and abolishing divisions. There was an underlying assumption that the success would be lasting and irreversible.

Ten years later, the degree of success and the sustainability of the education reform have been put to test. The most recent data shows that the vast majority of primary schools in Brčko District have been voluntarily re-segregated, marking a reverse development. The most recent data acquired at the District's Education Department (2018) indicate that in 2018/2019 school year thirteen out of fifteen primary schools in the District were largely mono-ethnic due to parents avoiding mixed classrooms.

The story of success was not internalized by local actors as it did not reflect their experience of supervision. Following the suspension of the supervisory regime, the

[51] Moore (2012a, b).

[52] Huterer (2017).

initial lack of local support re-surfaced and was reinforced by the feeling that citizens no longer had to obey the 'appointed foreigner'. In practice, this meant pursuing nationalist agenda and reversing reforms that were deemed undesirable.

5.2 Post-Conflict International Administration and Internationalized Territories: Brčko as a Model of Conflict Resolution

The international administration of territory, in which comprehensive administrative authorities are granted to international actors (sometimes on behalf of or with the consent of the UN) has recently re-emerged in the context of rebuilding (parts of) states after conflict.[53] The specific cases of international administration of Kosovo and East Timor, followed by international involvement in state-building operations in Iraq and Afghanistan, have reopened the debate on the scope, objectives and sustainability of international peacebuilding engagements. Along with the international supervision of the peace process in BiH, these four operations were specific in terms of the creation of international interim or transitional administrations with the task of overseeing the peace process. The power granted to international actors in a post-conflict context raised questions about the accountability, local ownership and appropriateness of internationalizing domestic institutions. The continuous expansion of peacekeeping mandates, which have gradually moved from *keeping* peace to *building* peace, had resulted in the complete take-over of administrative functions by international actors encompassing the commitment to engage in large-scale and comprehensive reforms in all governmental sectors and therefore significantly shifted the objectives of international administration over the years.[54]

The term 'international administration' describes the regime of administration of a territory conferred upon one or more states, or to one or more international organizations and essentially acts as the counterpart to the 'conventional' national or local administration.[55] Considering that international administrations are generally transitional and provisional in nature, the main feature is their non-elected or appointed character.

The following part will provide some context for international territorial administrations in order to examine the unique character of the international mandate in Brčko District. The focus will be placed on historical examples of international administrations that can serve to illustrate to what extent the engagement in Brčko could have been better planned and executed if the historical origins had been taken into account.

[53] De Brabandere (2009).

[54] De Brabandere (2009), p. 5.

[55] Ibid, p. 2.

The idea of placing cities under direct international supervision as a means of resolving territorial disputes can be traced back to the Congress of Vienna (1815) and the establishment of the 'Free City of Cracow' (also known as 'Independent Republic of Cracow').[56] The city and the surrounding areas were placed under the joint protection of Austria, Prussia and Russia and at the same time adopted a constitution granting it significant autonomy. The city enjoyed economic privileges and was declared a duty-free area thus turning it into a vibrant center of economic activity. Over the next decades, the city also became the center of the Polish political movement and, following the unsuccessful Cracow Uprising in 1846, the Free City was annexed by the Austrian Empire. The case of the Free City of Cracow set a precedent for international administration and became a reference point for later approaches.

Other notable cases of international administration were the cases of the assumption of administrative functions by the League of Nations in the Saar Basin and the 'Free City of Danzig'. In the aftermath of the Second World War, the UN also developed plans to administer the cities of Jerusalem and Trieste as the concept of international administration was seen as a way to resolve territorial disputes or to assist communities seeking self-determination in the decolonization process. A special case (*casus specialis)* of international administration was the division and administration of Germany by the Allied Powers in the immediate post-WW2 period.

In regards to the Brčko case, the 1947 UN General Assembly's Resolution 181[57] that proposed declaring Jerusalem an international city under United Nations Supervision, is particularly noteworthy. According to this plan, the city would become a demilitarized corpus separatum under a specific international regime. The UN would be granted a mandate to administer the city, under the supervision of the Trusteeship Council. A draft statute was adopted by the Trusteeship Council that also named the city Governor and formally placed the city under the administration of the United Nations. The Governor was granted the authority to protect the interests of the City and its citizens and regulate the external relations. The implementation of this plan was obstructed by the outbreak of hostilities in 1948 that left Jerusalem divided and essentially still disputed.

Around the same time, the city of Trieste was declared a 'Free Territory' as part of the 1947 Treaty of Peace with Italy. The territory was placed under the direct supervision of the UN Security Council with the intention of easing the tensions between Italy and Yugoslavia as both countries claimed ownership of the city. The Security Council approved the Statute and provided for the appointment of a Governor that was responsible for administering the Free Territory. The Security Council, however, never appointed a Governor because of conflicts of interest of its members and Trieste was consequently administered by the United States, the

[56] De Brabandere (2009).

[57] UN Resolution 181 (II) (1947).

United Kingdom and Yugoslavia until 1954 when it was formally divided between Italy and Yugoslavia.

Even though these two proposals were not implemented, they constitute evidence of the legal capacity of the UN and other international bodies to administer territories. These cases contribute to understanding early discussions about free territories and international administrations as a possible means of conflict resolution.

The establishment of Brčko District in 1999 breathed new life into the concept of internationalized territories. Considering that previous attempts to establish internationalized territories had either collapsed or never begun there was a heavy question mark hanging over the idea of revisiting this approach. In cases such as Cracow or Trieste, the objective of international administrations was not to implement a certain model of governance or re-build state institutions. Rather, these cases were concerned with solving territorial issues and finding mutually acceptable solutions. In many ways, the Brčko model surpassed the UN administration of territory considering that its status was expected to be indefinite and that the international engagement went beyond resolving a territorial dispute and it imposed a specific type of administration based on liberal peacebuilding principles. Brčko District was not envisaged as a sovereign state but at the same time, its relations with the central state government and the entities were precarious and complex, remaining essentially disputed.

The experience of Brčko District demonstrates that if supervisory regimes are to be revisited in other regions as a means of conflict resolution, they will need to be designed as long- term engagements without a predetermined exit date. The former Brčko Supervisor, William Farrand, repeatedly stated that their mission was compromised by public announcements of early withdrawal and the frequently expressed desire to leave Brčko as soon as possible. This had a profound effect on the way the local actors perceived international supervision. For the most part, it was understood as a 'waiting game' - a temporary stage that would soon be over and allow them to undo the imposed reforms. If this model is to be repeated in other areas, it is important to maintain a long-term international presence despite the costs of such engagement. So far, the District model was discussed as the potential solution for resolving the status of the oil-rich city of Kirkuk in Iraq and the disputed city of Mitrovica in Kosovo.[58]

The geopolitical climate of the 1990s and the strong interest in resolving the conflict in the Balkans created a unique set of conditions that allowed the Brčko Tribunal to adopt a robust approach and interpret its mandate flexibly. The Tribunal's task exceeded the territorial dispute and turned into a conflict management tool based on the need for pragmatic solutions. It is not likely that the Brčko Tribunal's approach would be effective in other disputes considering that it was the result of distinctive local and international setting.

[58] Binnendijk (2006).

6 Conclusion

The Brčko arbitration was a crucial part of the peacebuilding process in BiH and the solutions adopted by the Presiding Arbiter demonstrated the importance of tailored approaches in resolving complex territorial disputes. The establishment of condominium under international civilian supervision was an unorthodox approach that laid the groundwork for building multi-ethnic institutions and assisting the peace process.

The Tribunal's innovative approach is mirrored in; (i) using arbitration as a tool to monitor and manage the security situation on the ground; (ii) establishing an interim supervisory regime in the Brčko area to enforce the decisions of the Tribunal; (iii) granting extensive powers to the Supervisor who could issue binding decisions without local consent; (iv) adopting equitable solutions as opposed to purely legal provisions; (v) interpreting its mandate in a broad and flexible manner in order to assist the peacebuilding efforts.

While Brčko is a remarkably successful example of post-war peace-building in Bosnia, the success narrative has been tested with deterioration of ecnomic conditions, mass imigration, re-segregation of schools and escalation of political tensions in the rest of Bosnia and Herzegovina. None of the entities had ever given up their desire to incorporate Brčko into their territories, leaving the District locked in the position of a potenital conflict hotspot.

The scale of international intervention in Brčko was unparalleled and seemed to yield immediate success in terms of refugee returns, economic recovery, and integration programs. It was a testament to liberal peacebuilding success at a time when peace operations were under intense scrutiny due to a number of peacebuilding failures. The acceptance and implementation of the award was guaranteed by the presence of a large international military force (SFOR) as well as the Supervisor's stronghanded administration. While it can be claimed that the indefinite joint administration of Brčko has prevented further conflict and enabled multi-ethnic governance, this would not have been possible without strong international military and civil support. A number of authors (Parish 2010, Dahlman and Tuathail 2006) agree that Brčko remains a geopolitical space under construction and contestation. The sustainability of this model will depend not only on domestic politics but also on the shifting of international security priorities and the capacity of the international community to maintain its commitment to Brčko District.

References

Bildt C (1998) Peace journey. Weidenfeld and Nicolson, London

Binnendijk H (2006) Solutions for Northern Kosovo: lessons learned in Mostar, Eastern Slavonia and Brčko. National Defense University, Washington D.C.

Carter Center Report (2010) Approaches to resolving territorial conflicts: sources, situations, scenarios, and suggestions

Clarke HL (2005) Changes in the constitutional structure of Bosnia and Herzegovina. East European Studies Occasional Papers at the Woodrow Wilson Center No. 74
Dahlman CO, Tuathail G (2006) Bosnia's third space? Nationalist separatism and international supervision in Bosnia's Brčko District. Geopolitics 11(4):670–671
De Brabandere E (2009) Post-conflict administration in International Law. In: International Territorial Administration, Transnational Authority, and Foreign Occupation in Theory and Practice. Martinus Nijhoff Publishers, Boston
District's Education Department Report (2018). http://ob.bdcentral.net/Content/Read/ostala-obavjestenje-i-dokumenti
Duijentkunst B, Dawkins S (2015) Arbitrary peace? Consent management in international arbitration. Eur J Int Law 26(1):139–168
Farrand W (2011) Reconstruction and peace building in the Balkans: The Brčko Experience. Rowman & Littlefield Publishers, Inc.. ISBN 978-1-4422-1235-0
Final Award (1999) Arbitral Tribunal for Dispute over Inter-Entity Boundary in Brčko Area. Annex. March 5, 1999. Full text available at: http://www.ohr.int/?ohr_archive=Brčko-final-award-annex
Final Award (2007) Addendum. OHR. Available at: https://www.ohr.int/ohr_archive/addendum-to-final-award/
Final Award (2009): PCA optional rules for arbitrating disputes between two parties of which only one is a state. Available at: https://pcacases.com/web/sendAttach/18820
First Award (1997) Brčko Arbitral Tribunal for Dispute Over the Inter-Entity Boundary in Brčko Area Award. February 14, 1997. Full text available at: http://www.ohr.int/?ohr_archive=Brčko-arbitral-tribunal-for-dispute-over-the-inter-entity-boundary-in-Brčko-area-award
Geoghegan P (2014) Welcome to Brčko, Europe's only free city and a law unto itself. May 14, 2014. The Guardian. Available at: https://www.theguardian.com/cities/2014/may/14/brcko-bosnia-europe-only-free-city
Goertz G et al (2016) The puzzle of peace: the evolution of peace in the international system. Oxford University Press
Huterer D (2017) Ko ima priliku, otici ce. Voice of America. Available at: https://ba.voanews.com/a/iseljavanje-bh-gradjana-dijaspora-raseljenici-migracije/4092240.html
ILM (1968) The Indo-Pakistan Western Boundary (Rann of Kutch) between India and Pakistan (India, Pakistan) 19 February 1968 VOLUME XVII, pp. 1–576. Full text available at http://legal.un.org/riaa/cases/vol_XVII/1-576.pdf
International Crisis Group (2003) Bosnia's Brčko: getting in, getting on and getting out. ICG, Sarajevo/Brussels
Klemencic M, Schofield C (1998) Dayton in the balance? The continuing dispute over Brčko. Boundary Secur Bull 6(1):69
Landler M (2003) Rare Bosnia success story, thanks to U.S. Viceroy. June 17, 2013. NY Times. Available at: https://www.nytimes.com/2003/06/17/world/rare-bosnia-success-story-thanks-to-us-viceroy.html
Merdzanovic A (2015) Democracy by decree: prospects and limits of imposed consociational democracy in Bosnia and Herzegovina. Ibidem Press
Moore R (2012a) A message from supervisor Roderick Moore to the people of Brčko. Full content available at: http://www.ohr.int/ohr-offices/Brčko/gen-info/default.asp?content_id=47434
Moore R (2012b) Why I suspended the supervision in Brčko. Available at: http://balkans.aljazeera.net/vijesti/zasto-sam-suspendirao-superviziju-za-Brčko
Oner A, Kirbac A (2013) The role of the international community in Bosnia and Herzegovina: The case of Brčko District. Akademik Bakis Dergisi
Parish M (2010) A free city in the Balkans: reconstructing a divided society in Bosnia. I. B.Tauris & Co. Ltd, London
Secretary of State Madeleine K. Albright (2000) Remarks at inauguration of Brcko Statute, full speech available at: https://1997-2001.state.gov/statements/2000/000308b.html

Statistički godišnjak Jugoslavije (1991) Nacionalni sastav stanovništva – Rezultati za Republiku po opštinama i naseljenim mjestima 1991. In: Satistički bilten br. 234. Izdanje Državnog zavoda za statistiku Republike Bosne i Hercegovine, Sarajevo

Supplemental Award (1998) Arbitral Tribunal for dispute over inter-entity boundary in Brčko Area, Supplemental Award. March 15, 1998. Full text available at: http://www.ohr.int/?ohr_archive=arbitral-tribunal-for-dispute-over-inter-entity-boundary-in-Brčko-area-supplemental-award

UN Security Council Resolution 181 (II) (1947). Available at: https://documents-dds-ny.un.org/doc/RESOLUTION/GEN/NR0/038/88/PDF/NR003888.pdf?OpenElement

Vail T (2018) The Brčko arbitration: a process for lasting peace between non-state actors. In: Non-State Actors and International Obligations. Brill | Nijhoff, pp 313–341

Navigating the Intersection Between Islam, European Values, and the Integration of Muslims in Europe

Beata Polok and Mariana Dussin

1 Introduction

The ongoing debate surrounding the integration of Muslims in Europe, despite Islam's presence in the region for centuries, is a significant issue that Europe has been grappling with for decades. In Europe, Islam is associated with integration problems, exclusion, and lack of assimilation.[1] One of the key challenges in this integration process is the implementation of Muslim Personal Law and its implications for women's empowerment.[2] The topic of equality between women and men and the personal status laws in Islam is a subject of frequent debate and a "flashpoint for tensions between Muslims and the Western world".[3] It is often cited as a primary argument to highlight the perceived incompatibility of Islam with European or Western culture and human rights. European Court of Human Rights in the famous case, Refah Partisi v Turkey[4] clearly stated that Islam's position towards women is not in accordance with values represented by the European Convention on Human

[1] Kedikli and Mehmet Akça (2018), p. 9.

[2] Freedman (2007), pp. 29–44.

[3] Kren (2013).

[4] Refah Partisi (the Welfare Party) and Others v Turkey [GC] 41340/98, 41342/98, 41343/98 [13.2.2003]. In this case ECHR upheld the decision of the Turkish Constitutional Court dissolving a Turkish political party, which aimed to introduce Sharia law in Turkey.

B. Polok (✉)
Dar Al-Hekma University, Jeddah, Saudi Arabia
e-mail: bpolok@dah.edu.sa

M. Dussin
Swansea University, Swansea, UK

E. Omerović et al. (eds.), *Balkan Yearbook of European and International Law 2023*, Balkan Yearbook of European and International Law 2023,
https://doi.org/10.1007/978-3-031-69670-1_2

Rights.[5] On one hand, the Council of Europe asserts that "Muslims are at home in Europe" and recognizes the contributions of Islamic civilization to European culture.[6] However, when observing the increasing Islamophobia in Europe and the public discussions surrounding Islamic law, it appears contradictory to this stance.

This research paper aims to explore the interaction between Islam and European values in the integration of Muslims in Europe. It examines controversial aspects of Muslim Personal Law, such as polygamy, and the divisive issue of the "burqa ban." Furthermore, the paper explores the intricate connection between European values, human rights, and the complexities that emerge in the European context concerning identity, values, and discourse on rights. Before delving into these subjects, the article examines the essence of European values.

This paper seeks to answer the following question: How can the integration of Muslims in Europe be effectively facilitated while addressing the challenges associated with implementing controversial aspects of Muslim personal law, such as polygamy and Islamic customs regarding women's attire, in a manner that respects European values?

The paper starts by looking into the complex issue of Islamophobia in Europe. It highlights that Islamophobia has evolved from being primarily tied to immigration and refugees to encompassing government policies and public sentiments targeting Islamic identity. Despite the long history of Muslims in Europe, they are often seen as outsiders, and the implementation of Sharia law is viewed as conflicting with secular legal systems.

Moving forward, the authors examine the stance of the Council of Europe and the European Court of Human Rights regarding Islamic law. The Council of Europe's primary objective is to promote greater unity among its members and the realization of human rights and fundamental freedoms.[7] However, the organization's approach to Islam and, more specifically, to Sharia law appears contradictory, acknowledging disparities between Islam and European standards while seeking reconciliation, mainly by advocating for the elimination of Sharia law, which raises questions about the possibility of coexistence between universal values and Islamic values from its perspective. The analysis presented provides insights into the legal framework and its implications for the practice of Muslim personal law in Europe.

In the following section, the authors examine the specific issue of polygamy, which is widely regarded as discriminatory. Through the use of specific examples, the authors illuminate the complex tensions and challenges that emerge when attempting to strike a balance between upholding human rights and fostering integration.

Finally, the paper discusses the issue of "burqa bans" and the prohibition of wearing headscarves in Europe. This pressing issue highlights the potential

[5] Refah Partisi (the Welfare Party) and Others v Turkey [GC] 41340/98, 41342/98, 41343/98 [13.2.2003], para. 72.

[6] Ibid.

[7] Art.1 Statute of the Council of Europe https://assembly.coe.int/nw/xml/rop/statut_ce_2015-en.pdf.

hypocrisy in Europe. The authors argue whether "European values" truly exist and who should determine what these values entail. It is crucial to recognize that Muslims have transitioned from being considered "outsiders" to being part of the European community, and their laws, culture, and religion should be taken into consideration when defining "European standards." Additionally, the authors question the feasibility of establishing a singular set of European standards, as Europe is not homogenous, and neither is Islam. Consequently, claims made by the European Court of Human Rights that Islam is incompatible with the European Convention on Human Rights (and thereby "European values") may be regarded as stigmatizing.

2 Overview of Islamophobia and its impact on Muslims in Europe

Muslims have been present in Europe since the eighth century and have become integrated into European society.[8] E. Greble perceives the Muslim population as indigenous to Europe, emphasizing that, for example, Muslims have been living among multilingual and complex Christian groups in former Yugoslavia for centuries, which testifies to their openness and adaptability.[9]

In its fourteenth report on Islamophobia, the Organization of Islamic Cooperation (OIC)[10] finds that Europe (Especially the UK and France) accounts for most of the cases of anti-Muslim discrimination worldwide.[11] Interestingly, the report also indicates that the "central issue has moved far beyond immigration and refugees that used to dominate the political dynamics in Europe in the past 5 years. Instead, the recent trends show that the tension was dominated by government policies and public sentiments targeting Islamic identity"[12] This means that the current tension between Muslim and non-Muslim populations in Europe is centered around policies and attitudes directed towards the Islamic community rather than solely focusing on immigration and refugees as they did in the past.

In spite of the existence of fundamental rights that prohibit religious discrimination, several European countries have implemented legislation that specifically singles out and discriminates against the Muslim community residing within their territories. For instance, in 2007, Slovakia enacted a law that effectively rendered it extremely difficult for the Muslim community to be recognized as a legitimate

[8] Ahmad (1974/75), pp. 6–13.

[9] Greble (2021), p. 5.

[10] Fourteenth OIC Report on Islamophobia, Presented to the fourth Session of the Council of Foreign Ministers, Islamabad 2022, https://www.oci.org/upload/islamophobia/2022/14th_Annual_Report_on_Islamophobia_March_2022_r2.pdf.

[11] Report covered incidents of Islamophobic assaults and anti-Muslim hatred between December 2020 and January 2022.

[12] Ibid., p. 3.

religious group and enjoy the same rights as other religions in the country.[13] Numerous countries have also introduced "burqa bans," which prohibit the covering of the face in public places.[14] In Denmark, in 2018, under the umbrella of the "anti-ghetto" laws, individuals classified as "non-westerners" are subject to various restrictions.[15] Public figures, media, politicians, and often various institutions are playing a significant role in spreading the wave of hatred against Islam in Europe. Very recently, the French government imposed a ban on abaya in schools[16] and justified using rhetoric based on the extreme French version of secularism known as *laïcité*.[17]

The fear, hatred, and discrimination against Muslims are commonly known as Islamophobia.[18] Media and civil organizations report rising islamophobia in Europe in recent years and link it with the decline of liberal democracy in Europe.[19] Recently, The European Commission against Racism and Intolerance (ECRI) published its "General Policy Recommendation No. 5 on preventing and combating anti-Muslim racism and discrimination" in December 2021, which was adopted and later published on 1 March 2022.[20] The document is being considered the first official document issued by a European institution that "explicitly does not refer to the problem of Islamophobia as 'anti-Muslim hatred', thus psychologizing and downplaying the phenomenon, but explicitly speaks of 'anti-Muslim racism' and thus includes structural aspects of this phenomenon".[21] The rising Islamophobia in Europe is sometimes compared to the return to the Middle Ages when integration was considered a forced conversion from the minority religion to the majority.[22]

[13] Michaela Moravicikova (n.d.), 'Religion, Law and Secular Principles in the Slovak Republic. National Report: Slovak Republik' Strasbourg Consortium https://www.strasbourgconsortium.org/content/blurb/files/Slovakia.1.pdf, p. 615.

[14] For example, the recent ban was supported in referendum by 51.2% of the Swiss voters. See in: Switzerland proposes $1000 fines for breaking 'burqa ban', Al Jazeera, 12.10.2022 https://www.aljazeera.com/news/2022/10/13/switzerland-plans-1000-fines-for-breaking-burqa-ban.

[15] E. Barry and M.S. Sorensen, In Denmark, Harsh New Laws for Immigrant 'Ghettos' "The New York Times" (1 July 2018) https://www.nytimes.com/2018/07/01/world/europe/denmark-immigrant-ghettos.html.

[16] R. Bunyan, French schools send home dozens of Muslim schoolgirls for refusing to remove their abayas on first day of term - defying classroom ban on Islamic dress, "Daily Mail" (5 September 2023), https://www.dailymail.co.uk/news/article-12481907/French-schools-send-muslim-schoolgirls-home-wearing-abayas.html.

[17] Kuru (2008), pp. 1–19.

[18] See in: Marriam-Webster dictionary (n.d.) https://www.merriam-webster.com/dictionary/Islamophobia.

[19] Bayrakli and Hafez (2021), p. 8.

[20] Council of Europe (n.d.), ECRI General Policy Recommendation No. 5 (revised) on preventing and combating anti-Muslim racism and discrimination, Adopted on 8 December 2021 https://rm.coe.int/ecri-general-policy-recommendation-no-5-revised-on-preventing-and-comb/1680a5ae44.

[21] Bayrakli and Hafez (2021), p. 7.

[22] P. Goldschmidt (2018), With anti-Muslim laws, Europe enters new dark age, "Politico" 27.07.2018,https://www.politico.eu/article/with-anti-muslim-laws-france-denmark-europe-enters-new-dark-age/.

3 The Complex Relationship Between Islam and European Values

In Europe, Islamophobia is based on the assumption that Islam is contradicting European values. European values encompass freedom of expression, equality, protection of minorities, secularism, and individualization which emphasize personal choice in shaping beliefs, attitudes, and behaviors.[23]

European values are often seen as an expression of Judeo-Christian thought and the "Western cultural invasion", and therefore will never harmonize with the spirit of Islam.[24] There is a relatively strong inclination to consider Islam as a monolithic block and as a religious doctrine completely separated from the other two monotheistic religions, rather than looking at it with a more curious gaze seeking to unveil the commonalities between them.[25] Islam is rooted in Judaism and Christianity, just as Christianity is rooted in Judaism. Islam recognizes their messengers and prophets and upholds similar values and practices.[26] Islam, like Judaism and Christianity, has been increasingly challenged by the various industrial and technological revolutions that have accelerated exponentially due to the process of globalization and have profoundly and rapidly transformed countries and societies.[27] In addition to the above mentioned process of modernization, it has been contended that the Judeo-Christian values underwent a process of secularization and that the secularization of Europe is a core principle within the European human rights regime.[28]As a consequence, one of the pillars of democracy today is the secular character of the state. European policymakers consistently held the belief that Muslim legal concepts, as well as the Islamic framework governing family, property, and economy, were incongruent with their endeavors to modernize the state.[29] E. Greble asserts that the claim of Europe identifying itself as a secular entity is fundamentally flawed and can be labeled as a "myth" within the context of European secularism. Greble supports this argument by referencing the insights of anthropologist T. Asad, who

---

[23] Halman and Gevers (1997) pp. 1–29.

[24] El-Fadl (2009), pp. 113–178.

[25] Reducing Islam to a monolithic entity and refusing to understand its multiplicity is problematic. Even though Muslims around the world with undeniably have some shared core beliefs such as the five pillars of the faith, and shared religious scriptures (Quran), much is left to be commonly shared across Muslim countries and cultures. Many scholars have argued that Islam is not monolithic, that it encompasses various interpretations and schools of thought (a review of the existing literature and strong arguments for Islam multiplicity can be found in Syed and Pio (2018), pp. 599–611).

[26] Montville (2016), pp. 245–256. Common values and practices emphasized in the teachings of all three religions: love and compassion for others; justice and equality with a focus on treating others fairly and standing up for the rights of the oppressed; generosity and charity, and helping the less fortunate; the importance of repentance or seeking forgiveness for one's sins and forgiving others; the belief in the oneness of God, and the worship of a single divine entity.

[27] Halman and Draulans (2006), pp. 263–288.

[28] Gunn (2020), pp. 148–169.

[29] Greble (2021), p. 9.

maintains that the definition and understanding of Europe, as well as "Europeans", have been deeply influenced by the framework and conceptualization provided by Christianity since the very inception of the construct known as "Europe."[30]

Some European countries, however, seem to forget historical contexts and have put forth universalist and secular worldviews, resulting in the emergence of secular and individualist political and legal frameworks. They have implemented secularism, sometimes in extreme forms such as French laicism. These countries tend to disregard the notion that the universal and secular human rights they champion are, in fact, influenced and constrained by the unique historical backdrop of European Judeo-Christian worldviews. Paradoxically, while actively enforcing and endorsing these secular perspectives, they simultaneously contradict the very value of individualism they profess to uphold.

Importantly, the concept of universal human rights is often criticized for being Eurocentric.[31] According to M. Mutua, the endeavor to establish universal human rights standards can be viewed as a persistent effort to impose European values on a global scale, akin to the historical trajectory of Eurocentric colonialism where certain actors assume superior roles while others are relegated to subordinate positions. Due to this cultural and historical backdrop, the fundamental assertion of universality in the human rights movement is undermined. Mutua suggests that the challenges surrounding universalism are not only Western in nature but rather stem from a Eurocentric perspective.[32] The human rights regime is criticized for its Eurocentrism emphasis on individual rights, which are seen as reflecting Western values and priorities. This criticism suggests that the human rights framework may not fully consider the needs, perspectives, and cultural contexts of non-Western societies, leading to a lack of inclusivity and effectiveness.[33]

A. Sachedina points out that, at its core, the Universal Declaration of Human Rights is individualistic and secular, and therefore fails to make room for Islam.[34] From here, it is possible to assume that it is likely that it also fails to encompass and make room for other non-Judeo-Christian cultures that have not experienced similar processes and levels of modernization, secularization, and globalization, and therefore cannot fully be considered universal.

The discussion so far has demonstrated that in Europe (especially in the European Union), universalism, individualism, and secularization are considered to be key values in the management of the diversity of their country. But it also showed that despite claims of universalism and secularism, the Judeo-Christian historical and conceptual frameworks cannot be separated from European history, and from the

[30] Ibid.

[31] According to the Cambridge Dictionary Eurocentric means "seen from the point of view of Europe or European people; considering Europe or Europeans to be the most important" See in: Cambridge Dictionary. (n.d) https://dictionary.cambridge.org/dictionary/english/eurocentric.

[32] Mutua (2001), pp. 201–245.

[33] Interview with Huaru Kang "The Universality of Human rights" (2022) Geneva Graduate Institute https://www.graduateinstitute.ch/communications/news/universality-human-rights.

[34] Sachedina (2009), p. 11.

UDHR itself. On the one hand, Muslims and Islam seem to have been at the wrong receiving hand of such values, as demonstrated above. And, on the other hand, some observers[35] continue to argue that Muslims in Europe seemingly reap the benefits of the European notion of human rights. Indeed, in Europe, Muslims are supposedly free to profess their religion and enjoy freedom of opinion. As a result, some authors argue that since Muslims in Europe and other Western nations benefit from the equality and freedoms guaranteed in Western documents relating to human rights, it is only fair to require that they, in turn, respect the very European values that benefit them.

4 The Council of Europe's and European Court of Human Rights stance on Islamic Law

The Council of Europe, the anchor of democracy and human rights is known for its rather narrow[36] and dismissive view of Islamic law and sometimes seems to have contradictory views on Islam. For example, in 2010, the Council of Europe Parliamentary Assembly (PA) issued Resolution 1743 (2010[37]) in which it recalled its earlier Resolution 1464 (2005) on women and religion in Europe which highlighted that Muslim communities must abandon any traditional interpretations of Islam which deny gender equality and limit women's rights, both within the family and in public life." This suggests that the PA specifically condemns gender-discriminatory interpretations of Islam, rather than Islam as a whole. However, this statement may be unclear since Islam generally advocates for gender equality but certain provisions in Islamic law may appear discriminatory from a universal perspective.[38]

Further, Resolution 1743 states that traditional Muslim women are regarded as "of the subjugation of women to men, restricting the role of women within society, limiting their professional life and impeding their social and economic activities" and "could be a threat to women's dignity and freedom."[39] In this resolution, the PA astutely emphasized that a blanket ban on wearing the burqa and the niqab would infringe upon the rights of women who willingly choose to veil their faces. Such a

[35] The word observer/s is used throughout to express the academic and non-academic range of views that non-Muslims have over Islam and Muslims.

[36] Rehman (2011) pp. 37–51.

[37] Parliamentary Assembly, Resolution 1743 (2010) Final version, Islam, Islamism and Islamophobia in Europe.

[38] For example, the issue of equal rights to inheritance is a significant concern within the context of women's rights in Islam. During the 1993 World Conference on Human Rights in Vienna, American and European delegates called for Muslim countries to ensure gender equality in inheritance laws (Boyle 1995, p. 92; Weiss 2014, p. 585).

[39] Boyle (1995), p. 95.

prohibition would effectively curtail their freedom to exercise their rights to personal and religious expression.

The European Court of Human Rights (ECHR) is often considered the most important international human rights tribunal in the world.[40] The ECHR persistently holds the view that Sharia law is inconsistent with democratic values and the concept of the rule of law, and is contrary to fundamental human rights. In the famous judgment Refah Partisi v Turkey,[41] the court stated that "it is difficult to declare one's respect for democracy and human rights while at the same time supporting a regime based on Sharia, which clearly diverges from the Convention values, particularly with regard to its criminal law and criminal procedure, its rules on the legal status of women and the way it intervenes in all spheres of private and public life in accordance with religious precepts."[42]

In Molla Sali v Greece,[43] which was related to inheritance, the Court stated that only a compulsory application of Sharia law is discriminatory.[44] This could be perceived by many observers as an initial stride towards accepting the possibility of harmonizing Islam with European values. However, the latest Resolution issued by the PA in 2019[45] states that "various Islamic declarations on human rights adopted since the 1980s, while being more religious than legal, fail to reconcile Islam with universal human rights." The PA, in its 2019 resolution, also repeated the statement expressed in Refah Partisi, that the "institution of Sharia law and the theocratic regime was incompatible with the requirements of a democratic society."[46] The report titled 'Compatibility of Sharia law with the European Convention on Human Rights: can States Parties to the Convention be signatories to the "Cairo Declaration?"[47] prepared by the Committee on Legal Affairs and Human Rights, an

[40] Temperman et al. (2019), p. 2.

[41] Refah Partisi (the Welfare Party) and Others v Turkey [GC] 41340/98, 41342/98, 41343/98 [13.2.2003]. In this case ECHR upheld the decision of the Turkish Constitutional Court dissolving a Turkish political party, which aimed to introduce Sharia law in Turkey.

[42] Refah Partisi (the Welfare Party) and Others v Turkey, para. 72.

[43] Molla Sali v Greece 20452/14 [2018].

[44] For some commentators Molla Sali's case could have been the first step in changing image of Sharia law in ECHR perception (Gregor Puppinck, 'What Emerges from the Molla Sali v Greece Judgment' (Figaro Vox 26 December 2018), https://eclj.org/religious-autonomy/echr/charia%2D%2Dce-que-rvle-la-dcision-de-la-cedh.

[45] Parliamentary Assembly, Council of Europe, Resolution 2253 (2019), Sharia, the Cairo Declaration and the European Convention on Human Rights, http://assembly.coe.int/nw/xml/XRef/Xref-XML2HTML-en.asp?fileid=25353&lang=en. The standpoint on the incompatibility of Sharia and European human rights standards has also been confirmed in the following report: Antonio Gutierrez (2019), Compatibility of Sharia law with the European Convention on Human Rights: can States Parties to the Convention be signatories to the "Cairo Declaration"? (Doc. 14787) https://www.ecoi.net/en/file/local/1456044/1226_1547028478_document.pdf.

[46] Parliamentary Assembly, Council of Europe, Resolution 2253 (2019), Sharia, the Cairo Declaration and the European Convention on Human Rights.

[47] The Cairo Declaration of the Organization of Islamic Cooperation on Human Rights in Islam (1990) is an alternative or complementary declaration to the Universal Declaration of Human Rights.

organ functioning within the PA's institutional framework, states inter alia that the Cairo Declaration is in clear conflict with the ECHR and is more religious than legal.[48] The report also expressed "great concern that three Council of Europe member States—Albania, Azerbaijan, and Turkey—are signatories to the 1990 Cairo Declaration, as are Jordan, Kyrgyzstan, Morocco, and Palestine, whose parliaments enjoy partner for democracy status with the Assembly."[49]

The report revealed that Sharia law's regulations on divorce and inheritance proceedings are clearly in conflict with the provisions of the Convention, notably Article 14, which prohibits discrimination based on sex or religion, and Article 5 of Protocol No. 7 to the Convention, which ensures equality between spouses. Furthermore, it is highlighted that Sharia law contradicts various other articles and protocols of the Convention, including those safeguarding the right to life (Article 2), prohibiting torture or inhuman or degrading treatment (Article 3), guaranteeing a fair trial (Article 6), respecting private and family life (Article 8), upholding freedom of religion (Article 9), protecting property (Article 1 of Protocol No. 1, ETS No. 9), and banning the death penalty (Protocols Nos. 6, ETS No. 114, and 13, ETS No. 187). The PA criticized the existence of "Sharia courts" in the United Kingdom and the application of Islamic law in family matters in Greece as they are, according to the PA, very discriminatory towards women in family matters. The report recalled the Refah Partisi decision which stated that "the institution of Sharia law and a theocratic regime were incompatible with the requirements of a democratic society."

From the above-mentioned examples, it is evident that the PA has taken a clear stance against Sharia law. Indeed, on several occasions, the PA expressed concerns that Sharia law and its provisions, which are in clear contradiction with the European Convention on Human Rights, were being applied (officially and unofficially) in member States.[50] Therefore, the approach taken by the Council of Europe may appear perplexing and contradictory. On one hand, it acknowledges the disparities between Islam and European standards, underscoring their inconsistencies. On the other hand, it seeks to promote reconciliation between the two. The PA is concerned about islamophobia stating that: "The Assembly is deeply concerned about Islamic extremism as well as about extremism against Muslim communities in Europe. Both phenomena reinforce each other."[51] A further report from 2019 examined this approach and stated that the aim was to reconcile human rights principles with Islam. Authors suggest that the sole approach to reconciliation being discussed involves the removal of Sharia law, and reconciliation would only be viable if it

---

[48] Parliamentary Assembly, Compatibility of Sharia law with the European Convention on Human Rights: can States Parties to the Convention be signatories to the "Cairo Declaration"?, Report (Doc. 14787) 03 January 2019 https://assembly.coe.int/nw/xml/XRef/Xref-XML2HTML-en.asp?fileid=25246&lang=en.

[49] Parliamentary Assembly, Council of Europe, Resolution 2253 (2019), Sharia, the Cairo Declaration and the European Convention on Human Rights.

[50] Ibid.

[51] Parliamentary Assembly, Resolution 1743 (2010) Final version, Islam, Islamism and Islamophobia in Europe.

aligns with European values. The statements from the Council of Europe appear to contradict the notion of harmonization and coexistence between universal values and Islamic values. Essentially, according to the Council, reconciliation implies a request for Muslims "to be less Muslim".[52] The Council of Europe acknowledges the issue of Islamic radicalism, but the distinction between Islam and radicalism is a multifaceted and complex matter that extends beyond the scope of this paper. Defining what it truly means to be a "radical Muslim" is a nuanced undertaking, lacking a clear-cut answer. Subsequently, it is evident that the approaches adopted by numerous European countries do not facilitate reconciliation effectively. Instead, they attempt to strip European Muslims of their religious identity. Paradoxically, these measures, ostensibly implemented to safeguard basic human rights, end up infringing upon them. The subsequent sections of this research will delve further into this topic.

5 Polygamous Marriages in Europe: Human Rights, and Integration Challenges

Perhaps, one of the most controversial matters regarding the unequal position of women is the issue of polygamous marriages. It is well-known that Islamic law allows Muslim men to marry up to four wives.[53] Polygamy is widely being considered as a clear violation of human rights and deemed incompatible with public order.[54] The issue of polygamy however has often had a strong association with culture with some claiming that the practice is condoned by cultural norms and values.[55] Regardless of the fact that polygamy is considered a relatively rare phenomenon[56] in the world, it still causes quite a controversy among Europeans. In

[52] Nicolas Bauser, Confrontation of Islamic Sharia and Human Rights at the Council of Europe, European Centre for Law and Justice (2019) https://eclj.org/religious-freedom/coe/confrontation-de-la-charia-islamique-et-des-droits-de-lhomme-au-conseil-de-leurope.

[53] Qur'an 4:3 "If you fear that you might not treat the orphans justly, then marry the women that seem good to you: two, or three, or four."

[54] For example, in 2009 the Austrian Asylum court held that polygamous marriages were incompatible with the Austrian public order and did not recognize a polygamous marriage (13 November 2009, C9 317335-1/2008).

[55] Patel (2017), pp. 459–483.

[56] According to the Pew Research Centre Polygamy is rare and mostly confined to a few regions, especially in West Africa (Kramer S, PEW Research Center (2020) 'Polygamy is rare around the world and mostly confined to a few regions' https://www.pewresearch.org/short-reads/2020/12/07/polygamy-is-rare-around-the-world-and-mostly-confined-to-a-few-regions/.

However, it must be noted that the statistics of the PEW Research Center are missing data from several Muslim majority countries around the world. In addition, many African countries where polygamy is practiced may not hold records of polygamous unions and marriages as they do not have the administrative apparatus to record and monitor their population (they may not have records of marriages and birth, and may not conduct census). Although these facts might not affect

Italy, for example, at the beginning of the twentieth century, Muslims were not allowed to settle in Italy because their religion, especially the issue of polygamy was declared "against morality".[57]

Even though polygamy is in fact uncommon, some individuals view it as a means of demonstrating their loyalty to their particular interpretation of traditional culture, society, or religion. They perceive these aspects as being endangered by the increasing influence of globalization and migration patterns.[58] For example, Andreas Mölzer, an Austrian politician in a written question to the European Parliament claims that polygamy in Europe is indirectly supported as an example he gives France where Muslim immigrants can reunite with their second, third, or fourth wife. According to him, the number of polygamous marriages in France is 10,000 to 30,000.[59] In the answer provided, we can read that the reunification of third-country nationals is regulated by Council Directive 2003/86/EC of 22 September 2003 on the right to family reunification. According to Article 4(4), in the event of polygamous marriage where the sponsor already has a spouse living with him in the territory of a Member State, the Member State concerned shall not authorize the family reunification of a further spouse. It also provides that Member States may limit the family reunification of minor children of a further spouse and the sponsor. In addition, on their website, the French Senate clearly states that polygamy is illegal and punishable, however, it also expressed that there are ways for polygamous individuals to exist in all legality in the country: "However, religious or customary marriages, performed in France or abroad, are not taken into account in the definition of civil marriage. They therefore cannot support the accusation of polygamy. In French civil law, religious marriage is not recognized, only a civil marriage counts. It is therefore possible to live simultaneously with several wives, and as many children, without being married to them: this is neither legally reprehensible nor criminally reprehensible. You can therefore be "de facto" polygamous, without being in the least worried by the French authorities."[60]

Most European countries have a clear stance on the issue and do not recognize this type of marriage as a valid one and often penalize them.[61] Public opinion however argues that authorities often ignore Muslim migrant's polygamous unions—for example in cases of inheritance after a man dies the inheritance is distributed between two wives. In 2016, the German Justice Minister called for the total abolishment of polygamous marriages and said that "no one who comes here has the

---

the rarity of the occurrence of polygamous marriage, it still gives a partial figure on the actual occurrence of the practice of polygamy worldwide.

[57] Schmidt di Friedberg (2002), pp. 87–106.

[58] Zeitzen (2020), p. 165.

[59] European Parliament (2005), 'Polygamy in the European Union' Parliamentary Question to the Commission E-4761/05 https://www.europarl.europa.eu/doceo/document/E-6-2005-4761_EN.html.

[60] https://www.senat.fr/leg/ppl09-501.html#:~:text=En%20droit%20positif%20fran%C3%A7ais%2C%20la,%C3%A9tranger%2C%20est%20toujours%20en%20cours.

[61] Bigamy is a crime in several European countries.

right to put his cultural values or religious beliefs above our law".[62] Despite the fact that polygamous marriages are considered illegal in Europe, some countries still recognize the validity of marriages performed abroad. The issue of legality of polygamy is very complex and the validity of a marriage depends on various circumstances. As noted by M. Malik, in the scenario where a second marriage occurs in Europe after a previous marriage has already taken place in a country where polygamy is allowed, a conflict of rules arises. Rule 1 states that polygamy is completely forbidden, while Rule 2 states that polygamy is not prohibited. In Belgium, polygamy is contrary to the public order and prohibited (regardless of the fact that the country of origin might recognize polygamous marriages).[63] Therefore, only one spouse of a third country national can benefit from the right to family reunification. If two spouses apply for family reunification at the same time, the applicant will have to choose one.[64]

Recently the French Supreme Court held that polygamous marriage of non-French citizens is not automatically void under French law.[65] Under the French Penal Code, bigamy is punishable,[66] however, the global mobility of persons requires paying attention to the possible acceptance of polygamous marriages in the country.[67] In certain circumstances, if the second marriage was performed abroad, it can be recognized in France.[68]

The ECHR in the case Jehovah's Witnesses of Moscow v. Russia stated that polygamy is incompatible with the key principles underlying the Convention[69] and in the case Ivanov and Petrova v. Bulgaria[70] and Johnston v. Ireland[71] the court held that European society adheres to the principle of monogamy.

It should be also noted that from the legal perspective, the status of polygamy is not clear. As noted by J. Sandorski polygamous marriages previously have not only not been outlawed by international law but have been placed under protection on an equal footing with monogamous marriage, and the family formed on its basis is also

---

[62] Germany polygamy: Minister says migrants must abide by the law "BBC"15 June 2016. https://www.bbc.com/news/world-europe-36537305.

[63] Malik (2012), p. 149.

[64] European Commission (n.d.), EMN Ad-Hoc Query on Polygamous marriages https://www.refworld.org/pdfid/58ac4d2fd.pdf.

[65] Cour de cassation, civile, Chambre civile 1, 17 novembre 2021, 20-19.420, Publié au bulletin, https://www.legifrance.gouv.fr/juri/id/JURITEXT000044352185?isSuggest=true.

[66] French Penal Code. Article 344-20 (2000), Ordinance no. 2000-916 of 19 September 2000 Article 3 Official Journal of 22 September 2000 in force 1 January 2002).

[67] Marion Ho-Dac (2002), French Supreme Court Opens Door for Recognition of Foreign Bigamous Marriage, "Eapil", 6.01.2022, https://eapil.org/2022/01/06/french-supreme-court-opens-door-for-recognition-of-foreign-bigamous-marriage/.

[68] Ibid.

[69] Jehovah's Witnesses of Moscow and others v Russia (Application no. 302/02) (2010) par. 119.

[70] Ivanov and Petrova v. Bulgaria, (Application no. 15001/04) 2011par. 61.

[71] Johnston and others v. Ireland, (Application no. 9697/82) (1986), par 52 https://hudoc.echr.coe.int/eng#{%22itemid%22:[%22001-57508%22]}.

subject to protection.[72] The author notes that during the work on the UDHR, a clear proposal to establish a ban on polygamy emerged, but at that time, a decision was not made to regulate this issue in the Declaration.

Interestingly, it is not the fact of being in a relationship with more than one person that seems to be the biggest issue here, but the discriminatory character of polygamy and the fact that it is not possible for women to be in a relationship with more than one man. As mentioned by B. van der Sloot, from the liberal point of view there is no reason why three or more people could not live together and be bound married. According to the author, the prohibition of polygamy is similar to the prohibition of marrying closely related family members or the prohibition of gay marriages.[73]

There is also another dimension to polygamy, one that can be beneficial to men directly. Just as women are, men can also be forced into arranged marriages in their home countries, but would also want to have a spouse of their choosing. In their cases, "these young men are attempting to fulfill dual marital aspirations – they want a 'love match' of their own choosing, as well as to please their family and fulfill their filial duties by marrying the spouse selected for them."[74] Of course, a woman forced into a marriage by her family does not have the choice to use polygamy as an option, she either has to endure the unwanted union or seek divorce and the possible repercussions of either of these choices. Therefore, polygamy can be seen here as a clear advantage to a man in a similar situation of a forced marriage.

In Europe, polygamy is regarded as a threat to secular liberal nations.[75] In the eyes of many observers, as well as in the jurisdiction of the ECHR, polygamy is considered incompatible with the principle of equality between spouses and a clear example of discrimination against women. Some have even argued that from the perspective of universal human rights, polygamy violates women's dignity which, in this framework, is unacceptable.[76] What is however often missed is the fact that both recognition and non-recognition of the practice are potential sources of harm to women,[77] and by extension of the example above to men. In an international con-

[72] Sandorski (1986) p. 83. Later the Human Rights Committee took a clear stance on polygamous marriages by declaring them a violation of human rights and principle of equality of spouses (Human Rights Commission (HRC), General Comment no. 28, Equality of rights between men and women (article 3), U.N. Doc. CCPR/C/21/Rev.1/Add.10 (2000), par. 24).

[73] Van de Sloot (2014), p. 417. See in: Conor Friedersdorf, The Case Against Encouraging Polygamy, "The Atlantic" 9.07.2015, https://www.theatlantic.com/politics/archive/2015/07/case-against-polygamy/397823/.

[74] Charsley and Liversage (2013), pp. 60–78.

[75] Roodsaz (2023), pp. 181–197.

[76] Human Rights Commission (HRC), General Comment nr. 28, Equality of rights between men and women (article 3), U.N. Doc. CCPR/C/21/Rev.1/Add.10 (2000), par. 24. CEDAW (n.d.), General recommendation Nr. 21, par. 14. CEDAW, General recommendation nr. 29 on article 16 of the Convention on the Elimination of All Forms of Discrimination against Women (Economic consequences of marriage, family relations and their dissolution, par. 27.

[77] Avril Cryan, 'Does banning polygamy actually harm women?' (16 June Cryan (2017) "Irish Times" https://www.irishtimes.com/opinion/

text, those coming from a cultural background that does not endorse polygamy may believe that the most appropriate way to protect individual rights is to refuse recognition of polygamous marriages. On the other hand, individuals hailing from cultures that embrace polygamy may argue that respecting the validity of such unions is the optimal approach to safeguarding those rights.[78] "A state's refusal to recognize polygamy does not alleviate the harms associated with the practice. In fact, it denies women who are party to polygamous unions of their matrimonial rights, and thereby reinforces the associated harms."[79]

However, such claims can be considered culturally biased, since the definition of what is dignifying can be culturally charged. For example, as proved by C.M. Anderson in South African countries where polygamy is practiced, women are often financially dependent on men and prefer to become second or third wives rather than remain childless, divorced, or widows. The economic role of polygamous marriages can vary depending on the societal context in which they exist. A study conducted in South Africa revealed that women in polygamous marriages expressed support for the institution for several reasons. One significant factor was the necessity of having a male breadwinner within the household. Additionally, the economic advantages of having a co-wife were recognized, as she could contribute to the household income by caring for all the children and allowing another wife to seek employment outside of the home.[80]

While polygamy may be acceptable for women in other parts of the world, to choose polygamous marriages, such arrangements do not work well in Europe. As pointed out by M. Tiilikainen:

"In the countries of origin, women's dependence on men for material and relational well-being could make them agree to become a second wife (rather than remaining unmarried). Such gendered dependence most likely contributed to the relative stability of polygamous marriages, with all wives firmly anchored in the country-of-origin context. In comparison, immigrant women in Europe can often command a relatively high degree of self-determination, especially when they are descendants of immigrants (rather than migrants themselves) with European linguistic and educational skills. Such resourceful women may have relatively good options for leaving unsatisfying marriages. Thus, especially in a welfare state such as the Danish one, such women can survive on their own, even as mothers of young children, because they have money that they either earn or receive through social welfare."[81] Of course, in order to extend such an argument to the rest of the European member states, it implies that all member states have a well functioning welfare system that can provide decent living conditions to a single woman and her children once she decides to leave a polygamous arrangement because she cannot be granted

does-banning-polygamy-actually-harm-women-1.3121348.

[78] Ibid,

[79] Ibid.

[80] Anderson (2000), pp. 99–112.

[81] Tiilikainen et al. (2020), p. 90.

any rights otherwise. Another important dimension to take into consideration is the impact on children when breaking polygamous marriages (e.g. leaving the first or second wife and her children abroad because the marriage is not recognized). Indeed, research findings from around the globe have found that single-parent households, and specifically households without fathers, put the single-parent under a lot of difficulties that go beyond the financial aspects,[82] and also put children at risk by decreasing their academic performances,[83] diminishing their well-being including rising incidences of adolescent criminality, depression, eating disorders, teen suicide, and abuse.[84]

European states are currently grappling with the issue of polygamous marriages and lack a unified stance on how to address them. While recognizing the challenges associated with polygamy and its potential difficulty in being accepted within European societies, it is crucial to acknowledge that the primary victims in these situations are often the 'other' (not legally married in Europe) wives. Frequently, they find themselves abandoned with children in their husbands' countries of origin. Imposing stringent prohibitions on such marriages and failing to recognize the status of second wives, can be interpreted as a violation of human rights and a departure from the adherence to European values. Recognizing polygamous marriages has limitations on its application. It is important to note that polygamy is not mandatory for Muslim men; rather, it is an optional practice. Several Muslim countries do not permit unrestricted polygamy and have regulations in place. For instance, in some cases, a Muslim man must seek permission from his first wife before entering into a second marriage.[85] The Prophet Mohammed himself was in a strictly monogamous marriage to his first wife for 15 years until she passed. In addition, the limited practice of polygamy came to tackle the pre-Islamic practice of unlimited fornication outside of marriage, and specific responsibilities and requirements must be fulfilled by husbands to ensure equal treatment between his wives.[86] It was therefore in an effort to tackle immoral and harmful behavior that polygamy was made an option for Muslim men.

From the European perspective, the economic feasibility of such a model is questionable. It may be argued that allowing second wives, and their children, and granting them certain benefits would not be easily accepted in European societies. This, however, raises concerns about the financial burden of single-mother households on the welfare state, as well as the greater impact on children being raised in such households. Polygamy cannot be fully embraced in Europe and for a range of valid reasons. Even in countries where it is legally permitted, there are several restrictions

[82] Anderson (2003), pp. 121–152.

[83] Amato et al. (2015), pp. 191–202

[84] Singh and Kiran (2014), pp. 866–868,

[85] Food example Pakistan (See 6 Muslim Family Law Ordinance, 1961) In Turkey and Tunisia polygamy is legally prohibited (See also: Mir-Hosseini 2007, p. 1508).

[86] Qur'an 4:3 "If you fear that you might not treat the orphans justly, then marry the women that seem good to you: two, or three, or four.[4] If you fear that you will not be able to treat them justly, then marry (only) one".

in place. Nevertheless, a less concerned and relaxed approach to polygamy may be needed in Europe, as the practice is so rare, and some conditional legal acceptance could help alleviate the negative socio-economic impacts on already vulnerable populations such as women and children. While polygamy is often perceived as a rare phenomenon, it is important to acknowledge that each case is unique, thereby requiring individual analysis. The extensive attention given to the topic of polygamy may appear to exaggerate its significance. However, it serves as a compelling illustration of the contentious intersection between European and Islamic values. It is worth noting that even within the context of Islam, polygamy is not unrestricted, further emphasizing its limited occurrence.

6 Examination of the Controversial Issues of the Headscarf and Burqa Bans and Their Impact on Women's Rights

The issue of Muslim women's attire is certainly the most prevailing topic related to women's rights in Islam and a flagship example of conflicting cultural and religious values. The discussions related to the right of women wearing headscarves despite the passage of years did not lessen and still remain one of the most controversial topics. The two most important European courts—the ECHR and the Court of Justice of the European Union (CJEU) took a closer look and analyzed cases of burqa ban from different angles. In the case Sahin v. Turkey,[87] the ECHR found that Turkey's ban on headscarves in universities did not violate Article 9 (Freedom of thought, conscience, and religion) of the European Convention on Human Rights[88] because the ban was necessary to protect the "rights and freedoms of others" and to protect the "public order." In cases from Belgium, Dakir v. Belgium[89] and Belcacemi and Oussar v. Belgium,[90] the ECHR also ruled that Belgium's laws banning full-face veils did not violate Articles 8 or 9 of the Convention.

In the case S.A.S. v France,[91] the court ruled that face coverings may violate the rules of social coexistence because a visible face plays a fundamental role in all social interactions. It gives the opportunity to establish interpersonal relationships, which are deemed important in social life. For the French state, the barrier created by the face covering in public spaces carries a symbolic and dehumanizing violence

[87] Sahin v. Turkey, (Application no. 44774/98), (2005) https://hudoc.echr.coe.int/fre#{%22itemid%22:[%22001-70956%22]}.

[88] European Convention on Human Rights, (1950). https://www.echr.coe.int/documents/convention_eng.pdf.

[89] Dakir v. Belgium (Application no. 4619/12) (2017) https://hudoc.echr.coe.int/eng/#{%22itemid%22:[%22001-175139%22]}.

[90] Belcacemi and Oussar v. Belgium (Application no. 37798/13) (2017).

[91] S.A.S. v. France (2014) (Application no. 43835/11) https://hudoc.echr.coe.int/fre?i=001-145466.

that is in contrast with its social fabric[92] and can therefore be experienced as a violation of the rights of others to live in a public space that facilitates social life.

One of the most famous cases considered by the European Court of Human Rights was Dahlab v Switzerland.[93] Dahlab was a primary school teacher who was fired for wearing a headscarf. The ECHR agreed with the school management and considered the Islamic headscarf as a "powerful external symbol" that can influence young children. The Court also held that the Islamic outfit is a symbol imposed on women by Quranic regulations and, to its understanding, violates the principle of gender equality. Thus, the Court's ruling was based on compliance with the axiological axis built around the European system of human rights protection, which is primarily focused on tolerance, equality, and non-discrimination.

A number of cases were considered by the ECHR, and in almost every case, the court ruled that the state is entitled to restrict wearing Islamic headscarves if it is in contradiction with the protection of rights and freedoms of others,[94] values of the democratic society,[95] or is proportionate and aims to prevent social disorder.[96] Considering that, as stated above, this framework puts forth the protection of individual rights and freedoms with a focus on social justice and non-discrimination, it seems somewhat strange that the rights of others and values of tolerance, equality, and non-discrimination force women to not dress in a manner that they see fit as per their religious faith and personal conviction that being covered is better than not being covered. In order to protect the majority of women who prefer being uncovered and dressed in clothing that reveals their feminine forms for whatever ideological reasons, the ECHR decided to prevent women who do not follow a similar dress code. By doing so the ECHR contradicts the values that it protects and hinders the integration of the Muslims in Europe. Indeed, research shows that "the hijab is, of itself, neither liberating nor oppressive; the power relations invested in it are situational and contextual."[97] Therefore, the interpretation of the veil as a powerful external symbol or the face veil as a symbolic and dehumanizing violence is a European construction that directly affects women, especially women who are freely choosing to cover themselves out of their personal freedom. Such a construct shows a lack of tolerance towards those who do not adhere to mainstream codes, it deems them unworthy of being considered as equally free.

The issue of Muslim headscarves was also a subject debated in the Court of Justice of the European Union. For example, Samira Achbita v G4S Secure Solutions NV[98] held that a private company can set internal rules that prohibit the wearing of

---

[92] Ibid.

[93] Dahlab v. Switzerland (Application no. 65500/01) (2001).

[94] Kurtulmus v Turkey (2006) App No 65500/01 (ECHR, 24 January 2006).

[95] Leyla Şahin v Turkey (2005) App no 44774/98 (ECHR, 10 November 2005).

[96] Köse and 93 Others v Turkey (2006) App no 26625/02 (ECHR, 24 January 2006).

[97] Franks (2000), pp. 917–929.

[98] Samira Achbita, Centrum voor gelijkheid van kansen en voor racismebestrijding v G4S Secure Solutions NV Case no C-157/15 (ECJ, 14 March 2017).

any political, philosophical, or religious sign in the workplace, specifically the Islamic headscarf, and it will not constitute direct discrimination based on religion or belief according to EU anti-discrimination law. This was later confirmed in the 2021 case. The ECJ stated that employers can also prohibit wearing visible signs of political, ideological, or religious beliefs in the workplace and this includes also Islamic headscarves.[99] However, in another case, Asma Bougnaoui v. Micropole[100] concerned the client's wish that the employee should not wear a Muslim headscarf while performing her tasks. In the second case, the ICJ stated that the employer does not have the power to prohibit a Muslim from wearing a headscarf based only on a customer's wish or complaint.

In the most recent case from July 2023 Advocate General, in his opinion presented at the Court of Justice of the European Union[101] suggested that it is permissible for a public entity to forbid the display of any noticeable symbol representing political, religious, or philosophical beliefs in the workplace, as long as this prohibition applies universally. The municipality of Ans in Belgium implemented a ban on one of its female employees, prohibiting her from wearing an Islamic headscarf while at work.

In 2021, the Council of Europe released a video in which Muslim veiled women promoted a more tolerant inclusive society. This attempt to embrace a more diverse image of Europe was not well received by all member states. Finally, under pressure from the French government, the Council of Europe removed the video from the website.[102] As discussed in an earlier section of this paper, the same French State Council recently decided to uphold a decision by the French Ministry of Education to ban *abayas* from schools. Under the guise of the strict and ideologically charged French interpretation of the notion of secularism called *laïcité*, France once again put Muslim women under the spotlight and refused the diversity of its social fabric and the freedom of its citizens.[103]

According to numerous scholars, the act of wearing the Islamic headscarf, or hijab, does not possess a singular or static interpretation. Muslim women and girls opt to wear the hijab for a multitude of reasons, often characterized by conflicting and complex motivations. Other than religion, these reasons may encompass various aspects such as asserting personal autonomy, pursuing self-discovery and

---

[99] Judgment in Joined Cases C-804/18 and C-341/19, 15.07.2021 (n.d.) C-804/18 and C-341/19, 15.07.2021, https://curia.europa.eu/jcms/upload/docs/application/pdf/2021-07/cp210128en.pdf.

[100] Asma Bougnaoui, Association de défense des droits de l'homme (ADDH) v Micropole SA Case no C-188/15 (ECJ, 14 March 2017).

[101] Opinion of Advocate General Collins (Case C-148/22), OP v Commune Ans https://curia.europa.eu/juris/document/document.jsf?text=&docid=273313&pageIndex=0&doclang=EN&mode=req&dir=&occ=first&part=1.

[102] Nikolaj Nielse, Rights watchdog removes video of women in hijab, "EU Observer", 4.11.2021, https://euobserver.com/rule-of-law/153413. 2021 Islamophobia Report, p.14.

[103] France has been known to lead a fierce battle against the visibility of the practice of Islam under the principle of laïcité, first with a range of bans on headscarves, then a ban on the face-veil, then the burkini, and finally the abaya.

fulfillment, expressing resistance, and seeking liberation and freedom.[104] As rightly noted by M. Malik "in both the public debates about headscarves as well as sharia courts, non-Western religious difference is converted into 'barbarism' and a threat to liberal values."[105] As a result, European Muslim women become the targets of nationwide bans by member states, are discriminated against on the basis of their beliefs, religion, and origins, and are stripped of what they may believe is dignifying.

The prohibition of the burqa and the targeted scrutiny of women donning Islamic headscarves and other religious outfits, epitomize a profound paradox within Europe. Advocates of the ban contend that women should forsake their veils on the grounds of security, yet the sweeping impact of the COVID-19 pandemic has rendered this argument baseless and void. All members of society found themselves dutifully masked at all times in public spheres, yet, the sartorial choices of Muslim women have become a contentious issue. Furthermore, proponents of the burqa ban assert that it impedes integration when in actuality, it is these very bans and the singling out of Muslim individuals that obstruct the harmonious blending of cultures. The act of what one chooses to wear ought to remain a deeply personal decision, untainted by the intervention of the state. Just as there is room for discourse on the legality of for example polygamy, there should be no debate surrounding the hijab or burqa. These are choices imbued with personal agency, and upon examining the actions of European courts and the legislative landscape, one cannot help but perceive a targeted assault on Islam and an unmistakable display of Europe's hypocritical stance.

Imposing a burqa ban is clear evidence that European countries continue to have an ethnocentric understanding of human rights and that when confronted with an influx of exogenous populations they failed to apply human rights in a way that rightfully granted these rights to the newly added populations. Indeed, following the II World War and the adoption of the Universal Declaration of Human Rights in 1948, many European nations received large numbers of immigrants from various origins, which significantly altered their populations.[106] As a result, many European societies now include people from a wide range of ethnic, cultural, and religious backgrounds; however, many countries are still unwilling to consider this diversity and instead adhere to ethnocentric interpretations and applications of human rights that reinforce their superiority over others.[107] Consequently, despite the presence and application of human rights supposed to protect them in their personal choices and views, many Europeans are now finding it difficult to assimilate into the tightly ethnocentric social fabric of many European countries.

---

104 Danchin (2011) pp. 667–744.

105 Malik (2012), p. 140

106 Moniz (2023), p. 9.

107 Malik (2012), p. 140.

One of the most recent examples of such tightness is the series of French bans[108] targeting Muslim women's freedom of religion and expression. In September 2023, the French Minister of Education requested a ban on the wearing of the *abaya*, an outer garment similar to a long robe deemed traditional and cultural. This decision was contested by associations and moved to the Council of State who ended up rejecting the appeal. France is not the only country that enacted legislation aimed at reducing the visibility of Muslims and Islam in the public sphere. Many countries such as Switzerland, Netherlands, Belgium, Austria, Italy, Spain, and Denmark have banned either the headscarf or the face veil, or both. Such decisions may well be considered to infringe on the human rights of Muslim citizens across Europe, often creating a divide and tensions between Muslims and non-Muslims. Regardless, in a 2017 ruling, the European Union Court of Justice (ECJ) determined that EU companies can prohibit the headscarf on the condition that it is extended to all types of headwear that fall under the category of political, philosophical, and religious symbols.[109]

7 Conclusion

The Council of Europe has a complex stance on Islamic law, which has been a subject of examination. While it condemns gender-discriminatory interpretations of Islam, it acknowledges that certain aspects of Islamic law may be perceived as discriminatory. Similarly, the European Court of Human Rights consistently asserts that Sharia law is incompatible with democratic values, the rule of law, and fundamental human rights. However, there have been indications of a potential shift toward accepting the harmonization of Islam with European values. One such indication is the recognition that laws prohibiting the hijab may be discriminatory.

The Council's approach may appear contradictory, as it aims to reconcile human rights principles with Islam while simultaneously striving to eliminate or at least limit the application of Sharia law in Europe. It becomes evident that the only path for reconciling Sharia law with European values may be on European terms. It is

---

[108] See in: Law of 2004: Prohibition of the wearing of conspicuous religious symbols at school; Law of 2010: prohibition of the full veil in public spaces; Labor Law (amendment) of 2016: religious neutrality at work; Bill Eustache-Brinio of October 29: aims to ensure the religious neutrality of people contributing to the public service of education.

[109] 'The prohibition to wear any visible form of expression of political beliefs, philosophical or religious beliefs in the workplace may be justified by the need of the employer to present themselves in a neutral manner with regard to clients or prevent social conflicts. However, this justification must meet a real need of the employer and, within the framework of reconciliation of the rights and interests in question, the national courts may consider the context specific to their Member State and in particular more favorable national provisions in regarding the protection of freedom of religion.' See in: Cour de justice de l'Union européenne. (2021). Communiqué de presse n° 128/21. https://curia.europa.eu/ (Accessed 7 September 2023) https://curia.europa.eu/jcms/upload/docs/application/pdf/2021-07/cp210128fr.pdf.

apparent that Europe is grappling with contradictory opinions and a lack of clarity regarding its own values. The article highlights the significance of individualism as a key aspect of European values, yet it is not respected when it comes to the individual choice to wear the hijab. Consequently, Europe's discrimination against Islam can be seen as working against its own values and undermining them.

This paper looked at polygamy and how, in European discourse, it is frequently associated with gender inequality. Beyond this, it is also linked to the vulnerability experienced by women and children, especially single-mothers and their children, and the need to preserve a family (which used to be a leading value in most European countries). The article also tackled the decade-long and complex issues of Muslim women's choice of clothing and covering. Again, this demonstrates how specific stances, especially extreme ideological stances such as a universalist and laicized understanding of freedom, dignity, and diversity can impact European Muslim women.

The landscape of Europe has undergone a significant transformation, leaving behind the notion of a homogeneous Christian continent. In the past, immigrants were often treated as "outsiders" and struggled to meet the expectations of societal acceptance. However, the situation has changed, and Muslims in Europe are now fully integrated and should be recognized as genuine Europeans. This shift highlights the need to embrace respect for diversity as a guiding principle in understanding and respecting the different cultural practices and beliefs of Muslims. By acknowledging and valuing this rich cultural diversity, Europe can foster a more inclusive and harmonious society. A more relativist approach acknowledges that different cultures and religious traditions may have varying perspectives on human rights and legal systems. By recognizing and respecting these differences, the Council and ECHR can demonstrate cultural sensitivity and avoid appearing dismissive or hostile towards Islamic practices and values.

While the Council of Europe and the European Court of Human Rights frequently invoke slogans about "European" values, there is a lack of consensus on what these values truly represent. Europe is far from homogeneous, and different countries within the continent hold varying attitudes and perspectives on social issues. For instance, some countries have embraced same-sex marriages, legalized prostitution, and euthanasia, and have liberal abortion laws, while others, such as right-wing parties in Eastern European member states like Poland, are actively working towards banning abortion and promoting traditional gender roles. This diversity among member states makes it crucial to question who determines European values and to engage in inclusive dialogues that consider the multifaceted nature of Europe's cultural, social, and legal landscapes, without stigmatizing Islam and European Muslims because they are, in fact, still not considered after decades of presence, to be fully European.

Islamophobia exists in both Western and Eastern Europe, although it may manifest differently in each region. In Western Europe, there is a more visible Muslim population, and concerns about terrorism, immigrant crime, and gender oppression can contribute to Islamophobia. In Eastern Europe, where the Muslim population is smaller or almost non-existent, Islamophobia is often based on racial prejudice and cultural stereotypes. However, the European Islamophobia Report highlights that Islamophobia can be present even without a significant Muslim population.[110] Islamophobia in Eastern Europe primarily stems from racial prejudice; however, its influence is also expanding in Western societies. Eastern European Muslims are frequently perceived as outsiders, while the introduction of Sharia law is considered a direct threat to European values, sparking conflict with the secular legal system.[111]

It is also fully possible to look at Poland and be just as critical of its understanding and application of human rights. Poland's defense of the sanctity of fetal life, to the extent that doctors hesitate to perform abortions even in cases where the mother's life is at risk,[112] stands in stark contrast to the country's treatment of individuals, including children, who perish from hunger, cold, and thirst at the Polish-Belarusian border.[113] However, the Council and ECHR would rather discuss issues that stigmatize and marginalize a small portion of Europeans (5%).[114] This incongruity reveals a deep-seated contradiction in the notion of European values, suggesting a crisis of identity within the continent. While there is an outward expression of inclusiveness, non-discrimination, and human rights, the actions of individual European Union and Council of Europe member states often contradict these principles. Despite proclamations against discrimination, borders remain tightly closed, effectively blocking immigration for migrants from Asia and Africa. After the outbreak of the war in Ukraine, Europe welcomed a significant number of refugees from Ukraine with open arms. This gesture of acceptance is undoubtedly commendable. However, many observers have pointed out the presence of double standards. On one hand, we close our borders to migrants from Africa and Asia, effectively subjecting them to certain death in border forests. On the other hand, Europe opened its borders to Ukrainians because they were deemed more culturally fit.

It is essential to navigate the complexities and tensions arising from the divergent viewpoints present in European societies. Rather than relying on simplistic slogans, a nuanced approach that incorporates respectful dialogue can help bridge the gaps between different perspectives. Embracing inclusion means recognizing the full integration of Muslims in Europe and valuing their contributions to European societies. By doing so, Europe can move towards a more cohesive and progressive

---

[110] Bayrakli and Hafez (2015).

[111] Kalmar (2018), pp. 389–405.

[112] Human Rights Watch, Poland: Abortion Witch Hunt Targets Women, Doctors Criminalization, Pursuit of Alleged Offenders Violates (14 September 2023) Rights https://www.hrw.org/news/2023/09/14/poland-abortion-witch-hunt-targets-women-doctors#:~:text=Polish%20law%20now%20permits%20abortion,pregnant%20women%20refused%20terminations%20demonstrate.

[113] Agnieszka Pikulicka-Wilczewska, Fears of migrant deaths rise after bodies found in eastern Poland, "Reuters" (13 January 2023) https://www.reuters.com/world/europe/fears-migrant-deaths-rise-after-bodies-found-eastern-poland-2023-01-13/.

[114] Pew Research Center, Nov. 29, 2017, Europe's Growing Muslim Population, p.30 https://assets.pewresearch.org/wp-content/uploads/sites/11/2017/11/06105637/FULL-REPORT-FOR-WEB-POSTING.pdf.

future that respects the rights and identities of all its citizens, while celebrating the rich diversity which defines the continent.

References

Ahmad K (1974/75) Islam and the Muslims in Europe today. Eur Judaism 9(1):6–13

Amato PR, Patterson S, Beattie B (2015) Single-parent households and children's educational achievement: a state-level analysis. Soc Sci Res 53:191–202

Anderson CM (2000) The persistence of polygyny as an adaptive response to poverty and oppression in apartheid South Africa. Cross-Cult Res 34(2):99–112

Anderson C (2003) The diversity, strength, and challenges of single-parent households. In: Walsh F (ed) Normal family processes: growing diversity and complexity. The Guilford Press, pp 121–152

Barry E, Sorensen MS. In Denmark, Harsh New Laws for Immigrant 'Ghettos'. The New York Times (1 July 2018). Retrieved from https://www.nytimes.com/2018/07/01/world/europe/denmark-immigrant-ghettos.html

Bauser N (2019) Confrontation of Islamic Sharia and Human Rights at the Council of Europe. European Centre for Law and Justice. Retrieved from https://eclj.org/religious-freedom/coe/confrontation-de-la-charia-islamique-et-des-droits-de-lhomme-au-conseil-de-leurope

Bayrakli E, Hafez F (eds) (2015) European Islamophobia Report 2015. Seta

Bayrakli E, Hafez F (eds) (2021) European Islamophobia Report. Leopold Weiss Institute, Wien

BBC (2016, June 15) Germany polygamy: minister says migrants must abide by the law. Retrieved from https://www.bbc.com/news/world-europe-36537305

Belcacemi and Oussar v. Belgium (Application no. 37798/13) (2017)

Bougnaoui A. Association de défense des droits de l'homme (ADDH) v Micropole SA Case no C-188/15 (ECJ, 14 March 2017)

Boyle K (1995) Stock-taking on human rights: the world conference on human rights, Vienna, 1993. Polit Stud 43:92

Bunyan R(2023, September 5) French schools send home dozens of Muslim schoolgirls for refusing to remove their abayas on the first day of term - defying classroom ban on Islamic dress. Daily Mail

Cambridge Dictionary (n.d.) Eurocentric. In the Cambridge Dictionary. Retrieved from https://dictionary.cambridge.org/dictionary/english/eurocentric

CEDAW (n.d.), General recommendation Nr. 21, par. 14. CEDAW, General recommendation nr. 29 on article 16 of the Convention on the Elimination of All Forms of Discrimination against Women (Economic consequences of marriage, family relations and their dissolution, par. 27s

Charsley K, Liversage A (2013) Transforming polygamy: migration, transnationalism and multiple marriages among Muslim minorities. Global Netw 13(1):60–78

Council of Europe (n.d.), ECRI General Policy Recommendation No. 5 (revised) on preventing and combating anti-Muslim racism and discrimination, adopted on 8 December 2021, Retrieved from https://rm.coe.int/ecri-general-policy-recommendation-no-5-revised-on-preventing-and-comb/1680a5ae44

Cour de cassation, civile, Chambre civile 1 (2021, November 17). 20-19.420. Publié au bulletin. Retrieved from https://www.legifrance.gouv.fr/juri/id/JURITEXT000044352185?isSuggest=true

Cour de justice de l'Union européenne (2021, July 15) Communiqué de presse n° 128/21 [Press release]. Retrieved September 7, 2023, from https://curia.europa.eu/jcms/upload/docs/application/pdf/2021-07/cp210128fr.pdf

Cryan A (2017, June 16) Does banning polygamy actually harm women? Irish Times. Retrieved from https://www.irishtimes.com/opinion/does-banning-polygamy-actually-harm-women-1.3121348

Dahlab v. Switzerland (Application no. 65500/01) (2001)

Dakir v. Belgium (Application no. 4619/12) (2017). Retrieved from https://hudoc.echr.coe.int/eng/#{%22itemid%22:[%22001-175139%22]}

Danchin PG (2011) Islam in the Secular Nomos of the European Court of Human Rights. Mich J Int Law 32(4):667–744

El-Fadl KA (2009) The Human Rights Commitment in Modern Islam. In: Wanted: Equality and Justice in the Muslim Family (Malaysia)

European Commission (n.d.). EMN Ad-Hoc Query on Polygamous marriages. Retrieved from https://www.refworld.org/pdfid/58ac4d2fd.pdf

European Convention on Human Rights. (1950). Retrieved August 31, 2030, from https://www.echr.coe.int/documents/convention_eng.pdf

European Parliament (2005) Polygamy in the European Union: Parliamentary Question to the Commission. E-4761/05. Retrieved from https://www.europarl.europa.eu/doceo/document/E-6-2005-4761_EN.html

Fourteenth OIC Report on Islamophobia, Presented to the 4th Session of the Council of Foreign Ministers, Islamabad 2022:

Franks M (2000) Crossing the borders of whiteness? White Muslim women who wear the hijab in Britain today. Ethnic Racial Stud 23(5):917–929

Freedman J (2007) Women, Islam and Rights in Europe: Beyond a Universalist/Culturalist Dichotomy. Rev Int Stud 33(1):29–44

French Penal Code. Article 344-20. Ordinance no. 2000-916 of 19 September 2000. Article 3. Official Journal of 22 September 2000

Friedberg OS (2002) Being Muslims in the Italian Public Sphere: Islamic Organizations in Turin and Trieste. In: Shadid W, van Koningsveld P (eds) Intercultural Relations and Religious Authorities: Muslims in the European Union. Peeters, pp 87–106

Goldschmidt P (2018, July 27) With anti-Muslim laws, Europe enters a new dark age. Politico, Retrieved from https://www.politico.eu/article/with-anti-muslim-laws-france-denmark-europe-enters-new-dark-age/

Greble E (2021) Muslims and the Making of Modern Europe. Oxford University Press

Gunn TJ (2020) Do human rights have a secular, individualistic & anti-Islamic bias? Daedalus 149(3):148–169

Gutierrez A (2019) Compatibility of Sharia law with the European Convention on Human Rights: Can states Parties to the Convention be signatories to the "Cairo Declaration"? (Doc. 14787). Retrieved from https://www.ecoi.net/en/file/local/1456044/1226_1547028478_document.pdf

Halman L, Draulans V (2006) How secular is Europe? Br J Sociol 57(2):263–88. https://doi.org/10.1111/j.1468-4446.2006.00109.x. PMID: 16759195

Halman LCJM, Gevers JMP (1997) Exploring individualism in Europe. Results from the European value study 1990: Preliminary version (WORC Paper; Vol. 97.07.007/1)

Ho-Dac M (2002, January 6) French Supreme Court Opens Door for Recognition of Foreign Bigamous Marriage. Eapil. Retrieved from https://eapil.org/2022/01/06/french-supreme-court-opens-door-for-recognition-of-foreign-bigamous-marriage/

Human Rights Commission (HRC) (2000) General Comment nr. 28, Equality of rights between men and women (article 3), U.N. Doc. CCPR/C/21/Rev.1/Add.10, par. 24

Ivanov and Petrova v. Bulgaria (Application no. 15001/04) (2011), par. 61

Jehovah's Witnesses of Moscow and others v Russia (Application no. 302/02) (2010), par. 119

Johnston and others v. Ireland (Application no. 9697/82) (1986), par. 52. Retrieved from https://hudoc.echr.coe.int/eng#{%22itemid%22:[%22001-57508%22]}

Judgment in Joined Cases C-804/18 and C-341/19, 15.07.2021 (n.d.). Retrieved from https://curia.europa.eu/jcms/upload/docs/application/pdf/2021-07/cp210128en.pdf

Kalmar I (2018) Islamophobia in the East of the European Union: an introduction. Patterns Prejud 52(5):389–405. https://doi.org/10.1080/0031322X.2018.1512467
Kang H (2022) The Universality of Human Rights [Interview]. Geneva Graduate Institute. Retrieved from https://www.graduateinstitute.ch/communications/news/universality-human-rights
Kedikli U, Akça M (2018) Rising Islamophobic Discourses in Europe and Fight Against Islamophobia on the Basis of International Organizations. Mediterr J Soc Sci 9(1)
Köse and 93 Others v Turkey (2006) App no 26625/02 (ECHR, 24 January 2006)
Kramer S (2020) Polygamy is rare around the world and mostly confined to a few regions. Retrieved September 11, 2023, from Pew Research Center website: https://www.pewresearch.org/short-reads/2020/12/07/polygamy-is-rare-around-the-world-and-mostly-confined-to-a-few-regions/
Kren S (2013, February 20) The Islamisation of Spanish Jurisprudence: Spain Submits to "Adoption Jihad". Gatestone Institute. Retrieved from https://www.gatestoneinstitute.org/3595/spain-adoption-islam
Kurtulmus v Turkey (2006) App No 65500/01 (ECHR, 24 January 2006)
Kuru AT (2008) Secularism, state policies, and Muslims in Europe: analyzing French exceptionalism. Comp Polit 41(1):1–19. http://www.jstor.org/stable/20434102
Leyla Şahin v Turkey (2005) App no 44774/98 (ECHR, 10 November 2005)
Malik M (2012) The 'other' citizens: religion in a multicultural Europe. In: Zucca L, Ungureanu C (eds) Law, state, and religion in the new Europe: debates and dilemmas. Cambridge University Press, p 149
Merriam-Webster dictionary (n.d.), Retrieved from https://www.merriam-webster.com/dictionary/Islamophobia
Michaela Moravicikova (n.d.). Religion, Law and Secular Principles in the Slovak Republic. Strasbourg Consortium, Retrieved from https://www.strasbourgconsortium.org/content/blurb/files/Slovakia.1.pdf
Mir-Hosseini Z (2007) How the Door of Ijtihad Was Opened and Closed: A Comparative Analysis of Recent Family Law Reforms in Iran and Morocco. Wash Lee Law Rev 64:1508
Molla Sali v Greece 20452/14 [2018]
Moniz JB (2023) Secularization in Europe: causes, consequences, and cultural diversity. Religions 14(3):423
Montville JV (2016) The moral ties within the family of Abraham: a primer on shared social values in Judaism, Christianity, and Islam. J Ecum Stud 51(2):245
Mutua M (2001) Savages, victims, and saviors: the metaphor of human rights. Harv Univ Law J 42(1):201–224
Opinion of Advocate General Collins (Case C-148/22), OP v Commune Ans. Retrieved from https://curia.europa.eu/juris/document/document.jsf?text=&docid=273313&pageIndex=0&doclang=EN&mode=req&dir=&occ=first&part=1
Parliamentary Assembly (2019, January 3). Compatibility of Sharia law with the European Convention on Human Rights: Can states Parties to the Convention be signatories to the "Cairo Declaration"? Report (Doc. 14787). Retrieved
Parliamentary Assembly, Council of Europe (2019) Resolution 2253 (2019): Sharia, the Cairo Declaration, and the European Convention on Human Rights. Retrieved from http://assembly.coe.int/nw/xml/XRef/Xref-XML2HTML-en.asp?fileid=25353&lang=en
Parliamentary Assembly, Resolution 1743 (2010) Final version, Islam, Islamism and Islamophobia in Europe
Patel G (2017) How 'universal' is the United Nations' universal periodic review process? An examination of the discussions held on polygamy. Human Rights Rev 18(4):459–483
Pew Research Center (2017, Nov. 29) Europe's growing Muslim Population, p 30. https://assets.pewresearch.org/wp-content/uploads/sites/11/2017/11/06105637/FULL-REPORT-FOR-WEB-POSTING.pdf

Pikulicka-Wilczewska A (2023) Fears of migrant deaths rise after bodies found in eastern Poland, "Reuters" (13 January 2023). https://www.reuters.com/world/europe/fears-migrant-deaths-rise-after-bodies-found-eastern-poland-2023-01-13/
Puppinck G (2018, December 26) What emerges from the Molla Sali v Greece Judgment. Figaro Vox, Retrieved from https://eclj.org/religious-autonomy/echr/charia%2D%2Dce-que-rvle-la-dcision-de-la-cedh
Refah Partisi (the Welfare Party) and Others v Turkey [GC] 41340/98, 41342/98, 41343/98 [13.2.2003]
Rehman J (2011) The Shari'a, Freedom of Religion and European Human-Rights Law. Ir Stud Int Aff 22:37
Roodsaz R (2023) (Un)usual suspects: relational capacities and subjective transformations in polygynous and polyamorous practices in the Netherlands. Eur J Women's Stud 30(2):181–197
S.A.S. v. France (Application no. 43835/11) (2014)
Sachedina A (2009) Islam and the challenge of human rights. Oxford University Press
Sahin v. Turkey, (Application no. 44774/98), 2005. Retrieved from https://hudoc.echr.coe.int/fre#{%22itemid%22:[%22001-70956%22]}
Samira Achbita, Centrum voor gelijkheid van kansen en voor racismebestrijding v G4S Secure Solutions NV Case no C-157/15 (ECJ, 14 March 2017)
Sandorski J (1986) Międzynarodowa Ochrona Małżeństwa. Ruch Prawniczy, Ekonomiczny i Socjologiczny
Singh A, Kiran UV (2014) Effect of single parent family on child delinquency. Int J Sci Res 3(9):866–868
Switzerland proposes $1,000 fines for breaking 'burqa ban', Al Jazeera, 12.10.2022., Retrieved from https://www.aljazeera.com/news/2022/10/13/switzerland-plans-1000-fines-for-breaking-burqa-ban
Syed J, Pio E (2018) Unsophisticated and naive? Fragmenting monolithic understandings of Islam. J Manag Organ 24(5):599–611. https://doi.org/10.1017/jmo.2018.55
Temperman J, Gunn TJ, Evans M (2019) The European court of human rights and the freedom of religion or belief. Brill-Nijhoff
Tiilikainen M, Al-Sharmani M, Mustasaari S (2020) Wellbeing of transnational Muslim families: marriage, law and gender. Routledge, London
Van de Sloot B (2014) Between fact and fiction: an analysis of the case-law on Article 12 of the European Convention on Human Rights. Child Fam Law Q 26(4):417
Weiss A (2014) Interpreting Islam, Modernity, and Women's Rights in Pakistan. Springer
Zeitzen MK (2020) Polygamy: a cross cultural analysis. Routledge, p 165

Environmental Security as a New Challenge to International Relations and International Community

Mohamad Albakjaji

1 Introduction

Nowadays, the environment is considered as an important pillar in the international relations. This is due to the importance of environmental elements, and the international dimensions of these components that have become threatened by human action. Climate change, desertification, disruptions to water supplies, greenhouse gas emissions, and pollution in its various forms are examples of risks facing the environment. This made the environment the center of contemporary international politics.[1]

All of these thorny issues have become a challenge to international relations that have emerged and centered mainly on the Anglo-American system and the major industrialized countries. This made the issue of environmental protection a very complicated issue in international relations because of the bias of these forces to the option of industrial and economic development instead of focusing on the concepts and policies of environmental protection. However, due to environmental threats, which have come to affect the lives of societies, many civil organizations and social movements have had a significant impact on changing the pattern of international relations. So, the environmental issue has become a fundamental issue in formal deliberations of states and intergovernmental agencies. Environmental threats have become a threat to the international community as a whole, and this requires

[1] Albakjaji (2022), p. 83; See also Sosa-Nunez (2016), pp. 87–88.

M. Albakjaji (✉)
College of Law, Prince Sultan University, Riyadh, Saudi Arabia
e-mail: mabkjaji@psu.edu.sa

E. Omerović et al. (eds.), *Balkan Yearbook of European and International Law 2023*, Balkan Yearbook of European and International Law 2023,
https://doi.org/10.1007/978-3-031-69670-1_3

effective international cooperation between countries and a change in the traditional pattern of international relations.

The current paper is an attempt to answer the following research question: how does the environment change the dimensions/pattern of international cooperation and relations? For the research hypothesis, the research is based on the assumption that international relations are still devoid of any effective cooperation that would be able to meet the environmental challenges.

The researcher will use the doctrinal research method to discuss the topic. The researcher has used this method for many reasons. Firstly, one can get a deeper insight into the research question when reading and analyzing the related-sources topic. Secondly, through reading and analyzing the documents, the researcher will be able to provide some suggestions to develop the laws in the future. Moreover, the researcher will be better able to discover the inbuilt loopholes and gaps in the current situation. So, this work will draw the attention of the international community to the importance of the environment globally speaking as well as the necessity of adopting new rules, and new areas of cooperation.

To answer the above-mentioned question, the researcher will use primary legal research methods such as law texts. Moreover, to provide an in-depth insight and analytical discussion, the researcher will use secondary research sources such as academic papers, periodicals, and international, governmental and non-governmental reports.

2 The Environment as a New Term in International Relations

The current international deliberations and debates are centered on the issues of nature's influence on humanity and how human activities have negatively changed the natural conditions such as industrial pollution which may lead to social crises such as famine and social disaster.[2]

During the last 10 years, international debates have centered on the role of rich countries in shaping the future of the planet. The international community has currently failed to address the interrelated environmental problems.[3] So, will climate change lead to the adoption of new attempts and policies to counteract global warming, or is it likely that powerful countries and companies will oppose such measures, thus this conflict will erupt? Are we facing the environmental age?

---

[2] Dauvergne (2008), p. 3. This information is also available on: file:///C:/Users/USER/Downloads/Dauvergne_Preface_Introduction_ShadowsofConsumption_2008.pdf

[3] Galaz (2014), p. 7. Also, this information is available on: file:///C:/Users/USER/Downloads/9781781955543-GlobalEnvironmentalGovernanceTechnologyandPoliticsPlanetaryterraincognita.pdf

Environmental considerations are increasingly shaping new global policies and relations.[4]

In the first half of the twentieth century, there was no focus on the need for broad international cooperation on the level of the environment, and the environment was not a priority for civil organizations or policymakers. The matter was limited to the existence of bilateral or tripartite agreements in specific environmental fields such as the conventions on migratory birds which was between the US and the UK.[5] However, in the 1950s, concern for the environment at the international level became more important for academics and policymakers alike.[6] The motive behind this was industrial and economic development as well as local concern about the dangerous pollution associated with it, as well as the emergence of international organizations specialized in protecting the environment and increasing societal awareness about the risks that accompany industrial development, such as Greenpeace, World Wildlife Fund (WWF), Global Footprint Network, Friends of the Earth and so on.

Concerns for the environment emerged with the escalation of the Cold War, as well as with the attempts of powerful countries to control airspace, which led to a rise in the proportion of toxic gases in the atmosphere. This leads to confirmation that the environment is a global environment and is not confined to a specific geographical area, as winds transport toxic substances through the air to various regions around the world.[7] These concerns led to the emergence of the first global agreement to limit the spread of nuclear weapons,[8] which is considered the first global agreement to protect the global environmental atmosphere.

The scientific contributions had a great impact in guiding the international compass around environmental concerns where the emergence of meteorology associated with the invention of weather satellites has led to an increase in awareness about climate change.[9] Also, the invention of television and later on the Internet

---

[4] Radkau (2014), pp. 504–507.

[5] This information is available on the website of the Us Department of the Interior (n.d.): https://www.boem.gov/environment/environmental-assessment/migratory-bird-treaty-act-mbta.

[6] Brown (1954), p. 290.

[7] Soroos (1997), p. 360.

[8] The Treaty on the Non-Proliferation of nuclear weapons (NPT) (n.d.) is a landmark international treaty whose objective is to prevent the spread of nuclear weapons and weapons technology, to promote cooperation in the peaceful uses of nuclear energy and to further the goal of achieving nuclear disarmament and general and complete disarmament. The Treaty represents the only binding commitment in a multilateral treaty to the goal of disarmament by the nuclear-weapon States. Opened for signature in 1968, the Treaty entered into force in 1970. On 11 May 1995, the Treaty was extended indefinitely. A total of 191 States have joined the Treaty, including the five nuclear-weapon States. More countries have ratified the NPT than any other arms limitation and disarmament agreement, a testament to the Treaty's significance. This information is available on: Treaty on the Non-Proliferation of nuclear weapons (NPT) (n.d.. The United Nations/Office for disarmament affairs: https://disarmament.unoda.org/wmd/nuclear/npt/.

[9] Satellite Observations of the Earth's Environment (n.d.): Accelerating the Transition of Research to Operations. The National Academies Press. National research council of the national academies. https://nap.nationalacademies.org/read/10658/chapter/5.

made the world a small village which has facilitated the spread of environmental information easily all over the world. Moreover, the invention of modern technology had a major role in increasing societal awareness of the environmental damage caused by human activities, especially the effects of nuclear tests, which led to increased damage to the ozone layer.[10] In addition, scientific studies have proven that chlorofluorocarbons have caused a decrease in the level of ozone in the atmosphere, which increases the threat to life on the planet due to the increased burning of solar energy.[11] Also, academic and scientific studies on ultraviolet B radiation (UVB) and its risks to the ecosystem led international policymakers to adopt the Montreal Protocol of 1987, where these concerns raised by scientists and academics specialized in the environmental field were discussed.[12] Another example of scientific contributions to raising environmental concerns is academic research showing the dangers of smog from coal fires. These contributions prompted the government to adopt clean air policies in Britain.[13] Also, a book by Rachel Carson—the Silent Spring-(1962) showed the danger resulting from the use of pesticides on the environment and birds, and this in turn drew attention to the damages of the chemical industries and the need to adopt new legislation for them.

Concerns about the consumption of natural resources and the depletion of basic commodities due to the unbalanced overpopulation were and still are at the core of the concerns of countries at the geopolitical level.[14] Among the most important of these contributions is the novel by Thomas Malthus (1970) who raised the point of scarcity in commodities because of man himself where overpopulation will lead to economic disasters such as famines, increased demand for water and natural resources, and so on.

The contributions of Greenpeace and its use of modern technology, such as television footage, to prove pollution have fueled international debates about

---

[10] Albakjaji and Almarzoqi (2023), p. 4.

[11] Molina and Rowland (1974), p. 249.

Regarding the threat to the Ozone, argued that: Like an infection that grows more and more virulent, the continent-size hole in Earth's ozone layer keeps getting bigger and bigger. Each year since the late 1970s, much of the protective layer of stratospheric ozone above Antarctica has disappeared during September, creating what is popularly known as the ozone hole. The Antarctic hole now measures about 9 million square miles, nearly the size of North America. Less dramatic, but still significant, depletion of ozone levels has been recorded around the globe. With less ozone in the atmosphere, more ultraviolet radiation strikes Earth, causing more skin cancer, eye damage, and possible harm to crops. See: Sherwood Rowland (1996). This information is available one: https://nap.nationalacademies.org/read/9042/chapter/1.

[12] Litfin (1995), p. 251.

[13] In 1956, The UK passed the Clean Air Act which created smoke-free areas in the cities, and prevent people from burning the coal in domestic fires and in industrial furnaces as well. Martinez (1952). This reference is available on: https://www.britannica.com/event/Great-Smog-of-London.

[14] The impact of disasters and crises on agriculture and food security (2021). The report of Food and Agriculture Organization. This reference is available on: https://www.fao.org/3/cb3673en/cb3673en.pdf.

environmental policies.[15] In addition to the positive effects of satellite technology, which revealed the black cloud that covers space resulting from industrial pollution. All these efforts led to the adoption of environmental legislation in America and other countries,[16] and to the convening of the first Earth Summit in 1972 to discuss global concern about human activities and their impact on the environment and the planet.

3 Environment and Global Security

All these contributions had a significant impact on drawing the attention of international relations to the importance of the environment for future generations. The Stockholm Conference was held as the first global conference on sustainable development and environmental protection, and its primary title is «Only one land, so let's preserve it». The Warsaw Pact countries boycotted the conference, but few heads of state attended it. The issue pointed out is that rich countries always raise the issue of environmental protection to thwart the development process in poor countries. One of the most important outcomes of that conference was the establishment of the United Nations Environment Program to discuss how the United Nations should respond to future challenges. Accordingly, discussions on the laws of protecting waters, seas, and environmental bodies as a common human heritage led to an expansion of the scope of international concern on issues of the seas, oceans, land, space, and the outer atmosphere.[17] In the aftermath of the Cold War, scientific research emphasized that the resulting drop in temperature due to nuclear fallout could lead to a staggering loss of life, potentially even posing a «serious threat to human survivors and other species».[18] These researches and other initiatives have strived to make climate issues the top priority in international relations.

With the collapse of the Chornobyl reactor, fears of nuclear damage and its impact on the environment, especially the climate and the ozone layer, have increased.

---

[15] Deliani and Sugito (2021), pp. 5–7. Also this information is available on: https://www.e3s-conferences.org/articles/e3sconf/pdf/2021/92/e3sconf_iconard2021_04015.pdf.

[16] Although the United States adopted several laws before 1970, the most important laws came after this year. Endangered Species Act (ESA) (adopted in 1973). Hazardous Materials Transportation Act (HMTA) in 1974, amended in 1994. Marine Mammal Protection Act (MMPA) adopted in 1972, amended in 1981, 1984, 1988 and 1995. Noise Control Act (NCA) of 1972, amended in 1978. Pollution Prevention Act (PPA) of 1990, and others. This information is available on the website of Unites States Environmental Protection Agency (n.d.): https://www.epa.gov/enforcement/federal-facilities-and-other-environmental-laws-and-international-environmental.

[17] Vogler (1995), p. 8.

[18] Turco et al. (1983), p. 1283. Also, this information is available on: https://chuvaprataguerra.files.wordpress.com/2018/04/ttaps1983.pdf.

Scientific debates and initiatives paved the way for the huge United Nations Conference on Environment and Development in Rio de Janeiro in 1992, which adopted the United Nations Framework Convention on Climate Change (UNFCCC).

Although this agreement paved the way for applying the foundations of sustainable development, it did not achieve the desired goals because rich countries and major companies focused on business development instead of focusing on the requirements of sustainable development.[19]

In the past, the main concern of international relations was war—for colonial expansionist reasons—its impacts, and how to prevent the outbreak of conflict. Currently, international relations focus on the environmental conflict and the possibility of resource conflict as a source of war.

During the80s, fears increased about the effects of Chornobyl, desertification, climate change and its impact on weather fluctuations, the lack of water bodies, the lack of resources, and its impact on international security. This created a feeling of insecurity in many places around the world due to the conflict over natural resources. Accordingly, the World Commission on Environment and Development (1987) confirmed that mismanagement of resources and scarcity are the most important causes of conflicts in the world. Therefore, sustainable development is a necessity to avoid future conflicts. This led to the emergence of the concept of environmental security, which should be a source of cooperation and not conflict.[20]

Despite ongoing efforts by the United Nations to adopt legal frameworks to combat pollution,[21] these efforts face a common problem, which is the problem of law enforcement.[22]

In 2019 the United Nations issued the first reports on the assessment of the rules of the environmental laws and agencies. This report shed light on the fact that although there are various agencies and regulations, the failure to enforce such rules has hindered these efforts for providing a comprehensive protection of the environment.[23] Although such a report was focusing on the future of environmental protection, this is not surprising for lawyers who work in the area of international law. The lack of an effective enforcement mechanism is a challenging issue that weakens international conventions and agreements. This, in turn, constituted an obstacle to the implementation of an effective global policy.[24] This makes the international environmental law a set of theoretical points/provisions that only exist on paper.

---

[19] The Ecologist (1993). Also, This information is available on: https://wjsmith.faculty.unlv.edu/smithtest/The%20Ecologist%201993%20Whose%20Common%20Future.pdf.

[20] The study of environmental security revolves around a central idea that environmental problems — in particular, resource scarcity and environmental degradation — may lead to violent conflict between and among states and societies. Swatuk (2006), p. 203.

[21] United Nations Environmental Programme [UNEP], Environmental Rule of Law First Global Report (2019). https://wedocs.unep.org/bitstream/handle/20.500.11822/27279/Environmental_rule_of_law.pdf?sequence=1&isAllowed=y.

[22] Stulajter (2017), p. 325–326.

[23] Supra 21.

[24] Guzman (2011), pp. 15–17.

The UN report mentioned that although the UN supported states to enter into 1100 environmental agreements, neither the international support nor the national initiatives were able to establish governmental agencies with an effective power to implement laws, rules, and regulations. Only in 2017 more than 197 environmental defenders were killed.[25] What is most horrifying is that between 2002 and 2013 more than 908 environmental defenders and government inspectors were killed while carrying out their work.[26]

From a cultural and social side, the culture of environmental compliance is still weak. The UN report mentioned that the resistance to environmental regulations is growing. Some malpractices have been recorded against environmental activists. The report highlighted the frightening increase in the crimes of death or arrest threats against these activists.

This problem is double-sided. On the one hand, there are relevant international organizations such as the UN that lack effective executive tools to implement international rules related to the environment.[27] On the other hand, some states also suffer from lack of enforcement agencies within themselves and do not have the motivation to implement international environmental rules because they find such implementation expensive. Moreover, the non-compliance of other states with international regulations does not encourage others to implement them.

The issue is that the state sovereignty theory is still prominent in international relations. The interest of international community theory is not applicable when adopting new rules in the field of the environment. Because of this problem, the United Nations cannot force members to implement the relevant environmental agreements because most of them are voluntary, such as the Paris Agreement on Climate Protection. If the provisions of international environmental agreements were compulsory, the cost of non-compliance would be very high. This made countries demand that the implementation of the provisions of such agreements be voluntary. This makes the environmental threat a new challenge to the international community which needs to react in a different way to face such threats which could lead to the end of the planet one day.

[25] Jonathan Watts (2018). Almost four environmental defenders a week killed in 2017. The Guardian. This information is available on: https://www.theguardian.com/environment/2018/feb/02/almost-four-environmental-defenders-a-week-killed-in-2017.

[26] This information is available on the UN Environment Programme (UNEP) (n.d.): https://www.unep.org/news-and-stories/press-release/dramatic-growth-laws-protect-environment-widespread-failure-enforce#:~:text=Between%202002%20and%202013%2C%20908,197%20environmental%20defenders%20were%20murdered.

[27] Savaresi (2016), pp. 16–17.

4 Environment: As a New Threat to International Security

Security, the economy, and the environment have become issues at the top of the international relations agenda. It is assumed that natural resources shortage will certainly lead to conflicts. History proved that people always fight over natural resources.[28] That is why the environmental issues such as the issue of climate change was discussed in the Security Council in 2007. Environmental issues were also discussed more than once at the G20 summit. More importantly food security issues, sustainable management of natural resources and climate issues were discussed at the Davos conference in 2014. All these examples indicate that the environment is playing a prominent role in the international arena. Hence, the global environment and resources have become closely linked to security, which is the most important pillar of international relations.

Security in its broadest sense is preserving the acquired values of humanity and the feeling of security against violations those values. Thus, we must give people the guarantee to continue to enjoy these values, which are necessary for their survival and continuity.[29]

In the light of a world full of variables, security has become centered on cross-border phenomena. Environmental issues are the most important among these cross-boundary phenomena. For example, the risks associated with climate change, desertification, scarcity, and misuse of natural resources, and climate change have become cross-boundary phenomena that threaten the common values of human civilization and therefore global security.[30]

The industrial and technological revolution, the transition towards urbanization, the expansion of the use of transportation, and the increase in demand for food commodities are all factors linked to the high population increase that exceeds the quantities of available natural resources. This population increase and the accompanying increase in the demand for food commodities led to a shortage of water and exacerbated climate change and global warming and the problem of water scarcity. Recently, the concept of scarcity appeared, which coincided with the huge population increase. Therefore, international security became threatened due to the lack of water resources and their mismanagement. Here, new terms began to be used in international relations, such as environmental and water security, which are factors for protecting human security.

Environmental security, in its general sense, includes water security, energy security, and natural resources, as well as other human rights, such as the right to

---

[28] Dalby (2008), p. 264. Also, this information is available on: https://www.accord.edu.so/course/material/security-studies-328/pdf_content.

[29] Williams (2008), pp. 5–9. Also, this information is available on: https://www.accord.edu.so/course/material/security-studies-328/pdf_content.

[30] Pereira (2015), p. 194. Also, this information is also available on: https://www.researchgate.net/publication/283036911_Environmental_issues_and_international_relations_a_new_global_disorder_-_The_role_of_International_Relations_in_promoting_a_concerted_international_system.

life, health, education, food, and the right to have a family and a decent life.[31] These human rights are closely linked to the right to the environment.[32] At the international level, and during discussions between policymakers, the negotiations became focused on protecting the natural world and not deteriorating it to the extent that it would affect basic human rights, instead of focusing on national borders, state sovereignty, and state rights. Hence, new concepts emerged such as the need to focus on the security of individuals not only states. Social injustice and inequality between individuals resulting from the mismanagement of resources are all the result of a breach of global environmental justice.[33] Therefore, scarcity of resources, global financial crises, social inequality are all issues linked to environmental degradation that will endanger global security. As for the way to deal with this new threat, it is not clear yet, because countries are not used to dealing with such challenges.

Environmental threats are not confined to a particular country or region but are rather cross borders.[34] Thus, environmental protection requires a new type of international relations, which must focus on the development of individual cultures within local communities. Environmental security is not only associated with developing countries, but also includes developed countries. For example, the agricultural sector is a major source of income and stability in developing countries in Africa, Asia, and Latin America. This sector began to suffer from deterioration due to water scarcity, and climate change threatens the scarcity of water bodies resulting in the lack of agricultural areas. These factors will lead to the outbreak of wars as well as internal and regional conflicts. This will threaten societies and will have catastrophic effects on human rights. This frightening situation will have its effects on developed countries because poverty resulting from the loss of stability and work will push individuals into these societies to migrate to them. Certainly, this immigration has negative effects on the economies of America and Europe and will be a source of threat to the sovereignty of these countries. Hence, it can be said that poverty and environmental threats are the most important challenges facing international relations.

Among the risks that threaten international peace are environmental degradation and the economic crisis. Environmental degradation and climate change will lead to a lack of natural resources, which in turn will lead to financial and economic crises

[31] Schnurr and Swatuk (2012), p. 2.

[32] Meskic et al. (2022), p. 4.

[33] The report of the United Nations of Development Programme stated that: In many contexts "environmental degradation generates further poverty by the exhaustion of natural resources and creates prejudice to the exercise of basic rights. Poor and vulnerable communities suffer from various forms of environmental injustice, often unable to fight back and reverse trends which keep them mired in a state of exclusion. Without a paradigm shift in how natural resources and the environment are valued and governed, inequality will deepen and post-2015 development goals will be threatened, if not reversed. See: Environmental justice (n.d.): comparative experiences in legal empowerment. The report of the United Nations of Development Programme https://www.undp.org/sites/g/files/zskgke326/files/publications/Environmental-Justice-Comparative-Experiences.pdf, p. 5.

[34] Supra 1.

in the world.[35] The global recession will lead to the emergence of wars and regional conflicts and will lead to the emergence of tyrannical regimes. This explains the emergence of authoritarian political forces in Europe.

5 Environmental Security: The New Vouch for International Cooperation

In the light of a new world that will be governed by environmental changes, a new organization of international relations was necessary, which is not only based on states, state sovereignty, and state borders, but also on individuals and non-governmental institutions which must be involved in the decision-making process at the international level. This requires concerted efforts to find a solution to environmental problems, which are considered global problems. Problems that occur within a country will be transferred to the international space and vice versa. Therefore, the new organization of international relations must be based on the development of new knowledge about the political, economic, and social dynamics of the current world.

Considering that protecting the environment is a civilized necessity, the global mentality must be changed. So that it should focus on creating effective lifestyles based on the importance of protecting the environment.[36] Therefore, achieving the goals of the national interest is closely linked to the global interest, and vice versa whereas, local environmental crises must be addressed globally because environmental problems move from the local to the global sphere. So, that the northern part of the world cannot think arrogantly that it is the only one that can rid the world of its problems. Likewise, the southern section should not believe that its goals can only be achieved by cooperating with the countries of the south. Perhaps this cooperation will lead to the creation of a sustainable capitalism that can eliminate the current global division.[37] In the same way, solving environmental problems, and reaching the sustainable development should be through creating a global governance. For example, addressing the water scarcity crisis requires a global effective management of the causes that lead to this crisis, such as climate change, pollution, and population increase. However, in most international agreements that are related to environmental protection, we found that there is no serious political wish to protect the environment. This is reflected by the rule governing the issue of liability for the pollution. During the negotiation process, states push towards adopting general principles instead of adopting effective rules that may deter state parties from generating emissions and pollution. For discussing such a point in an-depth analysis,

---

[35] Pereira (2015), p. 198. This information is also available on: https://www.scielo.br/j/rbpi/a/kxF64drkXcz6QBT35kBVyvN/?format=pdf&lang=en.

[36] Ibid.

[37] Leggett (2013), p. 115.

the author will cover the issue of liability in the sea pollution as an example. Concerning sea pollution, it is clear that there is a lack of effective rules in the international agreements adopted for this purpose.

Theoretically, liability plays a very important role in any legal system including international law. Such a role is considered an essential guarantee for the application of these laws and regulations without violations. So, breaching the rules of responsibility will result in imposing compensations and reparations for the damages and injuries caused by the violation of national and international laws and regulations.

In practice, such rules are missing even if there are some rules on liability, however, such rules are not effective. For instance, the United Nations Convention on the Law of the Sea of 1982 has provided an independent section for the regulation of liability.

Section 9 of the chapter 2 includes some rules on protecting the sea against the pollution. Article 235 (2) stipulated that:

> States shall ensure that recourse is available in accordance with their legal systems for prompt and adequate compensation or other relief in respect of damage caused by pollution of the marine environment by natural or juridical persons under their jurisdiction.

Also, article 229 gives the injured persons the right to file a civil suit. Moreover, the third paragraph of the Article 235 invites States to cooperate in applying international law relating to responsibility and liability for the assessment of and compensation for damage and the settlement of related disputes, as well as to take procedures enabling the injured party to obtain satisfactory and effective compensation such as compulsory insurance or compensation funds.[38]

Article 232 added a new provision relating to liability:

> States shall be liable for damage or loss attributable to them arising from measures taken under section 6 when such measures are unlawful or exceed those reasonably required in the light of available information. States shall provide for recourse in their courts for actions in respect of such damage or loss.

This addition concerns liability for damages arising due to measures taken by states about intervention actions in areas beyond their national sovereignty. Thus, the sequence of articles setting out the rule of liability highlights the fact that the convention treats this question in a brief manner which is not appropriate to its importance in legal orders.

Also, in Article 235, the convention tries to distinguish the responsibility of States for its acts of sovereignty and its responsibility for the acts of natural and

[38] In the same sense the article 235 (3) provided that: with the objective of assuring prompt and adequate compensation in respect of all damage caused by pollution of the marine environment, States shall cooperate in the implementation of existing international law and the further development of international law relating to responsibility and liability for the assessment of and compensation for damage and the settlement of related disputes, as well as, where appropriate, development of criteria and procedures for payment of adequate compensation, such as compulsory insurance or compensation funds. See the International Convention of the Protection of the Sea (n.d.). https://www.un.org/depts/los/convention_agreements/texts/unclos/unclos_e.pdf.

legal persons, speaking about the subject of relevance to the jurisdiction of States (i.e., the responsibility of the States for the activities of its citizens), which is undesirable in international rules.[39]

Another gap in the convention is the use of imprecise terms. The convention established the responsibility of the states for the "damage caused by pollution of the marine environment by natural or juridical persons under their jurisdiction". In the absolute sense of the term, many questions arise because of the vague meaning of this term. Does that mean "subordination"? If so, what can we say about foreigners residing in that State? Will they be responsible for polluting the marine environment?! The convention fails to specify the legal relationship between States and the persons subordinate to them. Likewise, introducing texts talking about. "Civil liability" in articles that are not intended for this issue makes things vaguer, as is the case in article 229. Such texts must, a fortiori, be given to articles intended for the subject of civil liability, instead of introducing them into articles intended for repressive liability.

Furthermore, it adopts the theory of illegal actions as the origin of all international responsibility, at a time when many voices call for adopting the theory of risk because of the continuous increase in damages resulting from illegal activities, especially in the field of the marine environment.[40]

In conclusion, nothing new in this convention regarding the rules of international responsibility. On the contrary, it is vague, as we have found, in an unjustifiable way.

6 Conclusion and Findings

International cooperation should be the steering wheel for sustainable development. At present, it seems that the levels of international cooperation are not sufficient to meet the requirements of sustainability in the absence of international institutions supervising this matter.

For example, when it comes to the environment, the international community avoids establishing an international organization concerned with environmental affairs, and granting it a supreme authority that is higher than that of states. Climate agreements, for example, are applied voluntarily only without the existence of a supreme authority that has jurisdiction independent of the authority of states and has the power to enforce international environmental law.

It is assumed that the United Nations, as a university for the countries of the world, is the appropriate place to discuss environmental issues and related laws. That is why many bodies related to development were established, such as the Economic and Social Council and the United Nations Development Program, whose status was changed in 1992 to include sustainable development. This organization

---

[39] Abd Alwareth (2006), p. 151.

[40] Hashim (1986), p. 253.

recognized all countries, regardless of their size. Small states have the right to discuss and vote on international issues, even if in theory. But in reality, this international organization is not as effective as it should be when it comes to discussing sustainable development issues. The issues of sustainable development and global environmental security are issues of concern to people in the first place, and environmental security has become a human and social necessity not only an issue of states. This organization does not involve those who are concerned with environmental issues such as individuals and non-governmental organizations that were not party to any agreement on sustainable development and environmental protection.

The research demonstrated that there is no international consensus or wish to adopt obligatory rules in terms of environmental protection. This is clear when analytically discussing the effectiveness of the issue of responsibility for pollution in international agreements related to protecting the marine environment from pollution. If it was said that Agenda 21 recognized indigenous people, youth, women and their role in development, this matter does not go beyond theoretical points that were adopted as a matter of courtesy only without acknowledging their binding role in development issues, and this is considered a marginalization of them and not an acknowledgment.

The structure of the United Nations is essentially feudal. It includes more than thirty organs and sixteen agencies which are specialized in different fields such as education, labor, health, food, agriculture, telecommunications, and industrial development. However, if we examine these programs, we will find that they focus on sectorial development without sustainability.

Also, one of the obstacles that impede effective international cooperation is the variety of views on the difference in priorities between sustainable development and the protection of the environment.

When it comes to international cooperation, there is a big problem, which is the difference in visions and goals between the countries of the rich countries of the North sphere and the poor countries of the South sphere. The countries of the North do not want to make financial commitments that constitute an economic burden on them. Therefore, they do not wish to focus on binding themselves in sustainability agreements, but rather they wish to focus on issues of environmental protection such as climate change, water, biodiversity, and forests. Regarding sustainability, they want to define general principles rather than binding legal texts. Developing countries want to find international agreements between countries that focus on sustainable development and take into account the needs of each party. Fighting poverty and ignorance can only be achieved by concluding agreements to promote sustainable development in poor countries. According to their point of view, environmental problems are caused by consumption patterns in rich countries, which are abusive and non-rational. They also consider the unfair structure of the international system as one of the reasons that led to the absence of a comprehensive international agreement on development and the environment. Therefore, these fundamental differences between the two sides, it seems difficult to find solid cooperation between these countries. But with the emergence of environmental disasters that have threatened the world as a whole, it has emerged that environmental security will become the center of new international relations because environmental security is more comprehensive and requires the establishment of a new international relations system.

The study spots light on the fact that that global peace is closely related to environmental peace and security, as environmental threats can pose a global threat. This is a great opportunity for international cooperation. This made the environment a major focus in the new perspective of international relations, and an area for cooperation between states and individuals. An important conclusion was reached; the environment has become an influential factor at the global level. Environmental threats have proven that the world cannot be managed by one pole, but all countries in the North and South must cooperate to find effective governance of global environmental resources. And we saw that a country or a region is not able alone to solve intercontinental environmental problems. Here it is worth mentioning that globalization and the transformation of the world into a small village can be a field and opportunity for cooperation between countries to solve environmental problems. It has also been proven that economic development cannot be sustainable without adopting green economy policies, which will lead to the emergence of the term sustainable capitalism. Eventually, global division will be eliminated. Based on the above-mentioned findings, the research will shed light on the following recommendations, and suggestions:

1. The international law should be the main framework that should govern the issue of sustainable development. International law must be the umbrella for all international negotiations related to the environment and sustainable development.
2. With regard to international agreements, clear and unambiguous agreements must be adopted. The rules of responsibility must be clear and binding on parties. Moreover, such agreements must create an international instrument to supervise, and control the implementation of these agreements with a supreme authority.
3. The importance of establishing an international organization specialized in the field of environment and sustainable development, and granting it the authority to monitor countries with regard to relevant agreements. This organization must have binding authority
4. As the issues of sustainable development and global environmental security has become a human and social necessity and not only an issue of states, other actors should be involved in all international negotiations related to sustainable development and global environmental issues. Such actors may include individuals, civil actors, academics, and non-governmental organizations such as Greenpeace, and WWF, and others.
5. In international negotiations, the views, and approaches of states (north and south hemispheres) must be unified on the importance of the environment and sustainable development. It must be considered that providing sustainable protection for all environmental elements in each country will ultimately lead to providing sustainable protection for the global environment. Thus, achieving the goals of sustainable development is an urgent social and economic need. This

will lead to establish the base of environmental peace and security globally and nationally speaking.

Acknowledgements The author would like to thank Prince Sultan University for supporting this publication. Special acknowledgement is given to the Governance and Policy Design Research Lab (GPDRL) at Prince Sultan University (PSU) for their academic support to conduct this research and publish it in a reputable journal.

References

Abd Alwareth A-A (2006) The protection of the marine environment in international and national Legislation, Cairo. University Office, Cairo University, pp 1–286

Albakjaji M (2022) The responsibility for environmental damages during armed conflicts: the case of the war between Russia and Ukraine. Access Justice Eastern Eur 4-2(17):82–101. https://doi.org/10.33327/AJEE-18-5.4-a000444

Albakjaji M, Almarzoqi R (2023) The impact of digital technology on international relations: the case of the war between Russia and Ukraine. Access Justice Eastern Eur 2(19):1–17. https://doi.org/10.33327/AJEE-18-6.2-a000203

Brown H (1954) The challenge of man's future. New York: Viking. In: Thomas W (ed) Man's role in changing the face of the earth. University of Chicago Press, Chicago

Dalby S (2008) Security studies: environmental change. In: Williams PD (ed) Security Studies: An Introduction. Routledge, New York, pp 260–273. Also, this information is available on: https://www.accord.edu.so/course/material/security-studies-328/pdf_content. Accessed 12 Mar 2023

Dauvergne P (2008) The shadows of consumption: consequences for the global environment. MIT Press, Cambridge, pp 3–17. This information is also available on: http://mitp-content-server.mit.edu:18180/books/content/sectbyfn?collid=books_pres_0&id=7706&fn=9780262514927_sch_0001.pdf. Accessed on 12 Feb 2023

Deliani A, Sugito M (2021) E3S Web of Conferences 316, 04015. Greenpeace's role in pressuring the india government to overcome air pollution 2015–2018, pp 1–14. Also this information is available on: https://www.e3s-conferences.org/articles/e3sconf/pdf/2021/92/e3sconf_iconard2021_04015.pdf

Environmental justice (n.d.) Comparative experiences in legal empowerment. The report of the United Nations of Development Programme https://www.undp.org/sites/g/files/zskgke326/files/publications/Environmental-Justice-Comparative-Experiences.pdf. pp 1–34

Galaz V (2014) Global environmental governance, technology and politics: the anthropocene gap. Edward Elgar, Cheltenham, pp 1–15. Also, this information is available on: https://www.researchgate.net/publication/266259778_Global_Environmental_Governance_Technology_And_Politics_-_The_Anthropocene_Gap

Guzman A (2011) The consent problem in international law. Berkeley Program in L. & Econ. P, UC Berkeley, pp 1–63. Also, this reference is available on: https://escholarship.org/uc/item/04x8x174

Hashim S (1986) International responsibility for pollution of the marine environment. Ed. Dar Alnahda, Cairo, pp 1–634

Leggett J (2013) The energy of nations: risk blindness and the road to renaissance. Routledge, New York, pp 1–272

Litfin K (1995) Ozone discourses: science and politics in international environmental cooperation. Columbia University Press, New York, pp 1–257

Martinez J (1952) Great smog of London: environmental disaster. Britannica. This reference is available on: https://www.britannica.com/event/Great-Smog-of-London

Meskic Z, Albakjaji M, Jevremovic N, Omerovic E, Adams J (2022) Digitalization and innovation in achieving SDGs –impacts on legislation and practice. IOP Conf Ser Earth Environ Sci 1026:012061. https://doi.org/10.1088/1755-1315/1026/1/012061. p 1–11. Also, this reference is available on: https://iopscience.iop.org/article/10.1088/1755-1315/1026/1/012061/pdf
Molina M, Rowland F (1974) Stratospheric sink for chlorofluoromethanes: chlorine atom-catalysed destruction of ozone. Nature 249:810–812. https://doi.org/10.1038/249810a0
Pereira CJ (2015) Environmental issues and international relations, a new global (dis)order – the role of International Relations in promoting a concerted international system. Revista Brasileira de Política Internacional 58(1):191–205. This information is also available on: https://www.researchgate.net/publication/283036911_Environmental_issues_and_international_relations_a_new_global_disorder_-_The_role_of_International_Relations_in_promoting_a_concerted_international_system
Radkau J (2014) The age of ecology: a global history. Polity, Cambridge, p xiii-546
Satellite Observations of the Earth's Environment (n.d.) Accelerating the Transition of Research to Operations. The National Academies Press. https://doi.org/10.17226/10658. National research council of the national academies. https://nap.nationalacademies.org/read/10658/chapter/5
Savaresi A (2016) The Paris agreement: a new beginning? J Energy Natl Resources Law 34(1):16–26. Also, this reference is available on: https://www.tandfonline.com/doi/pdf/10.1080/02646811.2016.1133983?casa_token=jVe0FrZ3DLoAAAAA:MDkXXY8J92oIv1G3t_7LHTS1V5sxZRxrF7ilHF7QeaRVljc03ME2uLrSGRdmofWCYDA23P__J-k
Schnurr MA, Swatuk LS (2012) Towards critical environmental security. In: Natural resources and social conflict. Palgrave Macmillan, London, pp 1–14
Sherwood Rowland F (1996) Beyond discovery: the path from research to human benefit. The report of National Academies of Sciences, Engineering, and Medicine. In: The ozone depletion phenomenon. The National Academies Press, Washington, DC. https://doi.org/10.17226/9042. https://nap.nationalacademies.org/read/9042/chapter/1
Soroos MS (1997) The Endangered Atmosphere: preserving a global commons. University of South Columbia Press, Columbia, pp 1–360
Sosa-Nunez G (2016) Transversal environmental policies. In: Environment, climate change and international relations, pp 87–98. This information is also available on: https://www.e-ir.info/publication/environment-climate-change-and-international-relations/
Stulajter M (2017) Problem of enforcement of an international law analysis of law enforcement mechanisms of the United Nations and the World Trade Organization. J Mod Sci 33:325–335. Also, this reference is available on: https://www.jomswsge.com/pdf-79753-15801?filename=Problem%20of%20enforcementof.pdf
Swatuk LA (2006) Environmental security. In: Palgrave advances in international environmental politics, pp 203–236. Also this information is available on: https://www.academia.edu/380348/Environmental_Security
The Ecologist (ed) (1993) Whose common future? Reclaiming the commons. Earthscan Publications, London. This reference is also available on: https://wjsmith.faculty.unlv.edu/smithtest/The%20Ecologist%201993%20Whose%20Common%20Future.pdf
The impact of disasters and crises on agriculture and food security (2021). The report of Food and Agriculture Organization. This reference is available on: https://www.fao.org/3/cb3673en/cb3673en.pdf
The International Convention of the Protection of the Sea. https://www.un.org/depts/los/convention_agreements/texts/unclos/unclos_e.pdf
The Us Department of the Interior: https://www.boem.gov/environment/environmental-assessment/migratory-bird-treaty-act-mbta
Treaty on the Non-Proliferation of nuclear weapons (NPT). The United Nations/Office for disarmament affairs: https://disarmament.unoda.org/wmd/nuclear/npt/
Turco R, Toon OB, Ackerman TP, Pollack JB, Sagan C (1983) Nuclear winter: global consequences of multiple nuclear explosions. Science 222(4630):1283–1292. Also, this information is available on: https://chuvaprataguerra.files.wordpress.com/2018/04/ttaps1983.pdf

United Nations Environment Programme (UNEP) (n.d.) Dramatic growth in laws to protect environment, but widespread failure to enforce, finds report. This reference is available on the websites of the United Nations Environment Programme (UNEP): https://www.unep.org/news-and-stories/press-release/dramatic-growth-laws-protect-environment-widespread-failureenforce#:~:text=Between%202002%20and%202013%2C%20908,197%20environmental%20defenders%20were%20murdered

United Nations Environmental Programme [UNEP], Environmental Rule of Law First Global Report (2019). https://wedocs.unep.org/bitstream/handle/20.500.11822/27279/Environmental_rule_of_law.pdf?sequence=1&isAllowed=y

United States Environmental Protection Agency: https://www.epa.gov/enforcement/federal-facilities-and-other-environmental-laws-and-international-environmental

Vogler J (1995) Introduction. The environment in International Relations: legacies and contentions. In: The environment and international relations. Routledge, London, pp 1–21

Wattas J (2018) Almost four environmental defenders a week killed in 2017. The Guardian (Fri, 2 Feb 2018). This reference is available on: https://www.theguardian.com/environment/2018/feb/02/almost-four-environmental-defenders-a-week-killed-in-2017

Williams P (2008) Security studies: an introduction. In: Williams PD (ed) Security studies: an introduction. Routledge, New York, pp 1–10. Also, this information is available on: https://www.accord.edu.so/course/material/security-studies-328/pdf_content

Part II
European Law Section

Analysis of New Rule on Form of Power of Attorney in Serbian Law with Reference to Legal Approaches in Selected European Countries

Nikolina Miščević

1 Introduction

Until the entry into force of the Law on Amendments and Supplement to the Law on Obligations[1] in 2020 (LASLObl), in the law of the Republic of Serbia the parallelism of forms between the power of attorney and the contract concluded by the authorised person on behalf of the principal (main contract) was in force. Article 90 of the Law on Obligations from 1978[2] (LObl) stipulated that "the form prescribed by law for a contract or other legal transaction shall apply also to the power of attorney for concluding such contract, i.e., for undertaking that transaction." At the time of the adoption of this law, the following three forms were existent in Serbian legal system: real form, written form and signature verification performed by the court. With the development of modern technologies, the new electronic form of the contract has been introduced, which, under certain conditions, can replace the written form.[3] In addition, with the adoption of the Law on Notary Public Office in 2011[4]

[1] Law on Amendments and Supplement to the Law on Obligations (LASLObl), Official Gazette of RS, No. 18/2020.

[2] Law on Obligations (LObl), Official Gazette of SFR of Yugoslavia, No. 29/78, 39/85, 45/89—decision of Constitutional Court of Yugoslavia and 57/89, Official Gazette of FR of Yugoslavia, No. 31/93, Official Gazette of Serbia and Montenegro, No. 1/2003—Constitutional Charter and Official Gazette of Republic of Serbia, No. 18/2020.

[3] See more in Miščević (2019), pp. 1641–1661.

[4] Law on Notary Public Office (LNPO), Official Gazette of RS, no. 31/2011, 85/2012, 19/2013, 55/2014—other laws, 93/2014—other laws, 121/2014, 6/2015 and 106/2015. Implementation of

N. Miščević (✉)
Faculty of Law Novi Sad, Department for Civil Law, Novi Sad, Serbia
e-mail: nmiscevic@pf.uns.ac.rs

E. Omerović et al. (eds.), *Balkan Yearbook of European and International Law 2023*, Balkan Yearbook of European and International Law 2023,
https://doi.org/10.1007/978-3-031-69670-1_4

(LNPO), two new types of forms were introduced—a notary public record and a notary public confirmed (solemnized) private document, whereas the signature verification was transferred to the jurisdiction of notaries public instead of the court. After the introduction of new, stricter types of contract forms, the question arose whether it is necessary to maintain the rule on parallelism of forms of the contract and the power of attorney given for its conclusion. In other words, does the power of attorney have to be drawn up in the same form even in the case where the form of a notary public record or a notary public confirmed (solemnized) private document is prescribed by the law for a specific contract, or should it be allowed to draw up a power of attorney in a milder form?

The LNPO provides three types of notarial forms of obligation contracts: a notary public record, a notary public confirmed (solemnized) private document, and a notary public signature verification. All three types of forms imply the participation of a notary public as a holder of public authority, a neutral expert who acts in accordance with the principles of impartiality, independence, confidentiality, instruction, the principle of free access to the notary, *numerus clausus* and the principle of territoriality.[5] These types of notarial forms of obligation contracts differ from each other according to the degree of engagement of the notary public in the process of concluding the contract.

The least strict form is the notary public signature verification. This type of form had existed in the legal system of the Republic of Serbia even before the introduction of notary public profession, whereby the verification of signatures had been performed by the court. With this type of form, by adding an appropriate clause, the notary public confirms that the document was indeed signed by the person named in it as its signatory. On such occasion, the notary public does not examine the content of the contract, nor does he/she instruct the parties[6] about the legal scope of the contract they conclude. Therefore, the document containing the contract has the status of a public document only in the part where the signature is verified. This type of form is prescribed by law for the contract on conversion of a separate part of the building into a common part and the contract on disposal of common parts of the building,[7] contracts on transfer of shares between partners, contracts on transfer of shares in a limited liability company, contracts on transfer of shares in companies

---

the law began in 2014.

[5] See more in Miščević (2022), pp. 47–59.

[6] In the LNPO, the term "party" is used, by which the party in the formal sense is meant, that is, a person who declares his will before a notary public, either on his own behalf or on someone else's behalf. A party in the material sense is a person in relation to whom a declaration of will made before a notary public produces legal effect. Therefore, if one contracting party concludes the contract through an authorised person, the authorised person is considered a party in the formal sense, and his principal a party in the material sense. See more in Miščević (2022), pp. 145–146.

[7] See art. 6, para. 2 and art. 9, para. 3 and 4 of the Law on Housing and Maintenance of Buildings, Official Gazette of RS, No. 104/2016 and 9/2020—other law.

that are not public joint stock companies, memorandums of association, the contract on status change, etc.[8]

On the other hand, the notary public record and notary public confirmed (solemnized) private documents had not existed in the legal system of the Republic of Serbia before the adoption of the LNPO. A notary public record is a document about legal transactions and statements drawn up by a notary public.[9] It represents the strictest type of form which implies the highest degree of notary public involvement. With this type of contract form, the document is drawn up in its entirety by a notary public. He first examines the intentions of the contracting parties and establishes the facts and then formulates the text of the contract so that the legal goal the contracting parties are striving for can clearly emerge from it. On that occasion, the notary public is obliged to educate the parties about the legal scope of the contract which they are concluding, that is, to inform them of the legal consequences and risks arising from the contract they wish to conclude. In this way, he helps the contracting parties to conclude a contract that corresponds to their interests or not to conclude it if it is not in accordance with their interests or if it does not lead to the legal goal that they intend to achieve by concluding the contract. Consequently, the notary public record is intended for the contracts that carry the greatest risk or particularly severe legal consequences for one or both parties to the contract. The Serbian legislator opted for this type of form in contracts on transfer of immovable property of legally incapacitated persons, agreements on legal support, as well as in mortgage contracts or pledge statements that contain an explicit statement of the obliged person that he/she agrees to the direct enforcement be it by judicial or extra-judicial proceedings.[10]

A notary public confirmed (solemnized) private document is the second strictest type of form in the law of the Republic of Serbia. It differs from a notary public record in that the document is drawn up by the parties, whereas a private document drawn up in this way acquires the status of a public document upon its confirmation by a notary public. By solemnization, the notary public confirms that the content of the private document corresponds to the will of the parties. Like a notary public record, this type of form is separated from the others by the instructive function. During the solemnization, the notary public examines the content of the private document, establishes the facts, examines the intentions of the contracting parties, and makes sure that they are appropriately expressed in the submitted document. He examines whether the content of the document is adequate to produce the legal effect that the parties seek and instructs the parties about the legal scope and consequences of their declarations of will. The form of a notary public confirmed (solemnized) private document in Serbian law is prescribed in several laws for various

[8] See art. 97, para. 1 and 2, art. 175, para. 1, art. 261, para. 2, art. 264, para. 2, art. 491, para. 4, art. 492, para. 4 of the Companies Act, Official Gazette of the RS, 36/2011, 99/2011, 83/2014 (other laws), 5/2015, 44/2018, 95/2018, 91/2019, 109/2021.

[9] Art. 6 LNPO.

[10] See art. 82 LNPO.

contracts, amongst which are the contracts on transfer of immovable property,[11] mortgage contracts and pledge statements that do not contain an explicit statement by the obligated person that he/she agrees to the immediate enforcement, a contract by which real and personal servitudes are established,[12] a contract on the assignment and distribution of property during life, a lifetime support contract, a contract on the transfer of inheritance,[13] an agreement on the division of joint property of spouses, a marriage contract and a contract on the management and disposal of joint property.[14]

Depending on the degree of engagement of the notary public in the conclusion of a contract, the notary forms of the contract ensure a greater degree of protection of interests of the contracting parties, the public interest, or the interests of the third parties. However, the conclusion of a contract in a certain form is time-consuming, and implies financial costs, which represents an additional burden for contractors, and consequently can lead to a slowdown in legal transactions. Therefore, a deviation from the principle of informality should be reserved only for particularly justified cases when it is necessary for the protection of interests that may be threatened by the conclusion of a specific type of contract, i.e. for the fulfilment of certain legal and political goals. And even then, it is necessary to determine the optimal type of form that will be adequate for the achievement of the stated goals while preserving to the greatest extent possible the freedom of contract, not hampering the speed of legal transactions and taking care of the budget of the contracting parties.[15]

For the same reason, it is necessary to carefully approach the selection of the form in which the power of attorney should be given in order to conclude a certain contract. That is, it is necessary to examine whether the granting of the power of attorney in a less strict form enables the circumvention of the goal pursued by the legislator when prescribing the form of the main contract. Specifically, in judicial practice, the question arose as to whether a contract for which the form of a notary public record or notary public confirmed (solemnized) private document is prescribed by the law should be considered valid even when it was concluded based on a power of attorney on which only the principal's signature was verified.

---

[11] Contract on transfer of immovable property is the generic term for all the contracts by which ownership of an immovable property is transferred from one contract party to another with or without compensation, such as sale or a gift of immovable property.

[12] See art. 93, para. 2 LNPO.

[13] See art. 184, para. 1, 195, paragraph 1 and art. 231, para. 2 of the Inheritance Law, Official Gazette of RS, 46/95, 101/2003—decision of CC of RS and 6/2015.

[14] See art. 179, para. 2, art. 188, paragraph 2 and Art. 189, para. 5 of the Family Law, Official Gazette of RS, No. 18/2005, 72/2011, 6/2015.

[15] Miščević (2022), pp. 1–2.

2 Practice After the Adoption of the LNPO

Different answers to this question appeared in practice, usually in cases of conclusion of contracts on transfer of immovable property, in situations where the principal's signature on the power of attorney was verified by a diplomatic consular representation or a court. Namely, with the adoption of the LNPO, the rule requiring the form of signature verification for contracts on transfer of immovable property was derogated. Instead, the LNPO first stipulated the form of a notary public record for these contracts, whereas the amendment to that Law from 2015 stipulated the form of a notary public confirmed (solemnized) private document. The previously mentioned rule of the LObl on the parallelism of forms between the contract and the power of attorney given for its conclusion was still in force. This meant that the power of attorney given for the purpose of concluding a contract on transfer of immovable property had to be given in the same form. However, even after the beginning of application of the LNPO, diplomatic and consular representations continued the practice of verifying the principal's signature on the power of attorney for the conclusion of a contract on transfer of immovable property in the territory of the Republic of Serbia.[16] After that, notaries public refused to solemnize contracts on transfer of immovable property that were concluded on the basis of the power of attorney granted in this form.[17] The contractors filed objections to these decisions of the notaries public to the competent courts, which took different positions on this issue. According to one point of view, a power of attorney on which only the signature of the principal is verified by a diplomatic consular representation is valid, whilst, according to the other a power of attorney created in this way is null and void.[18]

In addition to the powers of attorney certified by diplomatic and consular representations, contracts on transfer of immovable property concluded in the territories of municipalities and cities where notaries public had not yet been appointed at the time of the conclusion of the contract also appeared problematic in practice. Until the appointment of notaries public in these territories, the confirmation (solemnization) of private documents was supposed to be performed by the basic courts in accordance with the law.[19]

[16] Đurđević (2016), p. 271.

[17] See decision of notary public N. Antić (Kruševac), OPU 138/2015, dated May 18, 2015; decision of the notary public D. Divac (Belgrade—Voždovac), OPU 281/2016, dated March 10, 2016; decision of notary public S. Soro (Novi Sad), OPU 802/2016, dated June 1, 2016. Listed according to Đurđević (2016), p. 271.

[18] See decision of the Basic Court in Kruševac, R-jb 1/15, dated May 29, 2015; decision of the Second Basic Court in Belgrade, R-jb 1/16, dated March 21, 2016; decision of the Basic Court in Novi Sad, RJB 5/16, dated June 3, 2016; decision of the High Court in Novi Sad, Gž.JB 1/2016, dated July 26, 2016. Listed according to Đurđević (2016), p. 271.

[19] Art. 9 of the Law on Amendments to the Law on Notary Public Office of January 22, 2015, *Official Gazette* of RS, No. 6/15.

One example of such a case is the contract on the gift of immovable property, which was concluded before the Basic Court in Trstenik. Namely, the court confirmed (solemnized) the contract on transfer of immovable property based on Article 9 of the Law on Amendments to the Law on Notary Public Office from January 22, 2015, because at that time there was still no notary public appointed in this municipality.[20] However, the special powers of attorney on the basis of which this contract was concluded were not drawn up in the same form, but the court only certified the signature of the owner on them. After that, court proceedings were initiated to determine the nullity of the contract on transfer of immovable property. In the court proceedings, it was emphasized that powers of attorney that were not granted in the required form are null and void, making the contract concluded thereupon null and void. In the first-instance proceedings, the Basic Court in Trstenik accepted the claim and declared the contract on transfer of immovable property null and void. In the explanation of the decision, the court referred to Article 90 of the LObl on the parallelism forms of power of attorney and the contract concluded thereupon and Article 93a of the LNPO on the solemnization of a private document. However, in the second-instance proceedings, the Court of Appeal in Kragujevac repealed this decision and referred it back to the first-instance court for a retrial. In the explanation of the decision, this court took the position according to which the subject contract on the gift of immovable property, as well as the powers of attorney, are valid and drawn up in the appropriate form. Nevertheless, the reasoning given by this court deserves criticism. Namely, the Court of Appeal first pointed out that at the time of the conclusion of the contract on the gift of immovable property in the area of Trstenik, there were no notaries public, and that their function was performed by the Basic Court. Also, it stated that the powers of attorney were authenticated by a judge who was authorized to perform solemnization in accordance with Article 93a of the LNPO, which then solemnized the contract on the gift of immovable property on the basis of the powers of attorney created in this way.[21] This part of the explanation of the judgment of the Court of Appeal seems contradictory. On the one hand, pointing to the absence of a notary public in the subject area at the time of concluding the contract leads to the conclusion that the court did not have the authority to solemnize the document, and that, until the appointment of a notary public, it should have performed the certification of documents in the same way as it has done before the implementation of the LNPO. On the other hand, emphasizing that the gift contract was solemnized in accordance with Article 93a of the LNPO, and that it was made in the appropriate form indicates that, according to the understanding of the Court of Appeal, the authority of the judge of the Basic Court to solemnize a private document is not disputed, in accordance with Article 9 by the Law on Amendments to the Law on Notary Public Office of January 22, 2015. Apart from the aforementioned contradiction, a special criticism should be given to the part of the explanation that states that the LNPO does not explicitly stipulate that the

[20] Verdict of the Appellate Court in Kragujevac GŽ-1756/17 dated April 27, 2018.

[21] *Ibid.*

power of attorney given for the purpose of concluding a contract for which the form of a solemnized private document is required must be drawn up in the same form.[22] At this point, the Court of Appeal completely ignored the general rule from then applicable Article 90 of the LObl on the absolute parallelism of forms between the power of attorney and the main contract when a mandatory form is prescribed for the main contract. In this way, this court also disregarded the part of the explanation of the first-instance decision in which this rule in addition to Article 93a of the LNPO was mentioned as the basis for decision-making.

The presented case shows the diversity of judicial practice, which encouraged the Serbian doctrine, as well as the legislator, to examine the need to maintain the rule on the unexceptional parallelism of forms of power of attorney and main contract. More precisely, it was indispensable to answer the question of whether it is necessary for the power of attorney to mirror the main contract in terms of form, and whether the valid issuance of the power of attorney requires it to be drawn up in the form of a notary public record, or a notary public confirmed (solemnized) private document. The answer lies in the answer to another question: whether issuing of a power of attorney in a less strict form can circumvent the goal, that is, the function of the form of the main contract.[23]

In order to answer this question, it is necessary to first present the different goals for which the legislator prescribes a mandatory form for a specific contract, i.e. the functions that the form should serve in a given case.

3 Functions of the Contract Form

According to the German author *Mankowski*, "dealing with the question of form in the first line means dealing with the purpose of the prescribed form."[24] Apart from the term "purpose of the prescribed form", the term "function of the form" is also used in theory, and their meaning is the same. They both denote the goal that the legislator strives to achieve by prescribing the mandatory form of the contract, that is, the task that the form should perform in a specific case.[25] As a rule, they are aimed at protecting certain interests. Therefore, one cannot talk about the form of power of attorney without considering its functions, but also the functions of the form of the main contract.

In legal theory, various functions of the contract form are mentioned. While some authors distinguish only two functions—evidential and protective, others list

[22] *Ibid.*

[23] See the Explanation of the Proposal for the Law on Amendments to the Law on Obligations.

[24] Mankowski (2010), p. 662.

[25] Miščević (2022), p. 70.

several different functions.[26] For example, *Mankowski* mentions as many as 14 different functions of form.[27] On the one hand, in order to determine the optimal type of form for a specific contract, it is important to make a more detailed distinction from dividing the functions of the form of the contract into protective and evidential. On the other hand, it is necessary to single out as independent only those functions, that is, goals that represent justified reasons for deviating from one of the most important principles of the law of obligations—the principle of informality. By applying the latter criterion, as well as by avoiding the separate allocation of functions that are already covered by some other function, the division stated by *Mankowski* is significantly narrowed, but it is certainly more complex than the dual division into evidentiary and protective functions. Thus, the independent functions of the form can certainly be considered to be the evidential function, the function of publicity, the function of control, the warning function, and the instructive function.[28]Amongst them, from the point of view of the topic of this paper, the warning function and the instructive function are the most important.

The *warning function* implies the protection of contractual parties from a hasty commitment. Namely, according to *Savigny*, "for legal transactions, it is preferable that contracts are not concluded hastily, but with careful consideration of the consequences arising therefrom."[29] This author states that the nature of a formal contract is aimed at "awakening reasonable consideration".[30] Similarly, *Jhering* speaks of the form as "an alarm clock for legal consciousness".[31] Therefore, by imposing a mandatory form for a certain contract, the contracting parties are given yet another chance to consider the importance and consequences of the contract when completing the required formalities and to soberly decide on its conclusion. Therefore, it can be said that the mandatory form of the contract does not necessarily mean only a limitation of the freedom of contracting, that is, private autonomy, but it can also

[26] More about the different understandings of the authors about the functions of the form see in Miščević (2022), pp. 70–97.

[27] Mankowski (2010), pp. 662–668.

[28] In addition, we can also talk about the functions of authentication and identification if they are viewed from the aspect of specific types of form, in e.g., in German law, which recognises a less strict form than the written one. Namely, the textual form from par. 126b of the German Civil Code implies only the legible expression of the content of the will in textual form with the name of the declarant and storage on a permanent data carrier. It does not contain the handwritten signature of the declarant of the will, and simply stating his name cannot provide a sufficiently strong and certain connection with the personality of the declarant of the will. On the other hand, in those systems in which the least strict type of form is a written form that also includes the handwritten signature of the declarant of the will, it can be said that there is no point in singling out the authentication and identification functions because they are already covered by the evidential function.

[29] von Savigny (1853), p. 219.

[30] *Ibid.*

[31] von Jhering (1926), p. 498. *Lorenz* also spoke about the function of the form to awaken legal awareness, encourage reasonable consideration and "enhance the seriousness of voluntary decision-making in accordance with the social significance of the decision." See Lorenz (1958), p. 393.

serve as a means of its protection.[32] For the same reason, it is said that the form of the contract "protects private autonomy from itself",[33] as well as that it protects "negative freedom of contract,[34] that is, the freedom of the parties not to conclude the contract. The warning function of the form can also be aimed at the protection of only one contractual party in contracts from which a significant risk or obligation arises for only one contractual party, such as e.g. the contract of guarantee or gift contract. This function can be achieved with any type of form since each formality to a certain extent influences the contracting parties to consider more carefully the importance and legal consequences of the contract they intend to conclude. However, the extent of the warning function depends on the strictness of the form. A stricter form implies more formalities, and thus more opportunities to prevent one or both parties from hastily entering into a contractual relationship.

The *instructive function* in the law of the Republic of Serbia can be realized only by the two strictest types of contract form—a notary public record and a notary public confirmed (solemnized) private document. When drawing up a notary public record or solemnizing a private document, the notary public, as a qualified, independent, and impartial expert, is obliged to provide the parties with the necessary information and instructions on the consequences of the contract they are about to conclude. Therefore, these types of forms are reserved for legal transactions with particularly high risk or serious legal consequences. The instructive function provides additional protection to the parties compared to the warning function. Moreover, the instruction provided by a notary public ensures that the warning function is exercised to the fullest extent. As stated before, the warning function means the protection of the contractual parties from hasty commitment. By imposing certain formalities, an effort is made to ensure that the parties make a thoughtful decision. For this reason, it is necessary for potential contractors to be familiar with the relevant facts, to understand the importance and legal consequences of the contract they conclude and the risks arising accordingly. In the case of certain contracts, the legislator estimated that it is not enough to provide the contractors with additional time, that is, the opportunity to consider the legal effects of the contract themselves and to decide on its conclusion. Namely, there are contracts which are particularly complex, carry particularly high risks or severe consequences that parties who do not have legal education are often unaware of. As a result, there is a significant probability that these parties, due to the lack of necessary knowledge and skills, conclude a contract which effect they do not want or that they formulate their declarations of will in a vague, imprecise manner. Consequently, the likelihood that such a contractual relationship will give rise to future disputes also increases. Therefore, in the case of such contracts, the legislator decides to ensure a clear picture and awareness of the contracting parties about the legal consequences and risks arising from the contract they wish to conclude by providing instruction from a notary public as an

---

[32] See more in Miščević (2022), pp. 15–17.

[33] Häsemeyer (1971), p. 172; Mankowski (2010), p. 665.

[34] Arnet (2013), pp. 403–404.

impartial expert. In this way, the equality of the parties is also protected, that is, it is prevented that the factual inequality between the contracting parties be transferred to the legal relationship based on the conclusion of the contract. Namely, there may be a factual inequality between the contracting parties as a result of significant differences in intelligence, knowledge or experience regarding the subject of the contract. With the participation of a notary public who adjusts the scope of instruction to the specific circumstances and needs of each party, it is ensured that both parties, with the necessary knowledge and understanding, effectively use the opportunity to participate in the formation of a legal relationship.[35] In this context, *Arnet* states that the warning function protects the freedom of a person not to conclude a contract (negative freedom of contract), and the instructive function protects the freedom to regulate one's own legal relationships (positive freedom of contract).[36]

4 Deviation from the Strict Parallelism of Forms of Power of Attorney and Main Contract: Arguments of the Doctrine and the Legislator

Considering the previously presented situation in practice that followed the introduction of stricter types of form in Serbian doctrine the question arose of whether the unexceptional parallelism of forms between the power of attorney and the main contract must be required even when one of the two strictest types of forms has been stipulated for the main contract. In Serbian doctrine only *Đurđević* dealt with the form of power of attorney and its relationship to the form of main contract in the context of introduction of new forms of contract into the legal system of the Republic of Serbia. He analysed this topic in the most detail, examining the possibility of achieving goals, i.e. examining the function of the form of the main contract in case of giving power of attorney informally or in a less strict form.[37]

In his work, *Đurđević* separately analyses each type of form that involves drawing up of a contract, examining their functions. Thus, for the ordinary written form, this author states that it primarily has the warning function and the evidential function. In order to achieve the warning function of the written form, according to the understanding of this author, it is necessary that the power of attorney is drawn up in the same form.[38] Namely, although the principal does not acquire obligations from the main contract by granting the power of attorney, he actually significantly narrows his influence on the creation of the main contractual relationship.[39] Until the moment of granting the power of attorney, only the principal reviews the

[35] Wagner and Knechtel (2007), § NO, Rn. 10.

[36] Arnet (2013), pp. 403–406.

[37] Đurđević (2016), pp. 293–306.

[38] *Ibid*, p. 295.

[39] *Ibid*, p. 296.

advantages and disadvantages of concluding the main contract and is the only one who decides whether to enter into a contractual relationship. After granting the power of attorney, this decision can be made by the authorised person. *Đurđević* points out that the *de facto* position of the principal is not significantly affected by the possibility of revoking the power of attorney. This is because the revocation statement is an addressed legal transaction. This means that in order to revoke the power of attorney, the principal must inform the other contracting party from the main contract about his decision to revoke the power of attorney. However, this is often not possible when the power of attorney does not precisely specify the person with whom the authorised person will conclude the main contract on behalf of the principal. For these reasons, according to *Đurđević*, it is necessary to provide protection against hasty commitment not only when concluding the main contract, but also when giving a power of attorney for its conclusion.[40]

In order to achieve the second function of the written form, the evidential function, it is necessary to provide a reliable proof of the existence and content of the contract, but also of the fact that the authorised person who concluded the contract really had the authority to establish a contractual relationship on behalf of the principal.

According to *Đurđević*, the consistent application of parallelism of forms between the main contract and the power of attorney is also necessary when the form of notary public signature verification is prescribed for the main contract. Namely, this type of form is most often prescribed for the contracts based on which the entry is made in the appropriate public register. It confirms that the contract was indeed signed by the persons indicated in the document as signatories. For this reason, signature verification is used to confirm the authenticity of the contract in a reliable way and also to prevent the misuse by falsification of signature of the contracting party. However, this protection would not be complete if it were allowed that contracts for which a form of signature verification is required be concluded on the basis of a power of attorney drawn up in an ordinary written form. Namely, in this case, by falsification of the signature of the power of attorney, it would still be possible for an unauthorized person to conclude the main contract and circumvent the purpose of its form.[41]

This author's opinion regarding the parallelism of forms of the main contract and the power of attorney is different regarding the two strictest types of forms, the notary public record and the notary public confirmed (solemnized) private document. Namely, he points out that these two types of forms are supposed to achieve additional goals compared to the form of notary public signature verification—the function of control and the instructive function.[42] Whilst the notary public is obliged to perform a limited control of the document during the verification of the signature, the instructive function can only be performed when concluding a contract in the

[40] *Ibid*, p. 297.

[41] *Ibid*, p. 300.

[42] *Ibid*, p. 302.

form of a notary public record or a notary public confirmed (solemnized) private document. Therefore, in the context of examining the existence of the need to grant a power of attorney in the same form, according to *Đurđević*, it is necessary to ask two questions. The first question is whether the instructive function from the form of the main contract is bypassed if the principal was not instructed about the consequences of the main contract when giving the power of attorney. Another question is whether he can at that moment be instructed at all on all relevant aspects of the main contract.[43] This author points out that the principal must rely on the ability of the authorised person and his duty to act with a required degree of attention and in accordance with the interests of the principal. According to his understanding, the notary public should not instruct the principal about the legal consequences of giving a power of attorney because they are widely known. On the other hand, a notary public cannot instruct him about the legal effect of the main contract because, as a rule, at the time of granting the power of attorney, many relevant circumstances of the main contract are not known. Since, according to this author, drawing up of a power of attorney in the form of a notary public record or a notary public confirmed (solemnized) private document does not achieve any additional legal and political goal, it is sufficient for it to be granted in the form of a notary public signature verification. In this way, it is avoided that the slowing down of legal transactions and considerable financial expenses for the notary public fees, as disadvantages of the two strictest types of forms be extended to the power of attorney without justifiable reason.[44]

The Serbian legislator accepted the understanding that *Đurđević* presented in his paper. This is evident from the provision itself, which was introduced by amending the LObl, but also from the explanation of the Proposal for the LASLObl in which the legislator almost completely took over the previously presented arguments from *Đurđević's* paper.[45] By this amendment, to the previously mentioned Article 90 of the LObl, which stipulated a strict parallelism of forms between the main contract and power of attorney, paragraph 2 was added which reads: "But, when the power of attorney is granted to conclude a contract or undertake any other legal transaction for which the form of a notary public confirmed (solemnized) private document or notary public record is stipulated, it is sufficient that the signature of the principal is verified by a notary public."

Thus, with this amendment to the LObl, the so-called modified parallelism of forms between the main contract and power of attorney has been introduced. According to the proposal presented by *Đurđević*, the amendment to the LObl deviates from the strict parallelism of forms in case when the form of a notarial public record or a notary public confirmed (solemnized) private document is required for the main contract. Also, according to this proposal, it is stipulated that in these cases

---

[43] *Ibid*, p. 304.

[44] *Ibid*, pp. 304–306.

[45] See Explanation of the Proposal for the Law on Amendments and Addition to the Law on Obligations from 2019. Available on the website: http://www.parlament.gov.rs/upload/archive/files/cir/pdf/predlozi_zakona/2019/2883-19.pdf.

it is sufficient for the power of attorney to be drawn up in the form of the notary public signature verification.

5 Form of Power of Attorney in German, Swiss and Austrian Law

Through the analysis of the way of regulating the form of power of attorney in the legal systems of some European countries, we have come across very different solutions. Whilst the strict parallelism forms between the main contract and power of attorney has been applied in Italy as was the case in Serbian law until the amendment of the LObl, in Germany, Switzerland and Austria the principle of informality of the power of attorney has been applied with various exceptions. In the following part of the paper the solutions of the latter countries will be presented, since the Serbian legislator took a more liberal approach to the form of power of attorney during the last amendment of the LObl. In this sense, possible shortcomings of such an approach, which are pointed out in the judicial practice and doctrine of these countries, will be considered, as well as the measures taken in order to mitigate or eliminate these shortcomings.

5.1 Germany

On the scale of different ways of regulating the form of power of attorney, the solution from German law stands on the opposite side in relation to the previously valid rule from Serbian law on the strict parallelism of forms of the main contract and power of attorney. Namely, in the German Civil Code (GCC),[46] in §167, paragraph 2 it is expressly stipulated that the principal's statement authorizing the authorized person to undertake certain legal transaction on his behalf does not have to be made in the form required for the given legal transaction.

This express rule on the informality of the power of attorney, regardless of the form of the main contract, has been the subject of analysis in German judicial practice and doctrine, most often in connection with the contracts on transfer of immovable property. In particular, the German authors dealt with the question of whether the informality of the power of attorney circumvents the purpose that the form of the main contract should serve. Critics of this rule point out that it is based primarily on the evidential function, and that the warning function of the form is not sufficiently

[46] German civil code in the version promulgated on 2 January 2002 (Federal Law Gazette [*Bundesgesetzblatt*] I page 42, 2909; 2003 I page 738), last amended by the Federal Law Gazette I, p. 3515.

considered.[47] Namely, the doctrine states that the warning function in certain cases cannot be realized by influencing the will of the authorized person because the consequences of concluding the main contract are not borne by him, but by the principal.[48]

In this context, there is an agreement in the doctrine and judicial practice that the effect of §167, paragraph 2 GCC should be limited, i.e. that in this case a teleological reduction of the aforementioned provision is required.[49] This means that the application of this rule shall be excluded in cases where the form of the main contract has a warning function, i.e. when it should provide protection against hasty commitment.

However, the exclusion of the application of the rule on informality of the power of attorney does not apply to all cases in which the form of the main contract has a warning function. Namely, in judicial practice, the application of §167, paragraph 2 GCC is excluded in the case of granting the irrevocable power of attorney. The irrevocable power of attorney does not exist in Serbian law, and in Germany this term refers to the case when the principal cannot unilaterally revoke the power of attorney, but a contract between him and the authorized person is required. In addition, it is accepted in judicial practice that the power of attorney must be drawn up in the form prescribed for the main contract even when it is not irrevocable, but the possibility of its revocation is actually significantly narrowed, e.g. by sanctioning the principle with a contractual penalty.[50]

The granting of an irrevocable power of attorney for the conclusion of a contract on transfer of immovable property for which §311b GCC stipulates the form of a notary public record is one of the examples of deviation from the informality of the power of attorney.[51] Some other contracts are also mentioned as potential examples of theological reduction of the §167, paragraph 2 GCC in case of granting of the irrevocable power of attorney because the form of a notary public record is also stipulated for these contracts and has the warning function. In this context it is also referred to the marriage contract that regulates the property relations of the spouses, the contract on the renunciation of inheritance that has not been opened, for which the form of a notary public record is also required, as well as the guarantee contract for which the law stipulates a written form. According to the understanding of certain authors, in order to fulfil the goal of a written form of guarantee, it is necessary to draw up the power of attorney in the same form as the main contract. In this way,

---

[47] Rösler (1999), p. 1150.

[48] Schubert (2021), §167, Rn. 19.

[49] Schubert (2021) §167, Rn. 19; Rösler (1999), p. 1150. According to *F. Bidlinsky*, the teleological reduction is applied "when the text of the regulation includes more than it is adequate for purpose." Bidlinski (2011), pp. 83–84. Similarly, *Vodinelić* states that it is used "when the text of the norm includes a case for which, however, its goal or reason (*ratio legis*) does not correspond. Then the opposite or otherwise different norm is applied to that case." Vodinelić (2014), p. 184.

[50] Schubert (2021) §167, Rn. 21. Rösler (1999), pp. 1151–1152.

[51] Brox and Walker (2014), p. 235, Rn. 544; Schubert (2021) §167, Rn. 21.

it is possible for the guarantor to be "clearly informed of the content and scope of the responsibility he undertakes".[52]

5.2 *Switzerland*

The form of power of attorney in Swiss law is not specifically regulated and is subject to the application of the general rule of informality of contracts from Article 11 of the Swiss Code of Obligations (SCO).[53] As an exception to this general rule, in some cases the form of power of attorney is specifically regulated. For example, the power of attorney for exercising the membership rights of shareholders and the power of attorney for a travelling salesman.[54] However, the form of power of attorney in these cases is regulated by special provisions, independent of the form of the main contract. Therefore, in these cases, there is no parallelism between forms of the main contract and the power of attorney. The only example of this parallelism in Swiss law is contained in Article 493, paragraph 6 SCO. According to this provision, the same form that is required for the guarantee is also required for the power of attorney that is given for its conclusion.

Apart from the specially regulated cases, the rule on the informality of power of attorney also applies when the power of attorney is given for the purpose of concluding a contract for which the form of a notary public record is required. This also applies to contracts on transfer of immovable property. Such a solution is accepted in Swiss judicial practice.[55] In Swiss doctrine it is also spoken about the informal power of attorney even in the case when the main contract is formal. In support of this opinion, the theory points out that the power of attorney can be revoked at any time, as well as that the terms of the form should be interpreted narrowly due to its flaws, because otherwise they would significantly slow down legal traffic and threaten legal certainty.[56]

Unlike German, the irrevocable power of attorney does not exist in the Swiss legal system. Even so, Swiss theory and judicial practice question the justification of the informality of power of attorney as well as the separate regulation of the form of power of attorney and the main contract. This is most often discussed in connection with the conclusion of contracts on transfer of immovable property.[57] Thus, some authors in recent literature point out that an informal power of attorney circumvents the goal that the legislator tries to achieve when prescribing the form of a

[52] Brox and Walker (2014), p. 235, Rn. 544.

[53] Part five of the Swiss Civil Code—Swiss Code of Obligations—SCO, Federal Gazette 1905 II 1, 1909 III 747, 1911 I 695 of 30 March 1911 (Status as of 9 February 2023).

[54] Cramer (2018), p. 282.

[55] See. decision of the Swiss Federal Court no. BGE 84 II 151 3 from 1.4.1958, BGE 99 II 159 dated 29.5.1973.

[56] Cramer (2018), p. 284.

[57] *Ibid*, p. 282.

notarial record for a specific contract. This goal is most often reflected in the protection of contractual parties from hasty commitments.[58] In this sense, *Giger* states that the informal granting of a power of attorney "practically excludes the protective function of the form that the legislator wanted to provide."[59] According to this author, the *ratio legis* of the provision requiring the form of a notary public record is "enabling prudent decision-making based on careful formation of opinion, taking into account all relevant facts.[60] When stipulating this form, the legislator had in mind the contracting parties themselves, and individual instruction, man-to-man.[61] Therefore, by transferring the authority to conclude a contract to an authorized person, the principal loses protection from his own haste, unless the power of attorney is also required in the form of a notary public record.[62] In this sense, supporters of this view believe that in cases where a notary public record form is required for the conclusion of a certain contract and when it is prescribed with the aim of protecting the contractor from hasty commitment, i.e. when it has a warning function, the same form should also apply to the power of attorney given for the purpose of conclusion of the contract.[63] If, on the other hand, this form is stipulated for a certain contract, but with the primary evidential function, then it is not necessary for the power of attorney to be drawn up in the form of a notary public record.

In an effort to find a compromise solution, in some cantons it is required that the power of attorney given for the purpose of concluding a contract for which the form of a notary public record is prescribed must be made in writing with the verified owner's signature. The problem, however, is not solved because the instructive function is missing.[64]

Authors who advocate the parallelism of forms between the main contract and the power of attorney try to limit the application of this rule only when necessary. Thus, *Cramer* states that the requirement of parallelism of forms should be limited to contracts where the form of a notary public record has a primary warning function, i.e. the protection against imprudence. Also, according to this author, this protection is needed only for those persons who get obligations from the contract. In addition, the circle of cases in which it is justified to insist on the parallelism of forms of the main contract and the power of attorney should be further narrowed down to natural persons. Namely, *Cramer* points out that legal persons do not need protection from haste because they usually act within the scope of their activity and with sufficient experience, and that the imposition of a form of notary public record for granting of power of attorney would be an additional administrative difficulty.[65]

[58] *Ibid*, p. 284 with further references.

[59] Giger (1997), p. 116, Rn. 186.

[60] *Ibid.*

[61] Giger (1997), p. 116, Rn. 186; Cramer (2018), p. 286.

[62] Giger (1997), p. 116, Rn. 186.

[63] Cramer (2018), p. 284 with further reference.

[64] *Ibid*, p. 287.

[65] *Ibid*, p. 278.

5.3 Austria

Unlike the SCO, the Austrian Civil Code (ACC)[66] contains a provision regulating the form of power of attorney. Namely, the § 1005 ACC states: "power of attorney agreement can be concluded orally or in writing". It follows that the power of attorney in Austrian law is informal.[67]

On the other hand, contrary to the solution from German law, there is no rule on the form of a power of attorney granted for the purpose of concluding a contract for which a certain form is required in Austria. In Austrian jurisprudence and judicial practice also, this issue has been discussed from the point of view of the possibility of fulfilling the goals, that is, the functions that the form of the main contract should serve. Thus, in Austrian law, the opinion is accepted according to which the power of attorney should be covered by the condition of the form of the main contract in cases where it primarily has a warning function. According to this, the power of attorney should be drawn up in the form required for the main contract, when it seeks to ensure the seriousness of the parties, and not just proof of existence and content of the contract.[68] The Austrian Supreme Court ruled on this issue for the first time in 1948 in connection with the marriage agreement.[69] § 1 of the Austrian Law on Request for Notarization of Certain Legal Affairs (Law on notarial acts-ALNA)[70] stipulated the form of a notary public record for this agreement. In its decision, the court took the position that the condition of form of the main contract should also apply to the power of attorney in case when the form aims to ensure the "seriousness of the will of the contracting parties" or to "encourage them to thoroughly consider the intended legal transaction".[71] From the quoted parts of the judgment, it can be seen that the court had in mind a form that has a warning function.

The amendment to § 69 Austrian Code on Notaries (ACN)[72] from 1962 stipulates that power of attorney for making notary public records must be a public document or a private document with the owner's signature verified by a court, a notary public or an Austrian representative office.[73] However, in a 1984 decision in a gift *causa*

[66] Austrian Civil Code from 1811 JGS Nr. 946/1811 last amended by Federal Law Gazette I Nr. 38/2023

[67] In a similar way, the general provision on the informality of the contract was formulated in the ACC. Thus, according to § 883 "A contract can be concluded orally or in writing; in or out of court, with or without witnesses. This difference in form does not make a difference regarding the obligation of the contract, except in cases determined by law".

[68] Rubin (2010), p. 24.

[69] Decision of the Austrian Supreme Court (OGH) no. 2Ob247/48 dated February 23, 1949.

[70] Austrian Law on the request for notarization of certain legal affairs (Law on notarial acts-ALNA), RGBl. No. 76/1871 from 1871, last amended by Federal Law Gazette I No. 75/2009.

[71] Decision of the Austrian Supreme Court (OGH) no. 2Ob247/48 dated February 23, 1949.

[72] Austrian Code on Notaries (ACN), RGBl. Nr. 75/1871 from 1871, last amended by Federal Law Gazette I Nr. 147/2022.

[73] This change was made by law published in the Federal Law Gazette No. 139/1962 of June 7, 1962.

mortis dispute, the Supreme Court took the same position as in the aforementioned decision from 1948. In this case too, the court considered that the power of attorney should have been drawn up in the form of a notary public record. According to the opinion of this court, it is not affected by the amendment of § 69 ACN from 1962 because this amendment does not imply that the accepted condition for drawing up a power of attorney for conclusion of a contract requiring the form of a notary public record should no longer be valid.[74]

In theory, however, there were different interpretations of § 69 ACN from 1962. According to one, with this amendment, the legislator wanted to derogate from the previously valid rules on the analogous application of the form of the main contract to the power of attorney when it was prescribed with the aim of protecting the parties from hasty commitment, i.e. when it had a warning function. Others, on the other hand, thought that the verification of the owner's signature mentioned in the amended provision was only a minimum condition for the form of a power of attorney, and that the rule on the analogous application of the form of a notary public record to the power of attorney is still valid in the case when the form of the main contract has a warning function.[75]

However, in 1993 there was a new amendment to § 69 ACN, which did not leave space for different interpretations.[76] Namely, in addition to paragraph 1 of § 69 ACN, paragraph 1a was added which stated that the power of attorney from paragraph 1 was sufficient for concluding legal transactions and making declarations of will, the validity of which requires the form of a notary public record. After this amendment to § 69 ACN from 1962, its validity became undisputed. Nevertheless, some authors in the Austrian doctrine express doubts about the correctness of this solution, that is, about its suitability to fulfil the warning function in contracts for which the form of a notary public record is stipulated.[77]

6 Concluding Considerations

Based on what has previously been said, it can be seen that the adequacy of the way of regulating the form of power of attorney both in the Serbian literature and the explanation of the amendment of the LObl given by the Serbian legislator, as well as in German, Austrian and Swiss doctrine and judicial practice was examined from the aspect of the function of form of the contract. It seems that all of them examinations start from the same criteria, and agree that informality, that is, a milder form of power of attorney, must not jeopardize the performance of the functions served by the form of the main contract.

[74] Judgment of the Austrian Supreme Court (ASC) No. 50b34/84 dated 26.06.1984.

[75] Schauer (1984), 185 and so on, with further references.

[76] This change was made by law published in the Federal Law Gazette No. 692/1993 of 13.10.1993.

[77] Rubin (2010), p. 25; Baumgartner and Torggler (2013) § 1005, 22, Rn. 25.

Nevertheless, Austrian, German and Swiss doctrine and judicial practise examine the adequacy of the rules on the informality of power of attorney from the aspect of the warning function. It can be said that they have a common position that the general rule on the informality of power of attorney should be deviated from in case when an informal or milder form of power of attorney would jeopardize the protection of the contracting party against hasty commitment, which the legislator tried to ensure with the mandatory form of the main contract. Therefore, it must not result in the principal establishing a contractual relationship through an authorised person without carefully considering the consequences of the contract and the risks arising therefrom.

On the other hand, the Serbian legislator, when evaluating the justification for changing the rules on parallelism of forms between the main contract and power of attorney, emphasized the instructive function. Thus, it concludes that drawing up a power of attorney in form of a notary public record or a notary public confirmed (solemnized) private document does not contribute to the instructive function. It is debatable, however, to what extent it is possible to separate the instructive function from the warning function. Namely, it was pointed out in the paper that the warning function can be achieved by any type of form to a certain extent. Each formality can be considered as an "alarm clock for legal consciousness" of the contracting party, i.e. a new opportunity to carefully consider the legal consequences of the contract, and to make a thoughtful, conscious decision on establishing a contractual relationship. However, in exceptional cases, in the case of particularly complex contracts, contracts that produce particularly difficult consequences for one or both parties or carry significant risks, the legislator stipulates a form that includes instruction by a notary public. It should ensure that the contracting parties really understand the significance and consequences of the contract before deciding on its conclusion. Therefore, it can be said that with the parties being instructed by an unbiased expert, the warning function is enhanced, performed in its full capacity. In this sense, the question arises whether by drawing up a power of attorney in a less strict form than the one prescribed for the main contract and by not instructing the principal, the warning function has been fully performed.

In the section on the arguments presented in Serbian doctrine in support of the introduction of the so-called modified parallelism between forms of power of attorney and the main contract, we saw that the impossibility of fully performing the warning function in the absence of the same form in the power of attorney was cited as a reason for retaining the parallelism of forms in the case when a written form is required for the main contract. In support of this position, it has been pointed out that by granting a power of attorney, the principal significantly limits his influence on the creation of the contractual relationship, and thus also limits the possibility of considering its suitability to his interests. Until the power of attorney is granted, the principal has a monopoly on being bound by the main contract, which he loses with this act because, apart from him, the contract can be concluded by the authorised person on his behalf. It is further concluded that due to the factual similarity between the granting of a power of attorney and the conclusion of the main contract, the principal should be protected from hasty commitment not only when concluding the main contract, but also when granting the power of attorney.

All the above mentioned arguments seem to be correct. However, limiting them only to a written form is disputed. The effect of granting a power of attorney on the principal's position when considering the compatibility of the contract with his interests, as well as on his impact on establishing a contractual relationship is the same regardless of whether and what type of form is required for the main contract.

In addition, the argument that is stated in the doctrine, but also in the explanation of the legislator for the amendment of the LObl, in support of the modified parallelism of forms, is that drawing up a power of attorney in the form of notary public record or notary public confirmed (solemnized) private document does not contribute to the instructive function. This is because at the time of granting the power of attorney, not all relevant aspects of the main contract that the notary public would instruct the parties about are known. However, as stated several times, the instructive function complements the warning function, i.e. the notary public's instruction serves to inform the parties by an impartial expert about the relevant facts, risks and legal scope of the contract so that they, with understanding and awareness of all the relevant circumstances, make a decision on concluding the contract. From this perspective, by applying the aforementioned argument of the doctrine and the legislator to the warning function and the written form, we come to the result that granting a power of attorney in the same form does not contribute to the fulfilment of not only the instructive, but of the warning function as well, since the principal at the time of granting the power of attorney is not aware of all the relevant aspects of the main contract that should be considered when deciding on the establishing of a contractual relationship. In this way, this argument cannot justify different treatment of types of forms on the criteria of instructive function as long as they primarily have the warning function for a specific contract.

Bearing in mind the abovementioned, it seems that the legislator has made a mistake when, while examining the need for parallelism of forms in case when the form of a notary public record or a notary public confirmed (solemnized) private document is required for the main contract, he focused exclusively on the instructive function, without taking into account the warning function, and that otherwise, the result of his analysis could have been different.

References

Arnet R (2013) Form folgt Funktion. Zeitschrift des bernischen Juristenvereins 149:391–414

Baumgartner A, Torggler U (2013) § 1005. In: Fenveyes A, Kerschner F, Vonkilch A, 3. Auflage des von Dr. Heinrich Klang begründeten Kommentars zum Allgemeinen Bürgerlichen Gesetzbuch, Wien

Bidlinski F (2011) Pravna metodologija (Legal methodology). CID, Podgorica

Brox H, Walker W (2014) Allgemeiner Teil des BGB. Vahlen, München

Cramer C (2018) Die Form der Vollmacht für öffentlich zu beurkundende Verträge. Aktuelle juristische Praxis - Pratique juridique Actuelle 3:281–292

Đurđević D (2016) Forma punomoćja *de lege lata* i *de lege ferenda* (Form of Power of Attorney *de lege lata* and *de lege ferenda*). Srpska politička misao 4:267–313

Giger H (1997) Schweizerisches Zivilgesetzbuch: Das Obligationenrecht – Die einzelnen Vertragsverhältnisse, Kauf und Teausch, Der Grundstückkauf, Art. 216-221 OR. In: Hausheer H (ed) Berner Kommentar, Nr. VI/2/1/3. Stämpfli Verlag AG, Bern, pp 113–131

Häsemeyer L (1971) Die gesetzliche Form der Rechtsgeschäfte – Objektive Ordnung und privatautonome Selbstbestimmung im formgebundenen Rechtsgeschäft. Athenäum, Frankfurt

Lorenz W (1958) Das Problem der Aufrechterhaltung formnichtiger Schuldverträge. Archiv für die civilistische Praxis 5:381–413

Mankowski P (2010) Formzwecke. Juristen Zeitung 13:662–667

Miščević N (2019) O elektronskoj formi ugovora u domaćem pravu (On the electronic form of contracts in domestic law). Zbornik radova Pravnog fakulteta u Novom Sadu 4:1641–1661

Miščević N (2022) Javnobeležnička forma obligacionih ugovora (Notary form of obligation contracts). Dissertation, Faculty of Law Novi Sad

Rösler P (1999) Formbedürftigkeit der Vollmacht- Eine Darstellung nach Fallgruppen. Neue juristische Wochenschrift 16:1151–1153

Rubin D (2010) Bevollmächtigung und formgebundenes Rechtsgeschäft. Ecolex 1:24

Schauer M (1984) Zur Formpflicht der Vollmacht bei der Schenkung. Österreichische Notariatszeitung, p 185 ff

Schubert C (2021) In: Säcker FJ, Rixecker R, Oetker H, Limperg B (eds) BGB § 167. Kommentar zum Bürgerlichen Gesetzbuch, Münchener

Vodinelić V (2014) Građansko pravo, Uvod u građansko pravo i opšti deo građanskog prava (Civil law, Introduction to civil law and the general part of civil law). Beograd

von Jhering R (1926) Geist des römischen Rechts auf den verschiedenen Stufen seiner Entwicklung. Zweiter Teil, Leipzig

von Savigny FC (1853) Obligationenrecht als Theil des heutigen Römischen Rechts. Zweiter Band, Berlin

Wagner K, Knechtel G (2007) NO online - Kommentar zur Notariatsodrnung. https://rdb.manz.at/document/1137_no_p0001

New ESG Obligations for Enterprises in Supply and Value Chains through Corporate Sustainability Due Diligence Acts in the EU and Germany

Darko Samardžić and Larisa Velić

1 Propagation of ESG

1.1 Incompliances and Changing Legislation

The attraction on ESG (Environmental, Social and Governance) has grown. In international law different conventions were agreed upon. A milestone was the United Nations (UN) Universal Declaration of Human Rights 1948. In 1998 the International Labour Organization (ILO) Declaration on Fundamental Principles and Rights at Work was adopted and amended in 2022. In parallel, climate change led to the Rio Declaration on Environment and Development in 1992. In 2003 the UN Convention Against Corruption was adopted. It was a new legal statement in international law showing the change of mind set. Further guidance was given by the UN Global Compact Principles (2000, latest edition 2004), the Guidelines on Business and Human Rights (2011) and Sustainable Development Goals (2015)[1] or the Organization for Economic Cooperation and Development (OECD) Guidelines for Multinational Enterprises on Responsible Business Conduct (2023).[2] The UN Global Compact[3] introduces corporate sustainability as operating business to grant at least minimum social and working conditions by providing ten guiding

[1] https://www.ohchr.org/sites/default/files/Documents/Publications/GuidingPrinciplesBusinessHR_EN.pdf.

[2] MNE Guidelines—Organisation for Economic Co-operation and Development (oecd.org). Guidelines for Multinational Enterprises on Responsible Business Conduct.

[3] https://www.unglobalcompact.org/what-is-gc/mission/principles.

D. Samardžić · L. Velić (✉)
Faculty of Law, University of Zenica, Zenica, Bosnia and Herzegovina

E. Omerović et al. (eds.), *Balkan Yearbook of European and International Law 2023*, Balkan Yearbook of European and International Law 2023,
https://doi.org/10.1007/978-3-031-69670-1_5

principles. At the core of the UN 2030 Agenda for Sustainable Development[4] are the 17 UN Sustainable Development Goals with its 169 targets.

In parallel, private organizations such as the International Organization for Standardization (ISO) have recognized a need for self-binding standards. Such standards are for instance, the ISO 26000 Guidance on Social Responsibility, the ISO 37001 Anti-Bribery Management System Standard, the ISO 37301 Compliance Management System Standard or the ISO 37000 Good Governance Standard. Such standards serve as guidance or certification basis for companies to proof the functioning of management systems. During a certification the adequacy and effectiveness of a management system shall be verified to provide assurance to business partners and customers. Finally, a certificate shall demonstrate good governance and compliance.

However, such international standards have not prevented inacceptable environmental and social incompliances in recent years. A few incompliances have become rather famous in public media. For instance, in 2010, the oil platform Deepwater Horizon exploded and caused the death of 11 workers. Over 87 days up to four million barrel of oil polluted the ocean.[5] The US Environmental Protection Agency filed complaints against BP and others. In 2015 the VW emission scandal was discovered by the US Environmental Protection Agency. The agency deemed VW as being responsible for disguising harmful emissions. VW was also reproached for cheating emission tests. VW used software in lab tests to show lower nitrogen emissions. In actuality, the nitrogen dioxide emissions were forty times higher when driving on public roads. Estimations were made that around 11 million cars of VW may be driving under falsified emission values. VW was only a prominent example of incompliances. Overall, enterprises are deemed as a crucial factor on a pathway to global warming, endangering the Paris climate goal of 1.5 degree.[6]

Globally, the guarantee of human rights protection in supply chains is doubted. In 2012, a fire destroyed the Tazreen factory for manufacturing clothes. The clothes were being produced in the name of different international enterprises registered in western or EU countries. Around 100 workers died. According to the authorities the fire was initiated in storage rooms on the first floor. The goods in the storage room were illegally stored there. This led to a lawsuit against Tazreen Fashions.[7] Dangers or warnings have not been taken serious enough or adequate means of escape were not given. In the following year the next human rights scandal happened. The Rana Plaza imploded. More than 1000 people died. These catastrophes were followed by further tragedies such as the Tampoco and MultiFabs factory fires in 2016 and 2017.

---

[4] https://sdgs.un.org/2030agenda.

[5] Deepwater Horizon—BP Gulf of Mexico Oil Spill | US EPA.

[6] UN climate report: It's 'now or never' to limit global warming to 1.5 degrees | UN News.

[7] Lawsuit against Tazreen Fashions (re factory fire in Bangladesh)—Business & Human Rights Resource Centre (business-humanrights.org).

To identify the reasons for incompliances it is crucial to capture the context of supply chains. In low cost countries manufacturing industries often are an extended workbench. Overall, the dependency is high. The clothing industry represents a dominant portion of exports. This industry relates up to twenty-five million people working directly or indirectly in this sector.[8] This indicates the dominance of profit over compliance. However, the mid- and long-term question is, how expensive or risky it is to take compliance lightly. Here we even have willful misconduct, not only negligence. Superiors were aware of the risks and have given instructions to the contrary. The governance and compliance management system have not been adequate and effective. It would be reasonable to use different instruments such as audits, resilience tests and certifications besides investments and trainings. External and internal controls are standard instruments of compliance for verification.

In many enterprises we do see that new ESG functions are introduced. To emphasize the importance of governance and compliance on human and environmental rights such functions often directly report to the executive board or the managing directors of an enterprise. For a long time ESG has been a communication and marketing issue without broad due diligence duties. Communication departments have taken over non-financial reporting responsibilities presenting a friendly picture. Single actions or projects such as the support of a school, the preservation of a forest or the installation of a water source served as social marketing for good corporate citizenship. Companies wanted to present their social goodwill. A good public image was accepted even if environmental and social breaches have taken place. Financial key performance indicators were generally dominant. Environmental and social aspects have not been integrated adequately and effectively. Therefore, the term greenwashing was invented to represent the discrepancy between needs and inappropriate actions.

For sure, the supply and value chain due diligence duties will increase obligations for organizations and their management. ESG and compliance will become focus topics of supervisory and executive boards who do want to avoid fines and liabilities.[9] Stakeholders and investors are already sensitive. Investments follow new ESG investment criteria, new transparency obligations and commitments. Here we also see new approaches by regulators requiring green investments.[10] Greenwashing doubts on investments may even have criminal consequences.[11] Citizens and consumers, in particular in the younger generation, have changed their investment attitude. Good corporate citizenship is not only a question of political correctness. Friendly communication and marketing are not accepted as viable any more.

[8] The Rana Plaza disaster—Case study—GOV.UK (www.gov.uk).

[9] Dörrwächter (2022), p. 1083; Ruland et al. (2022), p. 220027.

[10] BaFin—Fachartikel—Greenwashing verhindern: 'Greenwashing verhindern'(eng. 'Prevent Greenwashing'),

[11] Mosbacher (2023), pp. 14.

Greenwashing has become a characterization even in legal literature and associations.[12]

For enterprises, organizationally and procedurally this means that compliance and governance management systems have to be established or re-aligned. Risk management, audits and certifications will become standards. Operationally the effectiveness of whistleblowing, incident management, monitoring, reporting and continuous improvement is a key task for top management. Compliance accountability and liabilities will lead to increased attention. This awareness will rise even more, if authorities continue with their enforcement trends. Here, we want to focus on the EU corporate framework on due diligences in value chains and the supply chain act in the largest market in the EU, the German market, to show which actions are required in the future to establish adequate and effective compliance and governance management systems. Such duties demand adequate and effective risk management, knowledge building, incident solving, training, reporting, monitoring and continuous improvements. In Germany the crucial law is the GER ACDDO from 2021 (hereinafter referred to as 'GER ACDDO').[13] In the EU the Commission has made a proposal for the EU CSDDD 2019[14] (hereinafter referred to as 'EU CSDDD').[15] The focus is on obligations in supply and value chains according to the aforementioned two acts. Other supporting ESG acts in the EU will be referred to only for explanatory reasons, if necessary.

1.2 New ESG Trends in the EU and Germany

Environmental and social incompliances across countries, markets and continents show that supply and value chains have to be considered globally.[16] Different group of companies with complex corporate legal structures have entities and production facilities across the world or they follow other business models such as specific research and development, manufacturing or supply chain, service level or outsourcing agreements. For consumers, non-governmental organizations or authorities it is not always easy to identify single actions or processes in such complex supply and value chains. Hence, accountability cannot be identified easily. Principals of products and services are often companies from western countries or the EU only using manufacturing or service facilities abroad to lower costs and standards. Unethical behavior, incompliances or crisis in one part of the supply or value chain impact the rest of the world. Goodwill or self-commitment have not worked out.

[12] Driftmann (2022), p. 319; Keine Industrie vor "Greenwashing" sicher—Deutscher AnwaltSpiegel.

[13] Ger. 'Gesetz über die unternehmerischen Sorgfaltspflichten in Lieferketten v. 16.7.2021, BGBl. 2021 I 2959.

[14] European Union Corporate Sustainability Due Diligence Directive.

[15] EU COM 2022/71 final (Proposal for a DIRECTIVE OF THE EUROPEAN PARLIAMENT AND OF THE COUNCIL on Corporate Sustainability Due Diligence).

[16] Krause (2022), pp. 303.

The EU officially declared that voluntary self-commitments have not been effective. The reputation of the EU has been damaged.[17] It would be shocking if the EU as a community of values is not able to grant basic human rights.[18] Soft laws have not changed minds significantly.[19] International agreements were not effective enough.[20] Non-financial reporting standards were too soft.[21]

Hence, the EU has started different governance initiatives.[22] Two of the most remarkable initiatives are the Digital Decade and the Green Deal.[23] The EU sets further goals pressuring its member states. Independently of the UN international agreements, the EU has the goal to have market net-zero greenhouse gas emissions in 2050.[24] Climate neutrality is the goal for the whole community by 2050. Thus, the EU has recognized the need for a governance framework. Besides, more and more supply chain acts, and even more value chain acts, depend on a digital context.[25] To cover also the principals, not only the production facilities it is crucial to understand the procurement, logistics and accounting processes. Thus, digital, environmental and social ecosystems have to be seen holistically. Initiatives or soft law are gradually converted into binding or hard regulations.[26] In the meanwhile, more governance initiatives of the EU are transformed into EU legal acts with more binding character.

A further good sample for basic compliance legislation with measurable impact is the so-called EU Whistleblowing Directive.[27] Whistleblowers such as Eric Snowden regarding the US or Francis Haugen regarding Facebook have revealed the importance of transparency as general principal of law. The increased protection on whistleblowers has fostered the discovery of incompliances. Huge companies in the EU use leniency programs to reveal incompliances. For instance, the 'AdBlue'[28]

---

[17] The Study on due diligence, European Commission, Directorate-General for Justice and Consumers, Smit, L., Bright, C., et al., Study on due diligence requirements through the supply chain: final report, Publications Office, 2020, https://data.europa.eu/doi/10.2838/39830.

[18] Refer Explantory Memorandum of the Corporate Sustainability Due Diligence Directive, 2.

[19] Göpfert and Melles (2022), p. 2505.

[20] Fleischer (2022), p. 205.

[21] Schön (2022), p. 207.

[22] Schlacke (2022), p. 907; Brömmelmeyer (2022), p. 76.

[23] The EU Green Deal—A global perspective | EEAS Website (europa.eu)

[24] 2050 long-term strategy (europa.eu).

[25] Jacob (2019); Nemat et al. (2022), pp. 104.

[26] Herchen (2022), p. 3115; Göpfert and Melles (2022), p. 2505; Spießhofer (2022), p. 435; Fleischer (2022), p. 209.

[27] Directive (EU) 2019/1937.

[28] AdBlue is an exhaust fluid; within the process of catalyst, nitrogen oxide in the exhaust reacts with the ammonia and is transformed into nitrogen and water; refer What is AdBlue? AdBlue Diesel Exhaust | The AA.

decision of the EU Commission[29] was enabled by Daimler AG.[30] In 2015 Daimler AG acted as whistleblower reporting anti-competitive practices after participating in such practices since 2009. In 2009 Daimler AG agreed with BMW[31] AG and VW, Audi AG on the coordination of the development of selective catalytic reduction systems for diesel passenger cars including a specific size of AdBlue tanks for such cars. The consequence of Daimler's whistleblowing and the EU leniency program was that Daimler AG was not fined by the EU Commission. BMW AG received a fine of approx. EUR 373000000 and VW, Audi, Dr. Ing. h.c. F. Porsche AG in total approx. EUR 502000000. The EU Whistleblowing Directive has forced companies across the EU to implement whistleblowing systems. Such systems are part of compliance management systems. New employees, compliance officers, are hired with specific knowledge and status. Ideally, such compliance officers should be independent. Organizationally this means, that compliance officers should not be subordinated to other functions. In the spirit of the three-line model such functions as second- or third-line functions should be independent.[32] Generally, this understanding follows the idea of general principles of law such as the separation of powers, the rule of law or the principle of proportionality. Organizational independency is a basic condition. The constitutional ideas on institutions can be transferred teleologically. A hierarchical subordination of compliance functions does contain inherent risks. Compliance functions shall directly report to executive and supervisory board members. Clearing legal doubts or incompliances protects enterprises. Short term shocks, reflection and burdens are a supporting sequence of an improvement evolution.

The EU Commission emphasizes the need for climate regulations.[33] Enterprises should be aware of already existing governance frameworks on international level such as the UN Sustainable Development Goals.[34] The Green Deal is a further step on supranational level. This step was extensively communicated.[35] Moreover, legislators have started to adopt stricter laws and authorities are prepared to enforce rights more consequentially.[36] In the case of AdBlue the EU Commission took a remarkable legal interpretation of competition law in relation to environmental law.[37] Enterprises suspended competition in emission cleaning through AdBlue as

[29] Document 52021AT40178(02), Summary of Commission Decision of 8 July 2021 relating to a proceeding under Article 101 of the Treaty on the Functioning of the European Union and Article 53 of the EEA Agreement (Case AT.40178—Car Emissions).

[30] Aktiengesellschaft (eng. corporation).

[31] Bayrische Motorenwerke.

[32] Three-Lines-Model-Updated-German.PDF (diir.de).

[33] Regulation (EU) 2021/1119 ('European Climate Law').

[34] Refer Explantory Memorandum of the Corporate Sustainability Due Diligence Directive, 1.

[35] Communication from the Commission on the European Green Deal, COM/2019/640 final.

[36] Cappel and Hund (2022), p. 174.

[37] Document 52021AT40178(02), Summary of Commission Decision of 8 July 2021 relating to a proceeding under Article 101 of the Treaty on the Functioning of the European Union and Article 53 of the EEA Agreement (Case AT.40178—Car Emissions).

part of a collaborative agreement. Here, the green deal governance framework with its goals and principles served as interpretation basis for competition law. The Commission imposed a fine of approx. EUR 900 million on BMW and VW. From a compliance point of view, it is interesting to emphasize, that Daimler Benz was also part of the collaboration agreement. Nevertheless, Daimler Benz was not imposed by any fine due to its whistleblowing contribution. This shows that no cartel participant is safe. It is a question of risk or time who can escape and who has to pay. Stricter enforcement trends are visible across markets. For instance, in the US the 'Dieselgate' incompliance has provoked the US Environmental protection Authority to condemn VW.

The GER ACDDO and the EU CSDDD are remarkable examples of a new kind of governance. Due diligence obligations refer to human rights and environmental-related risks. This means that already risks trigger obligations. A violation is not needed. Partially, it is feared that enterprises will be impacted too much.[38] But the risk-based approach functions as a filter and action-plan, as basis for interpretation and setting priorities.[39] For enterprises it will be a question of adequate and effective governance, risk, compliance management systems, leadership and culture. Overall, we can see a new development of governance and compliance standards on human rights and environmental protection, either by the amendment of existing or the adoption of new regulations. Legislators proceed de lege lata as well as de lege ferenda. The ESG framework is growing. Organizations have to broaden, deepen their knowledge. All functions involved in ESG issues have to cooperate to assure a governance, compliance management system state of the art. Legal knowledge has to be combined with environmental, technological as well as organizational, supply chain expertise.

2 Subject Matter and Scope

In the GER ACDDO the scope is linked to specific conventions on the one side, on the other side to general risks. Formally, the German legislator refers to single conventions on the protection of human rights. These conventions are listed in an Annex of the GER ACDDO. But the scope of management duties is broader. Besides the single conventions, the legislator deems human rights risks already as trigger for management duties. This legislative technique reflects the increasing risk-based approach in regulations across all fields. The legislator has provided a catalogue of twelve numbers of human rights relevance in article two GER ACDDO. A risk is given if a sufficient probability exists that a risk may convert into a violation. For instance catalogue number seven contains the prohibition of unequal treatment in employment. Here a violation on the grounds of social origin or health status could

[38] DAV (2022), p. 909.

[39] Fleischer (2022), p. 213; Cappel and Hund (2022), p. 176.

be sufficient. However, a justification can be given by the requirements of the employment. Directors can explain actions or procedures by the nature, structure of an organization or other characteristics of the internal context.

The GER ACDDO refers to all steps within a supply chain used for the production of a good or the delivery of a service. In contrast to the EU CSDDD, the GER ACDDO distinguishes between direct and indirect suppliers. Direct suppliers are contractual partners. All other partners without a contractual relationship but necessary for supply are indirect suppliers. Here, we see a legal tradition being continued. Legislators still look at legal relationships. But supply chains are factual, economic, social and political relationships. If there is a chain of subjects each contribution needed shall be considered. Otherwise the formal legal view is not holistic and material. The legal view is no longer congruent with the factual, economic, social and political context in global markets. This becomes even more evident in value chains. Digital ecosystems are linked to the world wide web. The cyber space is not prevented by geographical or political boundaries. Data value chains can easily be influenced by parties all over the world. A distinction between direct and indirect suppliers fragments value chains. However, normatively the German distinction has to be considered. Single duties in the GER ACDDO only refer to own business areas or direct suppliers, not to indirect suppliers. The subject matter of the EU CSDDD is broader without such a distinction between direct and indirect suppliers. The directive stipulates obligations for actual and potential human rights and environmental adverse impacts, with respect to all operations. This also applies to value chain operations executed by suppliers based on established business relationship. The EU view is more holistic and effective. Crucial is not the contractual relationship, the legal view, but the factual business ties. If there is a certain business tie the parties have to be considered as cooperation partners within a value chain.

The GER ACDDO already applies since 2023 to enterprises with more than 3000 employees. As of 2024 all entities with more than 1000 employees have to apply the GER ACDDO. In the EU the scope is even extended. The EU distinguishes between EU-enterprises and non-EU-enterprises. For EU-enterprises the application is intended for entities with more than 500 employees plus a net global turnover which is higher than EUR 150 million. Reference points are annual accounts prepared for the previous year. For specific sectors such as textile, food or raw material industries the directive has already to be applied by companies with more than 250 employees plus a net worldwide turnover of more than EUR 40 million.[40] The EU CSDDD shall also apply to enterprises formed in third countries. Such non-EU-enterprises are in scope if they have a net turnover higher than EUR 150 million in the EU. Decisive is the previous financial year. In case of enterprises in specific sectors a net turnover which is higher than EUR 40 million is sufficient for application. At least half of the net worldwide turnover has been achieved in such specific sectors. To avoid uncertainties in case of counting employees the legislator acknowledges part-time and temporary employees such as full employees. Part-time employees

[40] Refer art. 2 b) i)-iii) EU CSDDD to see the complete list.

shall be deemed as full-time equivalent employees and temporary agency workers shall be treated such as workers employed directly.

The scope of the EU CSDDD is rather broad. It covers the complete value chain. It is remarkable that the EU uses the term value chain, not only supply chain. The traditional understanding of supply chains is focused on the supply of material goods. It is physical understanding from analogue markets. This does not fit to digital ecosystems, where data have a significant value. Thus, the term value chain is broader. It covers all actions related to production and services, in particular research and development, use, sale and waste management. In contrast to the GER CADDO, all actions are included upstream and downstream in established business relationships. Up- and downstream means that we do not only look at the supply side. Downstream business partners are included.[41] However, it remains challenging to understand what established business relationships are. Which criteria decide the moment of establishment? It may be helpful to look at French legislation.[42] France is a driver of environmental and social governance in Europe. The Commission may have used the *Loi de Vigilance* as guidance. The French commercial law relates to criteria such as duration, stability or regularity of trade relationships to determine an established business relationship.[43] This analogy is confirmed by article three lit. f) EU CSDDD. An established business relationship depends on its intensity or duration and which does not represent a negligible or merely ancillary part of the value chain.

The EU clarifies that the EU CSDDD is one regulation which has a mutual horizontal effect with other EU regulations strengthening ESG. Further relevant acts for the EU for instance are the Non-Financial Reporting Directive (NFRD),[44] the Corporate Sustainability Reporting Directive (CSRD),[45] the Sustainable Finance Disclosure Regulation (SFDR),[46] the Taxonomy Regulation,[47] the Directive on Preventing and Combating Trafficking in Human beings and Protecting its Victims,[48] Employer's Sanctions Directive,[49] Conflict Minerals Regulation,[50] Proposal for a Regulation Deforestation-Free Supply Chains,[51] proposal for a New Batteries Regulation[52] and the Sustainable Products Initiative to revise the current Eco-Design

[41] Bomsdorf and Blatecki-Burgert (2022), p. 141.

[42] Krause (2022), p. 307.

[43] Nietsch and Wiedmann (2022), p. 125.

[44] Directive 2014/95/EU.

[45] Directive (EU) 2022/2464; Kühnberger and Wohlgemuth (2022), p. 668; Schön (2022), p. 207.

[46] Regulation (EU) 2019/2088.

[47] Regulation (EU) 2020/852; Dreisigacker-Sartor and Ritter-Döring (2022), p. 422.

[48] Directive 2011/36/EU.

[49] Directive 2009/52/EC.

[50] Regulation (EU) 2017/821.

[51] EU COM (2021) 706 final.

[52] EU COM/2020/798 final.

Directive.[53,54] Additionally, the EU shows up the further governance framework on ESG such as the Action Plan on a Circular Economy, the Biodiversity Strategy, the farm to Fork Strategy, the Chemicals Strategy, Updating the 2020 New Industrial Strategy: Building a stronger Single Market for Europe's recovery, the Strategy for Financing the Transition to a Sustainable Economy, the Environmental Liabilities Directive,[55] the Fit for 55 Package, the EU Emission Trading System, the Carbon Border Adjustment Mechanism, the EU health and safety, and fundamental rights legislation, the EU Action Plan on Human Rights 2020–2024, the EU Strategy on the Rights of the Child and the EU Strategy on Combating Trafficking in Human Beings 2021–2025.[56] Besides the Regulations and Directives all other governance acts may be used for legal interpretation. This can be of importance for the evaluation of due diligence duties in corporate acts on supply and value chains.

3 Essential Corporate Due Diligence Duties in Supply Chains

Article three GER ACDDO summarizes the due diligence obligations specified in articles four to ten.[57] To stipulate proportionate duties the German legislator uses different criteria for appropriateness.[58] Appropriateness has to be interpreted in the light of proportionality and a risk-based approach.[59] This shows that each enterprise shall be treated proportionally in dependence of its circumstances, of the whole internal and external context of an enterprise. Comparably, the German legislator has listed indicators to be considered such as nature, extent of business activities or the ability to influence violation risks.

Article four GER ACDDO demands an appropriate, effective risk management system. This enables an enterprise to conduct a risk-assessment, to set priorities and build up structures accordingly. Basically, a compliance management system can be verified by two criteria, the adequacy and effectiveness. Adequacy refers to the set up and design of a compliance management system, while the effectiveness of a compliance management system requires that it works. It is remarkable, that the German legislator provides rather general scales for effectiveness. The legislator describes effectiveness abstractly by the need of identification or minimization of relevant risks. It is questionable if such an abstract explanation meets the spirit of effectiveness. The indefinite terms provide room for interpretation. It also has to be

[53] Directive 2009/125/EC.

[54] Refer Explantory Memorandum of the EU CSDDD, p. 3.

[55] Directive 2004/35/CE.

[56] Refer Explantory Memorandum of the EU CSDDD, p. 8.

[57] Schönfelder (2021), p. 119.

[58] Fleischer (2022), pp. 212, 214.

[59] Cappel and Hund (2022), p. 176.

asked if it is sufficient just to require a formal function within an organization such as one responsible person for human rights. What exactly is the empowerment of such a responsible person? Does such a responsible person have an own, direct reporting line to the executive board? Is such a responsible person independent in taking decisions and actions to mitigate risks? Is an adequate budget foreseen that can be used on own discretion to meet due diligence obligations?

Article six GER ACDDO requires preventive measures. Most of the measures are of general nature such as strategies, policies or trainings. The implementation of risk-based control measures is more measurable. We know that in parallel to the risk-based approach internal control systems serve as a building block of effective compliance management systems. Internal control systems also build bridges within the three-line model. The first, second and third line follow own responsibilities and principles. However, an organization has to be considered holistically and systematically. Internal controls serve as verification basis for all three lines. Here it would have been more helpful to get more governance on control fields, single controls or key performance indicators by the German legislator. The legislator could have used recitals or other explanations. Written reports for auditing compliance could be helpful as well know more about specifications of controls.

After a violation the German legislator requires imminent, appropriate remedial actions (article seven section one GER ACDDO). If a violation cannot end in foreseeable future, a concept has to be implemented for ending or minimizing a violation without undue delay. The concept must contain a concrete table and measures such as a temporary suspension of the business relationships while efforts are made to minimize a risk. As ultima ratio a termination of the business relationship is required (article seven section three GER ACDDO). This is required in serious cases, if a concept fails or there is no prospect of success through own influence. The effectiveness of a remedial action must be reviewed annually and ad hoc in significant cases.

In the GER ACDDO many duties specifically only refer to direct suppliers.[60] For indirect suppliers, article nine GER ACDDO serves as general clause. An enterprise must enable complaints procedure on indirect suppliers. If an enterprise gains substantial knowledge on indications for violation which have taken place at an indirect supplier, it must start a process of actions. The crucial criterion is substantial knowledge. Pursuant to article nine section three GER ACDDO this is the case if actual indications suggest that a violation may be possible. This threshold is rather low. Actual indications mainly enable a separation from opinions or rumors.[61] A risk analysis has to be carried out, a concept established and preventive measures prepared.[62] All actions follow the risk-based approach.[63]

60 Dohrmann (2021), p. 265.

61 Grabosch (2021a, b), p. 51.

62 Fleischer (2022), p. 209.

63 Fitzer and Gergen (2022), 327.

Overall, a holistic understanding of supply chains is required. Executive and supervisory boards shall establish adequate governance and compliance management systems integrating context, strategies, policies, risk assessments, actions, monitoring, reporting and improvement.[64] A risk-based approach will be the fundament for priorities and measures. Single strategies, procedures and mechanisms will be needed to establish transparency, to take care and mitigate risks. This includes a whistleblowing access, trainings, an incident solving mechanisms, investigations methods, certifications, audits or stress-tests. Set-ups have to be established to build up knowledge and power. There are principles which have to be assured such as independency, top down legitimation or professionality. Strong corporate governance and compliance functions have to be directly linked to the executive board or the managing directors. Compliance committees shall be established to enable an interdisciplinary information exchange among supervisory, executive board, governance and compliance functions.

Similar to the GER ACDDO the EU has summarized the duties in article six to eleven EU CSDDD. Diligence duties have to be stipulated in policies. Such duties shall describe the enterprise approach on due diligence. Minimum requirements are a a code of conduct comprehensible for employees and other group entities. Additionally, actions shall be foreseen to measure the degree of compliance internally as well as externally relating to established business relationships. In many organizations still a good, coherent corporate governance framework is missing. It is challenging to establish a stable, capable framework able to integrate cultures, to capture growth and changes adequately. To assure coherency it is important to provide a governance framework for all relevant functions. Furthermore, the business context such as the digital ecosystem changes risk and opportunities. Aspects such as cyber and data security, trade secrets and competition structures have to be realigned. The cyber space requires a holistic approach aligning different technological levels and cultures. Growth, mergers and acquisitions demand an integration of new units or functions. Hence, a value chain management system is needed to capture the complete internal and external context.

Pursuant to article six EU CSDDD companies shall take appropriate measures to identify actual and potential adverse impact. Following a risk-based approach risk firstly should be prevented, otherwise mitigated. Pursuant to the nature, complexity of an organization and its context, an action plan should be implemented. Such a plan should be measured by qualitative, quantitative characteristics to enable improvement. Such a plan requires a holistic stakeholder management. Business partner should give contractual assurances to comply with such duties. In particular, partners have to adhere to company's ethics and values, policies, strategies, leadership and culture.

Article eight EU CSDDD describes the treatment of actual adverse impact. Such impact has to be aborted. Otherwise this impact has to be mitigated to the extent possible. Companies shall take all appropriate measures. That means actions have

---

[64] Velte (2022), p. 63; Dörrwächter (2022), p. 1083.

to be assessed in the spirit of the principle of proportionality. Here, we again see that general principles of law are increasingly applied in private, economic law. Again, actions shall be proportionate in relation to the circumstances, the internal and external context of an enterprise. Proportionality may also require compensation of damages. The preventive approach is accompanied by repressive actions. A corrective action plan with clear goals, tasks, deadlines and performance indicators can serve as an adequate measure. If a concerned supplier is a small or medium sized company, it could be reasonable to provide support. This is logical if an established business relationship is given. Such relationships constitute rights and duties.

4 Effective Monitoring and State Authority Competencies

Enterprises shall conduct regular monitoring and assessments to find out the degree of compliance with own duties (article ten EU CSDDD). Such assessments shall take place at least annually. The EU legislator requires where appropriate, to use qualitative and quantitative indicators. Here, the legislator could have enumerated a few samples. This could support comparability and effectiveness. Acknowledged indicators could lead to a state of the art-understanding to assure a certain protection level.

Compliance documentation has to be available for at least 7 years (article ten EU CSDDD). Such periods are already known from financial reporting standards. However, it is interesting that transparency obligations are stipulated. An annual report has to be made available free of charge on the website of an enterprise.

Comparable to other legislative acts legislators have provide additional information on their understanding. We know this for instance from the ESG legislation in the EU, where the EFRAG is entitled to stipulated standards through delegated acts. For instance, the EFRAG has prepared ESRS for non-financial reporting. These delegated act proposals are rather broad and detailed describing due diligence obligations up to detailed reporting. Member states have adopted such a governance practice. The German legislator speaks about handouts. For instance, in article twenty GER ACDDO the German legislator announces cross-sectoral or sector-specific information, assistance and recommendations on compliance with the GER ACDDO.[65] For supply chain compliance the German legislator has declared Federal Foreign Office as competent authority. For legal interpretation this could be helpful, but also cause complexity. We do know that administration uses such authority guidance as basis for decision-making. From the perspective of equality this is a crucial basis because it can serve as scale for equal or non-equal treatment. Discrimination rights have to be observed. As far as such authority information do have a binding character courts have to take such guidance into consideration.

[65] Schmidt (2022), p. 217.

In article thirteen EU CSDDD the EU speaks about guidance. Here, the EU Commission provides the possibility to consult with the European Union Agency for Fundamental Rights, the European Environment Agency, and where appropriate with international bodies jointly with member states on due diligence obligations. To increase transparency, information and communication the EU pronounces the use of website platforms (article fourteen EU CSDDD) and the annual publishing of statements (article eleven EU CSDDD). It becomes evident that guidance is embedded in a bigger consultancy process. This could be time intensive. Besides the advantage of information exchange and transparency, the process requires the assurance of confidentiality and integrity.

5 Complaint Procedure

We know complaint procedures already as integral part of compliance management systems. The UN Guiding Principles on Business and Human Rights recommended such information or discovery mechanisms to be implemented.[66] Article twenty-three EU CSDDD refers to Directive (EU) 2019/1937, the well-known general Whistleblowing Directive. The German legislator has stipulated such duties explicitly in article eight GER ACDDO.[67]

The effectiveness of a complaint procedure depends on different pre-conditions and guarantees. Related people must have a right and easy possibility to access such a procedure. Integrity, anonymity and confidentiality have to be granted. Effectiveness also require that no disadvantage or punishment will be a consequence of a complaint. This is a triad of at least three duties. Undoubted, easy to understand explanation on the access and use of such a complaint procedure have to be publicly available. People shall not fear to complain. The idea of whistleblowing is characterized through anonymity. Experiences from the past have revealed improper investigations, tracking and pursuit. Insofar it is remarkable that the German legislator uses the term confidentiality instead of anonymity. Confidentiality here has to be interpreted teleologically. Full anonymity has to be granted. Otherwise the goal of the supply chain acts would be endangered. Finally, the avoidance of disadvantages is the most material point. This purpose has to be interpreted fairly. Effective protection has to be taken literally. Effective protection in its broadest understanding can mean that also relatives of a concerned person or supporters have to be protected. Furthermore, it can be demanded that the protection is not only extended to the target, but also to potential aggressors. Hence, protection against third parties has to be granted as far as proportional.

[66] un-leitprinzipien-de-data.pdf (auswaertiges-amt.de).

[67] Stemberg (2020), p. 85.

6 Supervisory Authorities, Concerns and Sanctions

In Germany the supervisory authority for monitoring and enforcement is the Federal Office of Economics and Export Control.[68] Traditionally, this authority is responsible for export control regulations. Thus, in term of supply chains this authority has been deemed as being competent for such purposes. Supervisory authorities monitoring and enforcement rights are stipulated in art. 12ff. GER ACDDO. The two-pillar approach consist of one pillar constituting an ongoing review and a second pillar following an event-driven assessment.[69] Article fourteen GER ACDDO entitles competent authorities to take actions ex officio or upon request. As far as it is necessary for the performance of such rights, authorities have access rights, to all buildings and offices as well as papers or information. To keep proportionality such visits shall take place during normal business times.

Sanctions are various and the GER ACDDO has to be interpreted jointly with different other acts. Article twenty-two GER ACDDO enables the exclusion from participation in a procedure for the award of a supply, works or service contract by the contracting authorities referred to in article ninety-nine and one-hundred Act Against Restraints of Competition. Article twenty-four section one Act on Corporate Due Diligence Obligations enables financial penalties up to TEUR 800. Article thirty section two sentence three Regulatory Offences Act remains applicable in case of article twenty-four section two sentence one number one and two. The Regulatory Offences Act, in particular articles nine, thirty, one-hundred thirty enables imposing fines on enterprises as well as on individuals. Legal entities with an average annual turnover of more than EUR 400 million may be punished with a fine up to two percent of the annual turnover (article twenty-four section three GER ACDDO). The turnover of a legal entity or association of entities is based on the global turnover of natural persons and legal entities as well as all associations of persons in the last three financial years preceding the decision by an authority insofar as the such persons and associations operate as an economic unit (article twenty-four section three sentence two GER ACDDO). Authorities may be even entitled to estimate such a turnover. The basis for the assessment of a fine is determined by the significance of the offence. Here, the authority has room for discretion. The law only provides samples of circumstances to be considered. These are for instance, the charge against the perpetrator, motives, objectives, effects of regulatory offences or previous regulatory offences (article twenty-four section four GER ACDDO).

The EU has established a two tier-sanction system of civil liability and public sanctions. In article twenty-two EU CSDDD civil liability is foreseen. Generally, member states have to implement a sanction regime (article twenty-one EU CSDDD). Regarding public support article twenty-four EU CSDDD demands member states shall ensure compliant public support. Enterprises which cannot

---

[68] Brouwer (2022), p. 137.

[69] Schmidt (2022), p. 216.

grant compliance with the duties stipulated in the EU CSDDD shall not receive public support.

7 Liabilities and Director's Duties

In article three section three GER ACDDO the German legislator emphasizes that violations of the GER ACDDO do not provide a legal basis to liabilities under civil law. At the beginning it was discussed to implement such a liability. From a civil law perspective the GER ACDDO should not serve as protection law in the meaning of § 823 German Civil Code.[70] In contrast to Germany, the EU CSDDD establishes civil liabilities in article twenty-two EU CSDDD. Member states shall ensure that companies are liable for damages if they are not compliant with articles seven and eight EU CSDDD. The EU Commission emphasizes that sustainability due diligence processes, actions and assurances have to be deemed as competitive advantage.[71] Consumers and investors already care for sustainable reputation. Meanwhile, incompliances have proven that voluntary self-commitments do not provide a guarantee. Insofar the legislative acts on sustainability provide legal certainty, legal security and confidence.

Director's duties are explicitly mentioned in articles twenty-five and twenty-six EU CSDDD. Directors have to consider consequences of their decisions for sustainability matters. The EU indicates the broad context and need of understanding value chains for internal organizational action and reaction such as a mitigation process.[72] This requires a thinking in scenarios and risk-assessment. Instead of thinking in single decisions, all business decisions have to be covered by a human and environmental rights mechanism, this means governance and compliance management systems including a whistleblowing system, incident management, investigation methods, reliable documentation, transparent reporting mechanism, open communication, effective trainings and continuous improvement. A management system can be divided into single elements and phases. For practical, effective implementation international standards may be used such as the ISO (International Organization for Standardization) 37,000 for governance or 37,301 for compliance. A compliance management system can be established in sequential steps. Firstly, context, culture and leadership have to be understood. This phase is characterized by a risk-based approach. Secondly, planning, support and operations are directed to daily compliance management. Incident management, awareness, training, documentation or reporting follow the principle of proportionality. Thirdly, assessments shall lead to continuous improvement.

[70] Schmidt (2022), p. 216.

[71] Refer Impact Assessment accompanying the Corporate Sustainability Due Diligence Directive, pp. 15, 23.

[72] Refer Explantory Memorandum of the Corporate Sustainability Due Diligence Directive, p.1.

8 Resumee

After the experiences of the last years we do see an increasing, unprecedent amount of new legislative acts on ESG issues, administrative acts and new enforcement trends by authorities. They do want to prevent violations of environmental and social rights. Moreover, good reputation and corporate citizenship are deemed as a competitive advantage and aspect of future viability. International conventions and self-commitments have not prevented such violations. Legislators have taken the next step to increase the protection and performance level. Compared to member states such as Germany, the EU is even stricter. The personal and material scope is broader, supply and value chains are in scope, both up- and downstream chains and civil liabilities are applicable. The GER ACDDO needs legal interpretation. This indicates the maturity level of the legislation requiring the application of traditional legal methodology combined with evolving knowledge on governance, risk and compliance. Indirect suppliers are not regulated in the same way as direct suppliers. Substantiated knowledge on risks is sufficient to initiate measures on indirect suppliers. Although, only single environmental conventions are explicitly mentioned in the GER ACDDO, specific environmental risks have to be considered only due to their qualification as such with the possibility to cause adverse impact. Adequate measures have to be taken. A violation of a right is not needed.

Overall, due diligence obligations have been increased and sanction regimes expanded, both for organizations and individuals. Looking at the different governance and compliance elements such as risk assessments, complaint procedures, internal control systems, monitoring and reporting duties it become clear that a holistic understanding is needed. Enterprises have to establish governance, risk and compliance management systems. It is not sufficient to advance single elements of management systems. Complex, global supply and value chain structures cannot be covered effectively by single approaches. Even if costs will rise, top management and responsible people have to assure adherence to the due diligence acts adopted.

The key is a risk-based approach and adherence to the prinicple of proportionality. Instead of proportionality legislators use different terms such as appropriatenes. Different wordings or systematic inconsistencies impede a proportionale application. Enterprise should not be forced to stop their business or become insolvent. It is a question of risk treatment, of setting priorities, taking appropriate actions and reporting. In so far, the legislators emphasize the well-known principle of proportionality. But if we look at the already existing audit and certification, governance and compliance standards, a governance for management systems exists. Management systems have to be adequate and effective. The term effective indicates, that management systems even proportionally designed, have to work in practice. The effectiveness test shows the results. Practically, this means that enterprises need competent people and sufficient process for implementation, execution and control. People have to be legally or comparably qualified, skilled in risk management, investigations, problem solving, applying IT systems, analyzing and exchanging data. A tone at and from the top has to be assured, authority and independency. An adequate organization only is one indicator. Working globally or in a matrix shows further challanges. Single people will not be able to oversee all supply and value chains, to understand all decisions, processes and systems. Compliance officers have to work with law, logistics, environmental, sales, marketing, procurement, supply chain and IT functions. Enterprises have to document their findings and actions and finally publish annual reports. Authorities are entitled to ask for reports, documents, interviews, to conduct investigations and to impose fines up to two percent of the annual turnover of an economic unit.

ESG and compliance requirements are not at the peak. To mitigate human, environmental and business risks regulations by authorities and in markets will increase, at least be complex and challenging. There is amutual effect among legislators, stakeholders, investors, clients and consumers to be compliant or even a good corporate citizen with positive social and environmental impact. Competition may benefit sustainable entrepreneurs. Reputation and quality of products and services will play a more dominant role.

References

Bomsdorf T, Blatecki-Burgert B (2022) Lieferketten-Richtlinie und Lieferkettensorgfaltspflichtengesetz. Zeitschrift für Rechtspolitik 2022(5):129–168

Brömmelmeyer C (2022) Nachhaltigkeit für Energieversorgungsunternehmen – Wie wirkt sich die Nachhaltigkeitsregulierung auf EU-Ebene auf die Energiewirtschaft aus? Energie- und Wettbewerbsrecht in der Kommunalen Wirtschaft 2022(3):75–117

Brouwer T (2022) Noch viele offene Rechts- und Auslegungsfragen zum Lieferkettensorgfaltsp flichtengesetz – Hinweise zum VCI-Diskussionspapier zur Umsetzung des LkSG. Corporate Compliance Zeitschrift 2022(5):125–164

Cappel A, Hund C (2022) Das Lieferkettensorgfaltspflichtengesetz – Ein Überblick über den Anwendungsbereich und die zentralen Regelungen. Zeitschrift für internationales Wirtschaftsrecht 2022(4):145–192

DAV, Deutscher Anwaltsverein, Ausschüsse Handelsrecht, Corporate Social Responsibility und Compliance sowie Menschenrechte (2022) Stellungnahme zum Vorschlag für eine Richtlinie des Europäischen Parlaments und des Rates über die Sorgfaltspflichten von Unternehmen im Hinblick auf Nachhaltigkeit und zur Änderung der RL (EU) 2019/1937. Neue Zeitschrift für Gesellschaftsrecht 2022(13):881–936

Dohrmann V (2021) Das deutsche Lieferkettensorgfaltspflichtengesetz als Vorbild für den europäischen Gesetzgeber? – Eine kritische Analyse. Corporate Compliance Zeitschrift 2021(6):265–312

Dörrwächter J (2022) Nachhaltigkeit und Gesellschaftsinteresse, Zu den Pflichten des Vorstands im Zusammenhang mit ESG. Neue Zeitschrift für Gesellschaftsrecht 2022(23):1081–1128

Dreisigacker-Sartor C, Ritter-Döring V (2022) Die europäische und finanzaufsichtsrechtliche Nachhaltigkeitsregulierung und ihre Auswirkungen auf die Immobilienbranche – Ein Überblick. Compliance Berater 2022(11):409–460

Driftmann F (2022) Das Phänomen des "Family Business Washing", Wenn das nicht belegbare Bild familienunternehmerischer Verantwortung zum bloßen Wertversprechen wird. Recht der Familienunternehmen 2022(7):297–344

Fitzer K, Gergen P (2022) Know your risks: Risiken managen und analysieren nach dem LkSG. Compliance Berater 2022(9):321–364

Fleischer H (2022) Grundstrukturen der lieferkettenrechtlichen Sorgfaltspflichten. Corporate Compliance Zeitschrift 2022(7–8):205–252

Göpfert B, Melles M (2022) Verantwortungsvolles unternehmerisches Handeln nach den OECD-Leitsätzen: Neue Juristische Wochenschrift 2022(35):2497–2576

Grabosch R (2021a) Grundlagen, Prinzipien und Begriffe. In: Grabosch R (ed) Das neue Lieferkettensorgfaltspflichtengesetz. Nomos

Grabosch R (2021b) Die Sorgfaltspflichten. In: Grabosch R (ed) Das neue Lieferkettensorgfaltspflichtengesetz. Nomos

Herchen H (2022) Die Transformation des deutschen Privatrechts. Neue Juristische Wochenschrift 2022(43):3105–3176

Jacob M (2019) Digitalisierung & Nachhaltigkeit. Springer

Krause R (2022) Das Lieferkettensorgfaltspflichtengesetz als Baustein eines transnationalen Arbeitsrechts – Teil I. Recht der Arbeit 2022(5):253–316

Kühnberger M, Wohlgemuth V (2022) Zum Stand der nichtfinanziellen Berichterstattung – Eine Skizze globaler Entwicklungen. Deutsches Steuerrecht 2022(13):633–680

Mosbacher A (2023) Kapitalanlagebetrug durch "Greenwashing". Neue Juristische Wochenschrift 2023(1-2):1–112

Nemat AT, Panzer-Heemeier A, Meckenstock C (2022) ESG 2.0 – Digitale Ethik als neue Dimension der Nachhaltigkeit. Zeitschrift für nachhaltige Unternehmensführung 2022(4):97–128

Nietsch M, Wiedmann M (2022) Der Vorschlag zu einer europäischen Sorgfaltspflichten-Richtlinie im Unternehmensbereich (Corporate Sustainability Due Diligence Act). Corporate Compliance Zeitschrift 2022(5):125–164

Ruland Y, Bürger C, Weber L, Kroth L (2022) Environment, social, governance – ESG-bezogene Haftungsrisiken Sustainable Finance, Greenwashing und Corporate Social Governance. Beck-Online, Newsdienst Compliance 2022:220027

Schlacke S (2022) Klimaschutz im Mehrebenensystem. Neue Zeitschrift für Verwaltungsrecht 2022(13):905–992

Schmidt F (2022) Die Durchschlagskraft des Lieferkettensorgfaltspflichtengesetz (LkSG) in der Schwebe – ein mahnendes Beispiel für zu hektische Gesetzgebung. Corporate Compliance Zeitschrift 2022(7–8):205–252

Schön W (2022) "Nachhaltigkeit" in der Unternehmensberichterstattung. Zeitschrift für die gesamte Privatrechtswissenschaft 2022(2):129–256

Schönfelder D (2021) Menschenrechtliche und Umweltbezogene Risiken. In: Grabosch R (ed) Das neue Lieferkettensorgfaltspflichtengesetz. Nomos

Spießhofer B (2022) Sustainable corporate governance. Neue Zeitschrift für Gesellschaftsrecht 2022(10):433–480

Stemberg C (2020) Die drei "Schlüsselkriterien" des Beschwerdeverfahrens nach § 8 Lieferkettensorgfaltspflichtengesetz. Corporate Compliance Zeitschrift 2020(4):85–124

Velte P (2022) Regulierung der *Sustainable Board Governance* – das fehlende Glied in der Kette des *"EU Green Deal"*- Projekts? Zeitschrift für Internationale Rechnungslegung 2022(2):47–91

The Crisis of the Rule of Law: "Chronicle of a Death Foretold"

Rosita Silvestre

1 Introduction

The crisis of the rule of law in the European Union has been a much-debated theme ever since the paradigm of illiberal democracies spread to some Member States of Central and Eastern Europe. After joining the Union, the approach of these States towards the European Union changed by throwing down the specter of nationalism and anti-Europeanism as an open challenge to the common European culture.

Such a crisis is associated with well-defined governmental actions, which rehabilitated the national sovereignty mantra, and which consisted of radical changes in constitutional arrangements, either through unpopular legislation or through distorting amendments to national Constitutions. Before Poland and Hungary became the driving forces behind the autocratic drift that seriously demobilised the European Union's forces to intervene, several other Member States had also claimed respect for national identities in the face of expanding integration in an attempt to preserve the internal order.[1] However, here the general concern escalated regarding the respect for democracy and for the founding principles of the Union, which have been accepted as preconditions for membership by virtue of Article 49 of TEU in conjunction with article 2 of TEU.

As of the first evidence of the crisis, two questions seem to be the most compelling: (1) Why is the clash between Central and Eastern members and the European institutions perceived more burdensome than in other countries where populism has

[1] See the examples of Germany and Italy, which through their Constitutional Courts have openly lashed out against the doctrine of European supremacy. For a complete analysis see Drinóczi (2020), pp. 106–112.

R. Silvestre (✉)
Consiglio Nazionale delle Ricerche-Istituto per la Bioeconomia, Rome, Italy
e-mail: rosita.silvestre@ibe.cnr.it

E. Omerović et al. (eds.), *Balkan Yearbook of European and International Law 2023*, Balkan Yearbook of European and International Law 2023,
https://doi.org/10.1007/978-3-031-69670-1_6

taken hold? and (2) Why has Europe allowed to be weakened by the challenges posed by its spread, instead of nipping it in the bud?

Going back in time, the establishment of the conditional regime based on the democratic identity common to the Member States has to be placed in the accession of the CEECs to the European Union. The preparation for the entry of the said countries into the European club was followed by a sudden process of transformation of values and by the abandonment of the old constitutional dimension in order to introduce the models typical of Western liberal democracies into the domestic systems.

In the context of the candidates' transformation, the primary goal of the Union was to assist the transfusion of democracy within national systems and, at this very moment, it has to reckon with the core of principles and values immanent in them, rooted as such in the national identities formed over a long history that separated the region from the rest of the Western world.

Needless to say, since intra-regional differences must be taken into account, a different picture of how the transition has occurred could be drawn for each country. For instance, in Poland in the pre-accession phase, the adaptation of the economic model to the free market was the priority.[2] Nonetheless, the roundtables taking place from '89 on the formation of the new Constitution, later ratified in '97, set off a straightforward constitution-making process; on the contrary, in other countries, the commitment of political forces to make the democratic transition palatable for entry into the European Union did not produce the expected results. One might think of Hungary, which, although it has been an example of a stable post-transition democracy, the populist and identity-based historical legacy, typical of the 1949 Constitution, was handed down in a text instrumental to the assertion of majority power.[3] Not to mention Slovakia, whose institutional framework was very unstable for a long time, with the characteristic of a strong depowerment of the Parliament, or Romania and Bulgaria, which adopted rough Constitutions, almost devoid of constructive dialogue among political actors.

It is therefore clear how the existing backgrounds may have launched "anomalous" developments in the socio-political framework of the said countries after their accession to the European Union. Besides, in the author's opinion, the slow dismantiling of democracy in Europe, which is threatening the European stability nowadays, is also rooted in the excessive confidence of the supranational authorities of being able to channel one value system into another, without taking into consideration that they originate from extremely different legal scenarios and, in addition, in their consequential inability to create an enduring protection network.

But not only. To date, what scholars continue to insist on are the effects of the phenomenon here analysed, ignoring its causes and neglecting that the inconsistency of the legal categories advocated during the pre-accession negotiations, such as common values, democracy, and the rule of law, generated an open space for

[2] On the Balcerowicz Plan see Sachs (1994), p. 267.

[3] Hungary's constitution has been amended nine times, according to the principle of two-thirds majority: the source on https://www.europarl.europa.eu/.

contents without defined boundaries, which cannot be prescribed in mandatory norms, and thus cannot set clear legal limits: neither was this so at the time of the negotiations nor is it currently.

In fact, given the vagueness of the terms of accession dictated by the European Commission under the supervision of the Council and the Parliament, the incisiveness of the monitoring activity conducted by the delegated institutions raised skepticism, whereas the assessment of candidates' respect for democracy and for the rule of law was just a manifesto. It is undeniable that in the pre-accession phase, the conditions architected by the European institutions to guide the candidates' transition turned into the imposition of structural competencies and institutional practices adapted to the *acquis communautaire*. After the accession, the controls loosened, as it was considered that once at the end of the negotiations for membership, the process was almost irreversible.

In view of this brief premise, in the present manuscript, it will be argued that *"the rule of law backsliding in the EU"*[4] depends on a number of contributing factors: not only the complex relationship between the Member States and the Union, custodians of differentiated identities, but also the institutional processes governed by the EU and the impact they have had on the democratic challenges tackled by the States. In light of this, the proposed work will be divided into a first part, where the interplay between the EU accession and the crisis of the rule of law will be debated. The second and the final parts will provide an attempt to relaunch the discussion on the provision of Article 2 of TEU, which has not only inaugurated the case-law before the Court of Luxembourg, but has also stimulated further insights, since up to now the importance of the values enshrined in it has been marginalised in view of their purely political nature.

2 The Constitutional Momentum of the Accession Phase. The Candidates' Status

The crisis of the rule of law in the Member States of Central and Eastern Europe stimulates the remarks on a value-driven dimension of domestic constitutions and on the adaptation of internal legal systems to that of the European Union prior to joining it. There are three stages that can be traced in the constitutional approach of these countries to the concept of transition during their gradual integration into the Union: the post-communist phase, from 1989, which marks the first tendencies towards liberal principles. At the same time, some traces of national identities as expressions of dissidence to the subtraction of sovereignty, well-know in the Soviet era, can be reported. The second phase has been labeled as the transition to the European Union, whose peculiarity has been the candidates'convertion to the liberal paradigm and their marriage with the liberal constitutionalism, following the

[4] On the process of democratic regression in the EU see Pech and Scheppele (2017), p. 7.

dominant models in the Member States. A third and final stage can be mapped out at the birth of illiberal democracies in the form of authoritarian/democratic hybrid-regimes, where the populist politics have jeopardised the democratic principles and human rights. As underlined by Bien-Kaczala, the dominant feature of this phase, which coincides with the post-accession up to present time, is the illiberalisation of the constitutions and the constitutionalisation of populist nationalism.[5]

Basically, it can be observed that the commitment to adopt a new constitutional *acquis* by the States has run in parallel with the promise of accession by the European Union, so the examination of the adaptation of national constitutional systems to the process of European integration and of the constitutional changes, which in fact are derived from the latter, are of strategic relevance for the purposes of this work.[6]

A. Di Gregorio has noted in *"The Fundamental Law of Hungary in the European context"*[7] that, with the fall of the Soviet regime, the States involved in this change have been primarily engaged in the rehabilitation of the respective legal systems in order to adapt them to the legal requirements of European conditionality, consisting, on the one hand, of the technical standards of accession, and of the European values and principles on the other. The result has been that the acquisition of these standards, and consequently the accession to the Union, has coincided with the imposition on the candidate States of compliance with permanent obligations, whose legal basis is enshrined in Article 2 TEU, and reinforced through the principle of sincere cooperation laid down in Article 4, par.3, TEU for protecting the execution of such obligations.[8]

Additionally, the risks of protectionist involutions have been avoided as a result of the post-Soviet *ordo constituens* definition in these countries, either through constitutional revision procedures, or through subsequent amendments which introduced European clauses, i.e., norms which transferred and/or delegated sovereign powers in accordance with constitutional principles, rather than protected these by safeguard clauses.[9]

In line with countries' rapproachement to other Member States, the growing interest over the time in making systems homogeneous is justified by the perception that the European integration has been a democratic choice needed to be protected, and around this intent a common understanding has undoubtedly developed between the governments of these countries and the European institutions.[10] Downstream of this political choice are the democratic traditions inspiring the transition and the experiences of pluralist democracies in the EU; the former have also been recalled

---

[5] Drinóczi and Bień-Kacała (2019), p. 1164.

[6] Morrone (2018) p. 7.

[7] Di Gregorio (2015), p. 258.

[8] Accession criteria (Copenaghen criteria) on https://eur-lex.europa.eu/; Resolution of the European Parliament (July 3, 2013) on the situation of the fundamental rights/ standards and practices in Hungary-pursuant to the european Parliament resolution of February 16, 2012.

[9] Di Gregorio (2004), p. 2067.

[10] Sadurski (2012), pp. 2–7.

by the Constitutional Courts in a friendly attitude, as seen in the first decisions on the adaptation to the European legal system.[11]

Having identified these aspects, there is no doubt that on a formal level the language of 1989 transition was a European language, which equipped the candidates with appropriate models for the entry into the Union, although, on its part, the latter conveyed the notion of membership through technical tools.

At the same time, the discussion relating to the diffusion of the Union's common values within the Central and Eastern States cannot be reduced to that formality. More specifically, the cultural and political traditions of these States have inspired the herein described constitutional developments.[12]

In fact, it cannot be neglected that the historical-cultural background of these countries neither belonged to the community of values promoted by the European Union, nor did it form its structure, other than the geographic one. A demonstration of what has just been stated is the so-called Visegrad Group, established in 1991, whose consolidation in terms of ethno-cultural stance represents a crucial instrument of interpretation of the value structures that governed the existence of the CEECs within the European Union. Despite the end of socialism, it is the core identity that has acted as the glue of the group, and which has been reproposed as a problem to solve for the European institutions.[13]

Leaving aside the specific experiences of such a coalition, at an overall glance, a number of reasons for the conflicting approach to the constitutional and European identity on the part of the CEECs can be mentioned, as the doctrine has illustrated.[14] There are two main ones: a) the impossibility for such States to reach full democratic maturity due to their communist past; and b) the absence of constitutional tradition, which has not made it possible to fully assimilate in a few years those concepts that in other European countries have matured over centuries of struggles for the limitation of power.[15]

In this regard, two concrete examples, *inter alia*, of the difficult shift highlighted up to now can be delineated. Those are Hungary and Poland, since the destruction of the very principle of majority democracy in these countries shattered the post-socialist constitutional architecture, imposed among the most suitable choices for a

[11] See for comparison Hungarian CC Decision 4/1997: in the event of a conflict between a domestic law that enshrines the protection of fundamental rights and international law, proclaims the harmonization of the domestic law with international obligations; Hungarian CC Decision 143/ 2010 on the Lisbon Treaty and Decision 22/2012 on the Treaty on Stability, Coordination and Governance; Polish CC—Ref. No. SK 26/08 on European Arrest Warrant (II) (October 5, 2010); Polish CC—Ref. No. K 32/09 on the Constitutionality of the Lisbon Treaty (November, 242,010). More than others, Polish jurisprudence assumes an open approach to the European model but by virtue of a precise European clause contained in the Constitution, counterbalanced by domestic principles and local constitutional values: see art 91. 3 Polish Constitution 1997 vs Czech Republic whose jurisprudence constitutional maintains a more critical attitude.

[12] Giaro (2017), pp. 23–38.

[13] Dangerfield (2008), p. 630.

[14] Blokker (2017), p. 14.

[15] Sadurski (2003-2004), Theme 2. See also Sbailò (2008), p. 35.

transitional context. Certainly, thanks to the transition of 1989, an overturning of values took place in both countries but in scenarios where the balancing of values was fluid.

Indeed, the transition in Hungary proved to be peaceful and gradual, taking up Western-style principles and institutions from the very first instances of democratisation.[16] Notwithstanding the centrality of institutional stability built on democratic bases[17] and the sympathetic, not violent, progression towards European law, Hungary is an example of a more tangible discontinuity between the constitutional models adopted at the time of the membership and once the relations with EU law strenghtened. Of course, from the first initiatives that led to the construction of the constitutional structure in Hungary, no attempt to consolidate relations with supranational institutions survived the advent of populism in the years following the obtaining of the member status. In fact, it had taken two decades for Hungary to consolidate its constitutional reality, when suddenly the plans, following the fall of the regime for a new Constitution, failed to materialise. Indeed, in the very short period between 1989 and 1990, after the ninth amendment, an entirely new Constitution was introduced. Immediately after the fall of communism and until 2011, Hungary was the only country in the former Soviet bloc that failed to adopt an innovative Constitution. The text ratified in 1949 survived until 2010 to any attempt at organic reform, while the country's accession to the Council of Europe in 1990 solved the problem of integrating Hungary into the community of democratic States. Consequently, one gets the impression that, when the sovereign movements managed to supplant the moderate parties in the government offices, through severe criticism to the European crises, they took hold solidly, after having proved to be a genuine alternative to those political forces that disrupted the post-transition reforms. In 2011, when the Constitution was codified, the governing majority, nationalist and populist, received all the electoral support and strength to be able to make the constitutional text an instrument of power for the executive and to remodel the relationship with the European institutions.[18]

On the other hand, in Poland, the 1997 Constitution encompassed the principle of State sovereignty, giving impulse to a legal order that revolved around this concept.[19]

The consolidation of constitutional changes in the country, which took place after the democratic transition, gave rise to a multifaceted system, in which national identity is intertwined with the supranational one and in which these are mutually supported through the inclusion in the Constitution of the international agreements, ratified as binding sources with *erga omnes* effects. Also, in terms of protection of rights, the Polish State has provided these with regulatory instruments aimed at

[16] Ganino (1996), p. 1 et seqq.

[17] Franceschi (2021), http://www.storiain.net/.

[18] Chronowski (2012), p. 119 et seq. See European Parliament (2011) Resolution n.2011/2655 (RSP) on the Revised Hungarian Constitution.

[19] Vella (2020), p. 105.

eluding authoritarian tendencies. Accordingly, the Constitution of 1997 adopted a democratic institutional framework and legitimised the integration process by circumscribing the limitations of sovereignty within the constitutional boundaries.[20] Thus, the immovability of the Constitution was the cardinal principle of the country's democratisation, so much so that, starting from 2015, in the absence of technical requirements for the initiation of the constitutional review procedure, the reform policy of the government party (PIS), has been implemented through legislation,[21] thus *de facto*, diverting the Constitution from its own authority and proceeding to the dismantling of the constitutional state *ab imis fundamentis*.

Beyond the political developments following the transition, the Polish dilemma lies in the fragmentation of civil society, which has made the country unstable, to the extent that political parties have continuously alternated in government since the Third Republic. On the contrary, Poland has boasted a solid parliamentary tradition, however changeable, given the succession of historical events. The impact of the actual authoritarian current, imperilling the cardinal principles of liberal constitutionalism in the Polish society, is out of control due to the deficiencies in the mechanisms of control and balance in the relations between the State powers and due to the deprivation of the Constitutional Court of its function as a counterweight to the political power.[22]

Outside the Visegrad group, but similarly and perhaps to a greater extent, in Romania and Bulgaria, the post-socialist transition was very difficult, although the two countries also adopted democratic constitutions. From the beginning, both faced the rise of illiberal democracies, which completely nullified oppositions and engaged political actors whose relationship to the communist past has remained ambiguous.[23] In fact, here the reform process was hampered by the limited capacity for action of democratic institutions and the absence of conditions necessary for the abandonment of the collectivist system in favour of the market system.

The transition in Slovakia is also worth illustrating, since the approach to democratic institutions suggested by the European Union was neither clear nor straightforward for this State. The most critical aspect concerned the complex relationship between political actors within the country and the precarious balance between the majority parties and the opposition, so much so that, on the formal level, democracy was an achievement within the Slovak system, but on the other hand, only a political bloc, that is, the liberal one, really embraced parliamentary democracy. Conversely, nationalist groups touted populism and the majority criterion. In this regard, an interesting interpretation has been provided by the politology literature, which has argued that, after the post-communist transition, consensual democracy has been

---

[20] Morrone, *ibidem*.

[21] Serowaniec and Witkowski (2021), p. 252.

[22] Polmonari (2021), https://massimedalpassato.it/.

[23] Rosanò (2022), p. 359.

lacking in the country, in the meaning of the absence of "socialised" political actors and of the absence of real equal participation in the reform process.[24]

And more, it cannot be overlooked that the confluence of European standards in the legal systems of the candidate countries was confronted with the limit of national sovereignty, which the countries of Central and Eastern Europe have been, in truth, quite fond of since the transition of 1989.[25]

Even the proclamation of constitutional identity by the government autorities, which apparently seems to be able to be explanted from the post-transition axiological fabric, has references to the transitional past and its partial settlement, as well as to the impulsive adaptation to Western values as a precondition for acceding to the Union. In this regard and once again, two historically dominant examples have served as a model. From the perspective of constitutional identity propaganda, it has been seen that in Hungary the obsession to protect *"constitutional identity"*, which experienced a greater homogenisation of identity radicalism in the text of the 2011–2012 Constitution, has some deep roots. Thanks also to the interventions of the Constitutional Court, the Constitution, already in force in Hungary before the current one (i.e., the one adopted in 1949 was extensively modified after the collapse of the communist regime), was adapted to the new political situation. The fear of *"majority oppression"* was a dominant feature throughout the transition phase; moreover, it was its peculiarity. However, this fear, resulting in actions to avoid unipolar systems of government, was subsequently revised with the *"tyranny of the majority nation"*, and this has corroborated Hungary's defense of its constitutional sovereignty in the European context.[26]

In the meantime, it is evident that the identitarian echo still resonates above all at the institutional level in Poland, since the introduction of pluralism, typical of liberal ideology, has collided with the traditional Polish Roman Catholic culture, which has not splintered its cultural outline and, moreover, has found a deep limit in it. At any rate, as one can notice, the 90's, marked by a strong de-sovietisation of institutions and society, were particularised by the transition to a hybrid system supported by an indicator of a feeling of strong ethnicisation: the recomposition of the Polish identity. This principle was reconsolidated only after the Soviet domination had ended and based not only on theory but on a strong pragmatism, which political parties also used, and around which it was not that difficult for autocratic fringes to be assembled.[27]

At the same time, European culture represented an opportunity for this country, since through the neoliberal model it first and foremost offered the prospect of possible economic development. Suddenly, the regained importance of national borders, as a cornerstone for the definition and consolidation of national identities, began to favour government reshuffles between more conservative parties.

---

[24] Malová and Rybář (2000), pp. 99–115.

[25] Kellermann (2001) p. 591. See also Chronowski (2009), p. 305 et seqq.

[26] Di Gregorio, *ibidem*.

[27] Anderson (1994), pp. 182–214.

3 The Decision-Making Process of the EU Institutions in the Accession Phase

The candidates' fragile constitutional systems made their very accession to the European Union incomplete, and the suddenness of the post-communist transformation process did not help to simplify the admission procedures. Neverthless, the spirit of democracy pervaded the sophisticated system of reforms engineered by the European institutions and the performance of the candidate countries, up until the signing of the accession Treaties.

To begin with, the pre-accession stage of the fifth enlargement was led by the democratic conditionality, which, albeit partially, had a predominantly political dimension, oriented to the EU's general stability and security.[28] Notably, the Copenhagen criteria and in particular the political conditionality were used to promote democracy in the Central and Eastern European countries through a norm- and form-driven process with the aim of changing institutional structures and the elite's attitude.[29] At the same time, the conditionality regime required the States' compliance with democracy and the rigid observance of such criterion was intended to be the precondition for a successful retention of the new political systems formed after the accession.

In principle, the enlargement developed along the main channels of Western liberalism: such as the common market, the electoral system, the horizontal accountability, as well as the external factors of democratic advancement (civil society first),[30] although the greatest efforts were invested at the economic level.

As a counterbalance, the democratic conditionality was based on the elaboration of more technical-legal instruments and an effective stratagem to ensure good practices by the candidates was the granting of financial aid and a massive programme of incentives.[31] The European institutions have taken the advantage of the promise of aid to reaffirm the importance of democracy as the inspiring principle of accession, thus stimulating the domestic reforms for the adoption of the internal market acquis, including the respect for the rule of law and human rights.[32] Even the so-called Copenhagen related documents, designed to guarantee the constant monitoring of the candidate countries' compliance with the Copenhagen criteria, played a key role in promoting the European democratic model. Notwithstanding the persistence in recalling this criterion, it should be noted how the mandatory nature of such a formula has faded over time.

---

[28] Giusti and Locatelli (2008), p. 282.

[29] Hughes et al. (2002), p. 2 et seq. See European Council (1993) Conclusions of the Presidency.

[30] Kochenov (2011), p. 4 et seqq.

[31] As example see the PHARE programme: Council of Ministers (EEC) Regulation n. 3906/89 on economic aid to the Republic of Hungary and the Polish People's Republic (December 18, 1989). See Sedelmeier (2011), p. 12.

[32] Kochenov (2008), p. 508 et seqq. See also Grabbe (2001), pp. 113–1131.

A first bottleneck in the accession procedure was the formalistic vision of the conditions for the candidacy, diluting thus all the remedies put in place to prevent deficiencies in the future Member States by merely launching control and surveillance procedures over them. The European Union's difficulties in identifying the most suitable interventions depended in part on the nebulosity of the demand for compliance with democratic requirements and the impossibility of implementing them, given the limitations in the structural conditions of these countries. As D. Kochenov has brilliantly argued in the work cited in the footnotes, the systematic pre-accession country assessment was not followed by an effective acknowledgment of the dysfunctionalities of the countries. To some of them the institutions conferred the status of special surveillance (see Slovenia and Czechia), for others, however, the request for compliance with the criteria was set at a lower threshold. Regardless of the regional peculiarities, the conduct of a neighborhood policy with future members, aimed at strengthening relations on an economic, political, strategic, and cultural level seems to have not been abandoned, debasing the function of the Copenaghen criteria as internal parameters for the management of the integration process.

This result is hardly surprising because the European Union has set up top-down mechanisms for the transmission of the EU's democratic principles, giving rise to a purely supranational administration of the process and to the search for a vertical dialogue with the hierarchical leaders of these States. This strategy, which might appear acceptable, in truth shows a gap in the political convergence of such countries to the European model, and hence in essence it has been fallacious. At this proposal, certain profiles of political conditionality gained in relevance, such as the institutional reforms in the candidate countries, where bureaucratic reforms have still remained the raw nerve of transition. And moreover, the costs of accession, which were not taken into a due consideration by the European institutions during the enlargement, were higher than economic benefits to such an extent that policy inputs proved to be ineffective at the bottom.[33]

On closer inspection of the institutional performance, the enlargement presented some defiances that were difficult to address. If the project of enlarging the common Europe was intended as a project that *in nuce* was supposed to keep Europe united on a political level and to incorporate energies at different levels, after the pre-accession phase, conditionality lost its central role in the discourse on membership. The doctrine held that in the second stage of enlargement, rather than being a process of real convergence and political homogenisation between the countries in Europe, Europeanisation[34] represented a theoretical model of economic and social transformation.[35]

And yet, it was impossible to slow down the differential results of the economic reforms implemented in the candidate countries. Examples are the effects of

[33] Matlak et al. (2018), pp. 6–18.

[34] On the concept of Europeanisation see Radaelli (2004), pp. 8–11.

[35] Dimitrova (2005), p. 8–15. See also Grabbe (2006), pp. 75–96.

cohesion policies, the differentiation in the adoption of the euro, as well as the regional development of individual countries.[36]

4 Rethinking the Remedies to Mend the Disruption of the Rule of Law: The EU Strategy in the Post-accession Stage

The accession prospects of the Western Balkans have motivated the European Union to significantly review its legitimacy *vis-à-vis* the Member States and to redefine the opportunities envisaged by the common European pact.[37] The *raison d'être* of the conditional criteria, drafted in the Eastern enlargement, is to be found in the specific objective of creating a homogeneous basis of values at the European level on which to inform the States' membership. After all, the inputs stemming from the intricate integration of the countries belonging to the Soviet bloc first and foremost revealed the need to preserve the community of values generated there. Under such pressures, a change in the decision-making process relating to the choice of the means by which to defend these principles quickly turned to be a European priority. In response to such an urgency, European leaders have not only identified the minimum democratic principles to be incorporated into the Treaties, but they also proceeded to foresee sanctions against the States that would not respect these principles. This purpose was unequivocal to such an extent that the European Commission began to engage in an intense search for a mode of governing the promotion and protection of the rule of law within the target area. As a demonstration of what was affirmed, the intention of the institutions to solve the problem of the acquisition of competences in the field of democracy, rule of law and human rights, as well as the entrustment of these competences to the bodies appointed, appeared clear. Nonetheless, the methods adopted at the institutional level for the refinement of the legal remedies that could potentially be activated in cases of non-fulfilment did not remain faithful to the original strategy, inasmuch as this only gave rise to the implementation of the regulatory powers of the Union. On the contrary, any enhancement of formal tools for the implementation of these powers was omitted. Yet once again, the regulatory gap, which had characterised the whole process, confined the rule of law and the annexed principles to the prerogatives of sovereign States. At the same time, the supranational entity continued to reserve the right to the monitoring of the States' compliance with the Copenhagen criteria.[38]

Added to this is the fact that, apart from the formal proclamations that the European legal system provides alternatively valid legal remedies to counteract the

---

[36] See in comparison Gergo Medve-Balint (2018) p. 108, Vukov (2018), p. 127, Verdun (2018), p. 143.

[37] Coman (2017), p. 264 et seq.

[38] Coman (2016), p. 6.

violations of the indicated principles, no *ad hoc* prescription is provided to remediate the threat to the rule of law. Indeed, the persistency of serious violations of democracy and the rule of law[39] across some European countries has shed a new light on the problem of the effectiveness of the legal means employed. One example is the post-accession plan drawn up by Brussels between 2012 and 2014 to create a reference framework *"to contribute to reaching the objectives of the Council of Europe, including on the basis of the expertise of the European Commission for Democracy through Law (Venice Commission)"*, which intended to make up for the political vulnerability evidently found since then. As if to compensate for the gap, the Court of Justice has intervened on several occasions by exploiting the instruments made available by the Treaties, through the most disparate interpretative experiments. In the jurisdictional context, the search for a case-by-case solution entrusted to the European judge seems to have surgically refilled the regulatory framework left fragmented by the legislator, to the point that the rule of law has been theoretically envisioned as a binding value within the Union and an integral part of its constitutional dimension.[40]

Thus, what we have been able to ascertain is that before and after the enlargement the results of the European action were not so dissimilar. Neither the pressure from the old Eastern candidates nor the menace of legal actions did spur any change. Nonetheless, alongside the application of the Copenhagen political criteria, the imposition of a new obligation on the adoption and implementation of European legislation and the Community acquis has materialised the institutions' change of strategy for new candidates with a view to strengthening the accession process. Possibly, the interaction between the international bodies specialised in strengthening the rule of law put forward a set of positive results as well as the sharing of efforts related to it between the Council of Europe, the Venice Commission, the European Commission for the Efficiency of Justice (CEPEJ), and other non-EU bodies.[41]

Along this positive trail, such activism managed to boost reforms in some new applicants, laying a more solid foundation for their membership.[42] As a matter of fact, the institutions initiated a discourse based on more solid and less precarious arguments with the Western Balkans countries, partially controverting the approach taken in the past enlargement. Then, in order to avert further risks of non-compliance with European standards by these countries, the European Union launched a policy which will lead to their gradual integration through horizontal strategies composed of bilateral negotiations, financial assistance, political dialogue and regional cooperation. In particular, candidates for membership will undergo merit and progress assessments throughout the entire pre-adhesion phase.

[39] De Wilde and Zürn (2012), p. 143 et seq.

[40] Pech and Kochenov (2021), p. 11. See CJEU, C-896/19 Repubblika [ECLI:EU:C:2021:311] (April 20, 2021); CJEU, C-204/21 R [ECLI:EU:C: 2021:593] (July 14, 2021).

[41] Closa and Kochenov (2016), pp. 17–19.

[42] Noutcheva and Aydin Duzgit (2012), p. 70. See also Papadimitriou and Petrov (2012), pp. 746–763.

On these bases, a focus has been placed on the re-evaluation of the role of the Parliament in the direction of facilitating bilateral relations and the democratisation of the pattern adopted as well as the procedures implemented.

5 Conclusions

In the previous paragraphs attempts have been made to highlight the complex process of dissemination of the very concepts of the rule of law and democracy during the fifth round of enlargement to the East, these principles being the constructive forces of the liberal European integration project.[43] It has been seen that the democratic transition of the Central-Eastern candidates was prodromal to their entry into the European Union and that the "democratic" rule of law was the pillar of the state model handed down to them by the European institutions, changing their political habits and legal customs.

In the context of the application of this principle, a serious vulnerability has emerged in the construction of the candidates' bureaucratic apparatus, whereas the need to guarantee respect for democracy and the rule of law has been proclaimed by the Commission in very general terms, without taking into account the internal institutional characteristics and the constitutional variables in force in each State. Indeed, the doubt is that the effort of the European institutions to promote democracy in Europe was aimed at consolidating an ideal type of a democratic State, given the theoretical nature of the common rules imposed for the respect of democracy. Consequently, the democratic conditionality seems to correspond to the imposition of an abstract political culture destined to stop with the attainment of the membership at the hands of the candidates.

One can well understand why it has been impossible for the European institutions to intervene directly on the state administrative system, due to the fact that the electoral system, the judicial organisation, and the media independence significantly prove that the respective discipline falls within the Member States' field of competence. And that given the limits to the power of action of the European Union, the criteria of conditionality have consisted mostly of political prerequisites for membership, which have not been legally viable and, consequently, only partially effective. At this point, it can well be considered that the current rise of illiberalism does not simply exemplify the crumbling of the European democratic basis, but it also highlights the scarce valorisation of democracy in its essential contents over the years and, subsequently, in the inadequate means of control on democratic principles.

That being stated, in this work three profiles of the EU unsuccessful pro-democracy programme have been identified. Firstly, the impression is that the institutions have ignored the potential of the Treaties, even neglecting the importance of Article 2 of TEU, which enshrines the rule of law together with respect for

[43] On the connection between enlargement and democracy, see Maresceau (2001), pp. 3–28.

democracy and human rights, and whose normative value could be clarified in a quality written source of primary law, so as to enhance its binding nature.

Secondly, the European dimension of the values promoted in the accession process (democracy, rule of law, human rights) has been emphasised only at a very advanced stage of integration, since the constitutional transition of the candidates, needed albeit complex, could not, at least in principle, be founded on homogeneous values, considering the regional traditions and that the most widespread instrument for the acquisition of the European language by the States has been the "imitation of the West".[44] Especially in the context of the 1993 applications, the dividing line between European values and constitutional traditions was never crossed, even though, after the democratic transition, they became both essential components of the European identity and together with the other Member States they form the unique and unchangeable heritage of the supranational pact. Arguably, the persistence of such dichotomy depends on the fact that the axiological profile of national subsystems, coexisting within the European legal system, differs from country to country.[45] As a consequence, the rule of law itself, as a basic principle of democratic systems, has had various manifestations,[46] strictly dependant on the domestic legal traditions. In the examined circumstances, at the mercy of continuous collisions, pluralism has evidently ceased to function.

The third and last theme is the European institutions' inertia in the legal strengthening of the democratic rules, which could have stopped and even anticipated the national intolerance towards them. Nonetheless, such an operation has been and still is very risky and it is not easy to do more than merely threat with sanctions or even veto the entry and, today even more so, given that it would contribute to the fueling of a scenario of conflicts within the European legal panorama. In fact, the counter-limits and the national identity are stratagems which the States oppose to safeguard national supremacy and which they opposed above all at the time after the end of Soviet socialism, when too invasive interventions by the supranational authorities fomented their hostile attitude towards Europe.

As evidenced, the results of such contributing factors are an inherent defect in the European bureaucratic machine and the repercussions are almost inevitable today, above all by virtue of the fact that the relations between executives have deteriorated.

Also, the objective of juridicalising the rule of law and democracy, demanding their observance on the basis of obligations of primary law,[47] seems for the moment impossible to achieve, considering that the constitutional tensions on the rule of law have corrupted the state of integration at an advanced level. Therefore, to prevent

[44] Claes (2019), p. 13.

[45] Brunet (2013), pp. 4–5.

[46] Heuschling (2002), pp. 1002–1005.

[47] See the case-law on article 2 TUE and the legal link with article 19 par 1(2) TUE on the effective judicial remedy inaugurated by Court of Justice with the ASJP judgment in C-64/16 Associação Sindical dos Juízes Portugueses (the 'Portuguese judges' case), [ECLI:EU:C:2018:117] (February 27, 2018).

the stop-gap measures adopted by the EU institutions from giving rise to unprecedented stagnation, the direct involvement of States through the principle of subsidiarity (Article 5.3 of TEU), which does not totally detract space to their national identity, could be an encouraging sign in the collective undertaking to preserve the unity in Europe.

References

Anderson J (1994) Religion, state and politics in the Soviet Union and Successor States. Cambridge University Press, p 236

Blokker P (2017) The evolution of constitutionalism in post-communist countries. In: Van Elsuwege P, Petrov R (eds) Post-Soviet constitutions and challenges of regional integration: adapting to European and Eurasian integration projects. Routledge, p 21

Brunet L (2013) The crisis of the EU enlargement. In: LSE Ideas, Special Report. London School of Economics and Political Sciences, pp 4–5

Chronowski N (2009) On the changing concept of sovereignty. In: 5th European Jurist's Forum Budapest

Chronowski N (2012) The new Hungarian fundamental law in the light of the European normative values. Revue Est Europa:111–142

Claes M (2019) How common are the values of the European Union? CYELP 15:VII

Closa C, Kochenov D (2016) Reinforcing rule of law oversight in the European Union. Cambridge University Press, p 356

Coman R (2016) Strengthening the rule of law at the supranational level: the rise and consolidation of a European Network. J Contemp Eur Stud 17:171

Coman R (2017) Central and Eastern Europe: the EU's struggle for rule of law pre- and post-accession 2017. In: The Routledge handbook of justice and home affairs research. Routledge, p 11

Council of Ministers (EEC) (1989) Regulation on economic aid to the Republic of Hungary and the Polish People's Republic n. 3906/89. https://eur-lex.europa.eu/

Dangerfield M (2008) The Visegrád Group in the Expanded European Union: From Pre-accession to Post-accession Cooperation. Sage J 22(3):630

De Wilde P, Zürn M (2012) Can the politicization of european integration be reversed? J Common Mark Stud 17:137

Di Gregorio A (2004) Riforme costituzionali ed integrazione europea: il caso dei nuovi membri dell'Est. Diritto pubblico Comparato ed europeo, p 2067

Di Gregorio A (2015) The Fundamental Law of Hungary in the European context. In: Hungarian Constitution and European law. Università degli Studi di Milano, AIR [Archivio Istituzionale della Ricerca], p 17

Dimitrova A (2005) Europeanization and civil service reform in Central and Eastern Europe. In: Schimmelfennig F, Sedelmeier U (eds) The Europeanization of Central and Eastern Europe. Cornell University Press, Ithaca, p 19

Drinóczi T (2020) Constitutional identity in Europe: the identity of the constitution. A regional approach. Cambridge University Press, pp 105–130

Drinóczi T, Bień-Kacała A (2019) Illiberal constitutionalism: the case of Hungary and Poland. Ger Law J 20:1140–1166

European Council (1993) Conclusions of the Presidency. https://www.consilium.europa.eu/

European Parliament (2011) Resolution on the Revised Hungarian Constitution. Strasbourg, 2011/2655(RSP). https://www.europarl.europa.eu/

European Parliament (2013) Resolution on the situation of the fundamental rights/standards and practices in Hungary -pursuant to the European Parliament resolution of 16 February 2012. Strasbourg. 2012/2130(INI). https://www.europarl.europa.eu/
Franceschi D (2021) Le democrazie fragili: Ungheria e Polonia, Storia in Network, http://www.storiain.net/
Ganino M (1996) Introduction to Ungheria, in Biscaretti di Ruffia. Costituzioni straniere contemporanee, Milano Giuffrè
Giaro T (2017) La cultura giuridica dell'Europa orientale. Fondamenti storici. In: Castorina E (ed) Servizi Pubblici, Diritti Fondamentali, Costituzionalismo europeo. Modelli di organizzazione dei servizi pubblici in Europa, Jean Monnet, p 15
Giusti S, Locatelli A (2008) L' Europa sicura. Le politiche di sicurezza dell'Unione Europea, I manuali. Egea spa, p 282
Grabbe H (2001) How does Europeanization affect CEE governance? Conditionality, diffusion and diversity. J Eur Publ Policy 6:19
Grabbe H (2006) The EU's tranformative power: Europeanization through conditionality in Central and Eastern Europe. Palgrave Macmillan, Basingstoke, p 231
Heuschling L (2002) Ètat de droit, Rechtsstaat, Rule of law. Dalloz, Paris, p 739
Hughes J, Sasse G, Gordon C (2002) Enlargement and European governance the ambivalence of conditionality: Europeanization and regionalization in Central and Eastern Europe. In: ECPR Joint Sessions Turin, 22–27 March Workshop. European Institute and Department of Government, London School of Economics
Kellermann A (2001) EU enlargement. The Constitutional Impact at EU and national Level, L'Aia TMC. Asser Press, p 604
Kochenov D (2008) EU enlargement and the failure of conditionality: pre-accession conditionality in the fields of democracy and the rule of law. KluwerLaw International, The Heague, p 358
Kochenov D (2011) Democratic conditionality in eastern enlargement: ambitious window dressing. Eur Foreign Aff Rev 16:589–605
Malová D, Rybář M (2000) The troubled institutionalization of parliamentary democracy in Slovakia. Politička misao 37(5):99–115
Maresceau M (2001) The EU pre-accession strategie s: A political and legal analysis. In: Maresceau M, Lannon E (eds) The EU's enlargement and mediterranean strateries, a comparative analysis. Palgrave, Basingstoke, p 25
Matlak M, Schimmefenning F, Woźniakowski T (2018) Europeanization revisited: Central and Eastern Europe in the European Union. European University Institute Robert Schuman Centre for Advanced Studies, p 161. https://doi.org/10.2870/675963
Medve-Balint G (2018) Implementing EU cohesion policy in the Eastern member states: quality of government balancing between equity and efficiency. In: Matlak M, Schimmefenning F, Woźniakowski T (eds) Europeanization revisited: Central and Eastern Europe in the European Union. European University Institute Robert Schuman Centre for Advanced Studies, p 108
Morrone A (2018) I mutamenti costituzionali derivanti dall'integrazione europea. Federalismi 20:27
Noutcheva G, Aydin Duzgit S (2012) Lost in Europeanization: the Western Balkans and Turkey. West Eur Polit 19
Papadimitriou D, Petrov P (2012) Whose rule, whose law? Contested statehood, external leverage and the European Union's rule of law mission in Kosovo. J Common Mark Stud 18:746
Pech L, Kochenov D (2021) Respect for the rule of law in the case law of the European Court of Justice: a casebook overview of key judgments since the Portuguese Judges Case, Swedish Institute for European. Policy Stud 3:12–234
Pech L, Scheppele KL (2017) Illiberalism within: rule of law backsliding in the EU. In: Cambridge yearbook of European legal studies, pp 3–47
Polmonari A (2021) La violazione dei diritti costituzionali in Polonia: aporie e anacronismi. Legali, Erudizioni
Radaelli C (2004) Europeanisation: solution or problem? EIOP 8(16):26

Rosanò A (2022) Not another EU report! Il meccanismo di cooperazione e verifica quale strumento di promozione dello Stato di diritto e i suoi effetti sul processo di allargamento, I Post di AISDUE, IV, Section "Atti convegni AISDUE", p 22
Sachs JD (1994) Shock therapy in Poland: perspectives of five years. In: The tanner lectures on human values. University of Utah, p 26
Sadurski W (2003-2004) The 'east' side of European constitutionalism. In: Constitutionalism in Europe, European Forum, academic year 2003–2004. European University Institute, Robert Schuman Centre of advanced studies
Sadurski W (2012) Constitutionalism and enlargement of Europe. Oxford University Press, Oxford, p 23
Sbailò C (2008) Transizioni costituzionali nell'era post-comunista. Pantarei Ed., p 135
Sedelmeier U (2011) Europeanisation in new member and candidate states. Living Rev Eur Govern 50
Serowaniec M, Witkowski Z (2021) The erosion of the legislative process in Poland. J Mod Sci 1:18. https://doi.org/10.13166/JMS/135046
Vella G (2020) Il processo di democratizzazione della Polonia tra consolidamento e battute di arresto. In: Un'analisi alla luce dell'evoluzione politico-istituzionale. Pisa University Press, p 183. https://core.ac.uk/
Verdun A (2018) Europeanization and Euro adoption. In: Matlak M, Schimmefenning F, Woźniakowski T (eds) Europeanization revisited: Central and Eastern Europe in the European Union. European University Institute Robert Schuman Centre for Advanced Studies, p 143
Vukov V (2018) Europeanizing development: EU integration and developmental state capacities in Eastern Europe. In: Matlak M, Schimmefenning F, Woźniakowski T (eds) Europeanization revisited: Central and Eastern Europe in the European Union. European University Institute Robert Schuman Centre for Advanced Studies, p 127

Part III
International Law Section

The Legitimacy Crisis in International Investment Law: Towards an Overcoming?

Georges Philippe Zakhour

1 Introduction

1. Over the past 25 years, there has been a notable transformation in the resolution of disputes related to foreign direct investments.[1] Due to the necessity of attracting international capital, and the very limited nature of guarantees offered to private investors who submitted complaints to domestic courts,[2] many States have opted to resolve their disputes related to foreign investments through arbitration founded on investment treaties—also known as arbitration without privity.[3] As an indispensable institution today, the International Centre for Settlement of Investment Disputes (ICSID) was established under the auspices of the World Bank by the Washington Convention of 1965.[4] Although relatively inactive for an extended period, the ICSID has recently gained significant prominence due to

[1] Behn et al. (2022); Zakhour (2019); McLachlan et al. (2017); Sornarajah (2017); Collins (2016); Kinnear et al. (2015); Dolzer and Schreuer (2012); Bungenberg (2012); Newcombe and Paradell (2009); Binder et al. (2009); Reinisch and Knahr (2008); Muchlinski et al. (2008); Subedi (2008); Weiler (2005).

[2] Schreuer et al. (2009), pp. 5–6.

[3] Paulsson (1995), pp. 232–257; Werner (1997), pp. 5–16; Ben Hamida (2005), p. 599; Crépet Daigremont (2007), pp. 453–516; Pinna (2008), p. 6; Nolan and Sourgens (2010).

[4] Schreuer et al. (2009), pp. 2–4.

G. P. Zakhour (✉)
College of Law, Prince Sultan University, Riyadh, Saudi Arabia
e-mail: gzakhour@psu.edu.sa

E. Omerović et al. (eds.), *Balkan Yearbook of European and International Law 2023*, Balkan Yearbook of European and International Law 2023,
https://doi.org/10.1007/978-3-031-69670-1_7

the rapid proliferation of international investment agreements, securing a central role in resolving disputes between States and investors.[5]

2. In fact, a new generation of bilateral investment treaties (BITs) has emerged.[6] The decisive impact of the BIT program launched by the Reagan administration has led to the signing of 45 treaties. This American-born initiative was recognized and supported by successive governments, including President Clinton's Democratic administration. Despite the slim odds of success predicted by analysts, this groundbreaking program has shown unwavering growth over the years.[7] During the early 1990s, most of the BIT models proposed by countries of the Organization for Economic Co-operation and Development (OECD) embraced the American model concerning the resolution of investment disputes.
3. The American contribution to international dispute resolution, which played an essential role in shaping and expanding International Investment Law, is nonetheless open to numerous criticisms.[8] This ongoing legitimacy crisis has its roots in how BITs were initially established: Western countries initiated these treaties to protect their investors in other countries, especially in the Global South. However, a shift occurred when countries from the Global South started using these treaties to protect their own investors, altering the traditional use of these agreements. The crisis deepened when Western nations realized that these treaties, originally intended to safeguard their interests, were now being used against them by investors from the Global South. This unexpected use of BITs prompted Western countries to reconsider how these treaties function in the global economic system, leading to a reevaluation of the fundamental principles and ideas behind these agreements. At the heart of this crisis is a substantial change in how BITs are utilized. Initially designed to assist Western investors, these treaties underwent a significant transformation as the Global South became more

---

[5] Shihata (2009); Leben (2003) pp. 197–386.

[6] Sacerdoti (1998), pp. 251–460.

[7] McKinstry Robin (1984), pp. 931–958.

[8] Schill (2017), pp. 649–672; Balchin et al. (2010), pp. 1–10; Juillard (1994), p. 75; Leboulanger et al. (2006), p. 351; Brower and Schill (2008), p. 473: « *The rise of investment treaties and investment-treaty arbitration has attracted critical attention from the users of the dispute settlement mechanism (that is, investors and host states) as well as various interest groups that claim to represent « civil society » and the « public interest. Although these critical voices vary in the specific points they raise and in the tone in which they raise them, they have contributed to a considerable amount of literature intimating that investment law may be in a veritable « legitimacy crisis* »»; Alfaro and Lorenti (2005), p. 2; Audit et al. (2004), p. 191; Kentin (2007), pp. 629–667; Sornarajah (2003), p. 209: « *Since protection has been the main thrust of the dispute settlement provisions, there has been a definite movement towards the creation of an automatic and unilateral right of recourse to arbitration created in the foreign investor. The right has led to concerns that there is a considerable erosion of sovereignty involved as a result of such provision* »; Mann (2003), p. 215: « *The IIAS have become a charter of rights for foreign investors, with no concomitant responsibilities or liabilities, no direct legal links to promoting development objectives, and no protection for public welfare in the face of environmentally or socially destabilizing foreign investment [...] international investment law is a system of corporate rights without responsibility or liability* »; Anderson and Grusky (2007, April); Ben Hamida (2008), p. 999.

involved. However, despite the serious legitimacy crisis currently afflicting this discipline (1), the undeniable fact remains that this crisis can indeed be overcome (2).

2 The Legitimacy Crisis in International Investment Law

4. Numerous criticisms have been made against the evolution of International Investment Law. These opposing arguments have been seen on both the substantive (2.1) and the procedural levels (2.2).

2.1 *Opposing Arguments on the Substantive Level*

5. On the substantive level, criticisms have been directed towards BITs, primarily due to the imbalance favoring investors, where the rights granted to them often lack corresponding duties.[9] These critiques argue that Foreign Investment Law was primarily conceived to safeguard the rights of investors.[10] Indeed, as Professor Patrick Juillard aptly notes, this discipline can only be comprehended as biased, unfair, and imbalanced. This imbalance arises from the fact that the rights protecting investors from potential State actions outweigh the rights safeguarding host States from investors.[11] He further argues that the fundamental imbalance results from BITs being inherently unequal, not placing the investor and the State on equal footing.[12] Professor Philippe Fouchard shares a similar perspective, highlighting that host States find themselves in a position of inferiority, as their interests are given lower priority.[13]
6. Furthermore, at the political level, certain American congressmen invoked the principle of State sovereignty as an argument against the legal regime governing international investments. As conflicts involving State interests emerged within the North American Free Trade Agreement (NAFTA) framework, these deputies sounded the alarm during the August 5, 1999, session of Congress: *«We must stand together to protect the sovereignty of American laws. We should not allow*

---

[9] Audit et al. (2004), pp. 191–194.

[10] Poulsen (2015); Juillard (1994), p. 75; Audit et al. (2004), p. 191; Fouchard (1999), pp. 481–482; Brower and Schill (2008), p. 474: « *The perceived unevenness created by a regime that protects property, investment, and foreign investors without sufficient regard to other non-investment-related interests of host states* ».

[11] Juillard (1994), p. 75.

[12] Audit et al. (2004), p. 191.

[13] Fouchard (1999); Brower and Schill (2008), p. 474: « *The perceived unevenness created by a regime that protects property, investment, and foreign investors without sufficient regard to other non-investment-related interests of host states* »; Poulsen (2015).

American taxpayer dollars pay American lawyers to help a foreign corporation fight American state laws in court. Support this important amendment! ».[14] They argued that the current legal framework for International Investment Law violates State sovereignty and consequently obstructs public legal entities from implementing measures in their best interests.[15]

7. In the same vein, Georges Kahale strongly criticized International Investment Law noting that « *most of us intuitively sense that the drafters of these 3000 treaties had little or no idea that fair and equitable treatment meant anything other than the minimum standard of treatment under customary international law* ».[16] Indeed, the United States, Canada, and Mexico were disconcerted by the extensive interpretation of the standards of fair and equitable treatment by certain arbitrators. As for the Most Favored Nation Clause, Georges Kahale describes it as a « *"magic wand" that allows "one bad treaty" to provide protections "never imagined for virtually an entire world of investors* ».[17]
8. Taking these criticisms into consideration, several amendments were introduced, including the addition of a dedicated chapter addressing investors' obligations.[18] Certain countries, deeming these modifications insufficient, have gone even further by terminating their investment agreements, absolving themselves of international obligations. For instance, The Republic of Venezuela denounced the BIT it had concluded with the Kingdom of the Netherlands in 2008. In March 2014, amidst a mounting global backlash against BIT provisions, Indonesia disclosed its intention to terminate all 67 of its BITs upon their renewal.[19] Since then, it has terminated BITs with more than 20 countries. Similarly, in 2017, the Ecuadorian President formalized Ecuador's withdrawal from all its BITs concluded with 16 countries.[20] This action aligns with the position of the Ecuadorian

[14] (1999) Congressional Record H7367-02, pp. 1–18, especially p. 2. [https://www.congress.gov/crec/1999/08/05/CREC-1999-08-05-pt2-PgH7367-2.pdf].

[15] Rubins (2006), p. 243.

[16] Kahale (2014, April 11), p. 2.

[17] *Ibid.*

[18] UNCTAD (2016), p. 110; Hepburn and Kabra (2017), pp. 95–114.

[19] Peterson (2015, November 20).

[20] The International Institute for Sustainable Development (2017), p. 18: « *Ecuadorian President Rafael Correa formalized Ecuador's withdrawal on May 16, 2017 from bilateral investment treaties (BITs) concluded with 16 countries: Argentina, Bolivia, Canada, Chile, China, France, Germany, Italy, the Netherlands, Peru, Spain, Sweden, Switzerland, the United Kingdom, the United States and Venezuela. Ecuador previously denounced nine BITs in 2008 (with Cuba, the Dominican Republic, El Salvador, Guatemala, Honduras, Nicaragua, Paraguay, Romania and Uruguay) and one in 2010 (with Finland). With the new denunciations, Ecuador has completed the process of withdrawal from all of its BITs. While the treaties with the Dominican Republic, Guatemala and Uruguay are no longer in force, all others are subject to survival clauses ranging from 5 to 20 years. The recent denunciations follow the recommendation of CAITISA, an audit commission composed of government officials, academics, lawyers and civil society groups that examined Ecuador's BITs between 2013 and 2015. CAITISA's 668-page report (of which drafts were leaked in January 2016) was officially published and presented to President Correa on May 8, 2017. For CAITISA President Cecilia Olivet, "the auditing process revealed that these treaties*

Constitutional Court, which considers that the provisions of several BITs were unconstitutional.[21]

9. More recently, in 2020, the majority of European Union Member States opted to terminate all intra-European Union BITs.[22] This decision stems from the judgment issued by the Court of Justice of the European Union (CJEU) in the *Slovak Republic v. Achmea* case, ruling that the provisions of these BITs were incompatible with European Union law.[23]

   In the ever-evolving landscape of international investment, the *Achmea* ruling stands as a landmark decision that has reverberated within the European Union, sparking a fundamental shift in its approach toward BITs and Investor-State Dispute Settlement (ISDS) mechanisms. The European Union's assertion that BITs are inferior, as evidenced by the aftermath of the *Achmea* case, emphasizes palpable hostility within European Union law toward ISDS. This pronounced change in perspective can be traced back to the realization that investment arbi-

---

not only failed to attract additional investment or advance the country's development plan, they also diverted millions of dollars of government money to fighting costly lawsuits." She added: "We hope other governments will learn from Ecuador's example and review their own investment agreements to find out if they are truly beneficial to their citizens." Several other developing countries—including Bolivia, India, Indonesia and South Africa—have terminated their BITs, or indicated their intention to renegotiate or terminate them, as part of a growing effort to reform and rebalance the international investment regime ».

[21] UNCTAD (2010), p. 1: « *In 2010, Ecuador's Constitutional Court declared arbitration provisions of six more BITs (China, Finland, Germany, the UK, Venezuela and United States) to be inconsistent with the country's Constitution»*.

[22] (2022) Agreement for the Termination of Bilateral Investment Treaties Between the Member States of the European Union, EU Doc. A/T/BIT/en 1 [https://eur-lex.europa.eu/legal-content/EN/TXT/PDF/?uri=CELEX:22020A0529(01)].

[23] Case C-284/16, *Slovak Republic v Achmea B.V.*, EU:C:2018:158 (CJEU, March 6, 2018). The *Achmea* decision, delivered by the CJEU, had a significant impact on BITs by effectively disregarding certain provisions. The case centered on a dispute between the Dutch company Achmea and the Slovak Republic under a BIT between the Netherlands and Slovakia. The crucial aspect of the *Achmea* decision was the CJEU's ruling that an arbitration clause in the BIT, enabling investors to bring claims against a host State through international arbitration, was incompatible with European Union law. The CJEU asserted that the arbitration clause undermined the autonomy of European Union law by establishing a parallel system of dispute resolution outside the European Union 's judicial framework. Essentially, the CJEU deemed that the arbitration mechanism in the BIT contradicted the principles of the European Union legal system. It argued that the arbitration tribunal, composed of individuals outside the European Union 's judicial structure, posed a risk to the uniform interpretation and application of European Union law. The CJEU concluded that such arbitration clauses within BITs were inconsistent with the European Union legal framework and, therefore, should be disregarded. By invalidating the arbitration clause in the *Achmea* case, the CJEU essentially ignored the dispute resolution mechanism established in the BIT. This decision conveyed a clear message that arbitration clauses in BITs involving European Union member States would not be recognized, contributing to the perception that BITs were being undermined within the European Union legal context. The rationale behind this stance was the determination that arbitral tribunals constituted under intra-European Union BITs lacked the essential independence and impartiality required to interpret and apply European Union laws. For more in-depth information about the European Union Law, please refer to Samardžić and Meškić (2017).

tration has encroached upon domains that traditionally fell within the purview of European Union courts. The European Union's reluctance to embrace ISDS can be perceived as a strategic move to safeguard its own interests. As investment arbitration gained prominence, the European Union seemingly saw a potential diminution of its authority in resolving disputes that would have otherwise fallen under the jurisdiction of European Union courts. In the complex arena of international relations, where every actor seeks to assert and safeguard their interests, the European Union's stance reflects a broader battle for jurisdiction and influence. This shift has not unfolded without controversy. Investment arbitration bodies argue that the European Union's position breaches the spirit of BITs, creating tension in the delicate balance between international investment protection and the regulatory autonomy of States. The dispute becomes emblematic of a broader struggle: a clash of interests where entities, be they States or international institutions, navigate the intricate terrain of legal frameworks to protect what they perceive as their interests.

In navigating this complex landscape, there emerges a compelling argument for establishing a hierarchical framework of international laws that all countries can collectively endorse. Such a framework would seek to harmonize the interests of States, investors, and international institutions, creating a shared understanding of the rules governing international investments. This approach recognizes the inherent tensions but aims to build a cooperative environment where disputes can be resolved through a universally accepted legal hierarchy, providing a more stable and equitable foundation for the future of International Investment Law.

2.2 *Opposing Arguments on the Jurisdictional Level*

10. On the jurisdictional level, criticisms were primarily targeted at the ICSID. In fact, the arbitral tribunals operating under its auspices tend to favor the rights of private investors over those of the States involved, as highlighted in *El Paso Energy International Company v. The Argentine Republic* case: « *the investors will not use appropriate restraint — and why should they? — if the ICSID tribunals offer them unexpected remedies. The responsibility for showing appropriate restraint rests in the hands of the ICSID tribunals* ».[24]
11. The primary criticism frequently directed at the investment arbitration process pertains to the possibility that arbitrators may deem States responsible for taking actions in the vital interest of their nations. Consequently, such measures

[24] *El Paso Energy International Company v. The Argentine Republic,* ICSID Case No. ARB/03/15, decision on jurisdiction (April 27, 2006), para. 82. Some argue that multinational companies are exploiting Bilateral Investment Treaties (BITs), originally designed to safeguard foreign investors, to bypass domestic laws and regulations. Refer to Gaillard (2017), pp. 17–37, for further insights.

should, under no circumstances, lead to financial sanctions against States that have acted in the public interest.[25]

12. Given that transparency is a crucial element in all legal systems, additional criticisms have been aimed at the inconsistency of case law,[26] the perceived lack of arbitrators' independence and impartiality,[27] and the absence of an appeal process.[28]
13. These observations were reiterated in Georges Kahale's aforementioned article, where he highlighted that transnational arbitrators often lack adequate training in international law and may have additional interests that do not necessarily

---

[25] Waren (2001), p. 10986.

[26] Bernasconi-Osterwalder and Rosert (2014, March 12), pp. 15–16; Franck (2005), p. 1584: « *Without the clarity and consistency of both the rules of law and their application, there is a detrimental impact upon those governed by the rules and their willingness and ability to adhere to such rules, which can lead to a crisis of legitimacy. Legitimacy depends in large part upon factors such as determinacy and coherence, which can in turn beget predictability and reliability. Related concepts such as justice, fairness, accountability, representation, correct use of procedure, and opportunities for review also impact conceptions of legitimacy. When these factors are absent, individuals, companies and governments cannot anticipate how to comply with the law and plan their conduct accordingly, thereby undermining legitimacy* ».

[27] Rao (2021), Article 105980: « *It is often argued that arbitrators, as ad hoc appointees, may be incentivized to vote in biased ways that enhance their career and financial prospects. For example, as investor-state arbitration can be initiated only by investors, arbitrators may favor claimant investors over respondent states to enhance the attractiveness of investor-state arbitration to potential claimants and increase reappointments as the total number of cases grows. [...] these arbitrators are considered likely to favor their appointing party out of gratitude or self interests to generate more future appointments* »; Cleis (2017), pp. 1–187; Mainguy (2017), p. 8; Muchlinski (2008), p. 683: « *There is a real danger that arbitral tribunals, seeing themselves bound by the limits of the treaties upon which their jurisdiction is based, will feel understandably compelled to give a very narrow interpretation of the nature and scope of the IIA obligations to the exclusion of interests other than those of the investor as an alleged victim of regulatory malpractice. If they do not offer a creative interpretation of IIA obligations, which allows for the balancing of investor expectations with those of the wider society in which they operate and which, as argued above, must act as a formative influence of investor expectations, then arbitral tribunals risk being perceived as upholding an increasingly unjust and biased system of existing pro-investor BITs and other IIAs* »; Schultz and Dupont (2015), pp. 1147–1168; Simmons (2014), pp. 152–153: « *Critics argue that arbitration, as compared to dispute resolution in courts, is unsuitable for such public law disputes because arbitrators are privately contracted by the parties to specific disputes and do not hold, like tenured judges, a public office* »; Cazala (2016), p. 919; Malintoppi (2008), p. 829: « *The debate triggered by recent challenges contributed to amending the ICSID Rules at least by expanding the scope of the arbitrator's declaration upon appointment and imposing a continuing duty to disclose. Nonetheless, it may still be necessary to consider enacting a code of ethics for investment arbitrators under the guidance and leadership of ICSID. Too much is at stake in this type of arbitration to continue to ignore the need for a comprehensive solution to the issue of conflicts of interest in investment arbitration* ».

[28] Some argue for the reform or replacement of ISDS mechanisms with a more balanced system. This may include the establishment of an appellate mechanism to ensure consistency and predictability in arbitral awards. See Schultz and Dupont (2015), pp. 1147–1168; Bernasconi-Osterwalder (2015), p. 7; Simmons (2014), pp. 12–46; Williams (2003), pp. 251–276; Redfern (2005), pp. 665–675; Lowenfeld (2002), pp. 1–7.

align with their role as arbitrators.[29] The author adds that the professional profile of the arbitrators could influence their decisions: « *in that environment, arbitrators are actually encouraged to trade points as if they are bargaining in a Turkish bazaar, acting more like party representatives negotiating a settlement than arbitrators deciding a momentous legal controversy* ».[30]

14. Similarly, Georges Abi Saab, the arbitrator overseeing the *ConocoPhillips Petrozuata B.V., ConocoPhillips Hamaca B.V. and ConocoPhillips Gulf of Paria B.V. v. Bolivarian Republic of Venezuela* case, expressed his views as follows: « *I don't think that any self-respecting Tribunal that seriously takes its overriding legal and moral task of seeking the truth and dispensing justice according to law on that basis, can pass over such evidence, close its blinkers and proceed to build on its now severely contestable findings, ignoring the existence and the relevance of such glaring evidence. It would be shutting itself off by an epistemic closure into a subjective make-believe world of its creation; a virtual reality in order to fend off probable objective reality; a legal comedy of errors on the theater of the absurd, not to say travesty of justice, that makes mockery not only of ICSID arbitration but of the very idea of adjudication* ».[31]
15. As a consequence, these underlying issues have inevitably prompted certain countries to denounce the Washington Convention.[32] The Republic of Bolivia became the first country to take this step in 2007, followed by the Republic of Ecuador in 2009, and Venezuela in 2012. Another wave of rejection has been observed in certain Latin American countries that have launched a project to establish a regional system for the resolution of conflicts related to foreign investments.[33] Other economic powers, including Brazil, India, and South Africa, have never even joined the ICSID Convention. Some countries have also modified their constitutional standards. For instance, the Constitutions of the Republic of Ecuador and the Republic of Bolivia have been amended to consider the arbitrability of disputes related to foreign investment as unconstitutional.[34]

---

[29] Kahale (2014, April 11).

[30] *Ibid.*, p. 2.

[31] *ConocoPhillips Company et al vs. Bolivarian Republic of Venezuela,* ICSID Case No. ARB/07/30, Dissenting Opinion of Georges Abi-Saab (March 10, 2014), para. 67.

[32] Garibaldi (2009), pp. 251–278; Tietje et al. (2008); Tzanakopoulos (2011), pp. 75–93; Castro de Figueiredo (2009), pp. 1–22; Gaillard (2007), pp. 1–3; Fouret (2008), pp. 71–87; UNCTAD (2010), pp. 1–11; Schreuer (2010), pp. 353–368; Nolan and Sourgens (2007), pp. 1–52.

[33] This project has been founded by The Bolivarian Alliance for the Peoples of our America (ALBA).

[34] UNCTAD (2010), p. 1

3 The Overcoming of the Legitimacy Crisis in International Investment Law

16. Some experts argue that the critics' attacks on the discipline were excessive and unfounded. Recent statistics, supported by a consensus among scholars (3.1), suggest that overcoming the crisis is possible through the implementation of necessary reforms (3.2).

3.1 Statistics in Favor of the System's Survival

17. Despite a widespread false statement, recent statistics have found that States have been the major beneficiaries under the ICSID, rather than private investors. In fact, considering the 2023 statistics, out of the 890 concluded ISDS proceedings, about one-third were decided in favor of the State, while only a quarter ruled in favor of the investor with monetary compensation awarded. The rest were resolved amicably or discontinued.[35]
18. Furthermore, the legitimacy crisis that the ICSID has undergone seems to have had no effect on its activity, as reflected in the annual report for 2022: « *By the end of FY2022, ICSID numbered 164 signatories to the ICSID Convention, of which 157 were Contracting States to the Convention. Membership has been expanding since ICSID's establishment in 1966, reflecting its global relevance as the only institution with a primary mandate to support the resolution of international investment disputes. The Kyrgyz Republic is the newest Contracting State, having deposited its Instrument of Ratification of the ICSID Convention with the World Bank on April 21, 2022* ».[36] During this particular year, 48 new cases were registered by the ICSID, indicating a considerable increase in the number of claims.[37] As for the total number of cases handled, the Centre administered a record of 346 ICSID cases.[38]
19. The aforementioned statistics found favorable support from Jan Paulson, who concluded that criticisms directed at investment arbitration are misdirected: «

[35] UNCTAD (2023), p. 79.

[36] ICSID (2022a), p. 13.

[37] ICSID (2022b), p. 22.

[38] ICSID (2022a), p. 22: « *ICSID is the premiere global institution for the resolution of investment disputes, having administered the vast majority of all known international investment cases. The 2022 fiscal year saw strong demand for ICSID's services—with 50 new cases registered and a record 346 cases administered by ICSID. Additional highlights in FY2022 include: § A record number of concluded proceedings, as ICSID continues to work with tribunals and parties to reduce the time of cases § The second highest number of hearings held in a single fiscal year, over 90% of which were held remotely § The third highest number of procedural orders and decisions issued in a single fiscal year, and § A notable forty-two nationalities represented amongst the appointments made to ICSID cases* ».

Criticism of international tribunals on the ground that they impede democratic policies – whether protection of the environment or the labour market – is misdirected. International tribunals do not establish policy. They give effect to international agreements. To deny the authority of international tribunals is to deprive states of the power to make meaningful promises ».[39] Additionally, according to Christopher Schreur's predictions, this discipline of foreign investments will remain steadfast, with international investment arbitration continuing to be the preeminent mechanism for dispute resolution: « *Investment arbitration is likely to remain the most important form of dispute settlement in the relationship of host States and foreign investors for some time. A number of shortcomings have emerged over the years and the initial enthusiasm for investment arbitration has given way to a more sober assessment. But it is an exaggeration to speak of an acute crisis or a backlash* ».[40] As for the claims that arbitrators may strategically render decisions in biased ways with the goal of encouraging reappointments, Maria-Nicole Cleis rejects them by exploring, in her recently published book,[41] how the independence and impartiality of ICSID arbitrators have consistently been upheld.

3.2 Recommended Reforms

20. « *The fear against abuse cannot be a proper ground for refusing to engage in an effective dispute settlement mechanism. [...] If procedures are vulnerable to abuses, anti-abuse mechanisms should be introduced. An effective dispute settlement mechanism should not be abandoned for fear of abuses* ».[42] Therefore, despite the complexity of reforming Foreign Investment Law, which requires a delicate balance between the rights of investors and the regulatory authority of host States, implementing reasonable amendments can contribute to overcoming the legitimacy crisis.
21. On the substantive level, Foreign Investment Law should strike a balance between protecting the rights of foreign investors and respecting the sovereign right of States to regulate in the public interest. As a result, BIT's provisions should clearly indicate that the right of States to regulate in the public interest is preserved. This could involve clarifying the scope of ISDS mechanisms to prevent abuse and overreach. To achieve this result, some clauses such as the Fair and Equitable Treatment Clause or the Most Favored Nation Clause[43] must

[39] Paulsson (2005), p. 164.

[40] Schreuer (2011), p. 802.

[41] Maria Nicole Cleis asserts that the ICSID Convention guarantees impartial decision-making. See Cleis (2017), pp. 1–187.

[42] Kodama (1999), p. 49.

[43] Zakhour (2023a), pp. 38–52; Zakhour (2023b), pp. 53–71

be reviewed and amended to thwart foreign investors from exploiting them to obtain excessive benefits.[44]

22. In addition, to rectify the imbalance prevailing within Foreign Investment Law, it would be advisable to impose obligations on foreign investors, who often exclusively benefit from rights. While foreign investments significantly contribute to the economic development of the host State, they can also potentially cause damage to the environment, social rights, and public health.[45] Generally, BITs do not address the liability that investors could incur in exchange for the rights granted to them. Therefore, it would be appropriate to advocate for the inclusion of treaty provisions pertaining to environmental, social, and public health protections. Reforms in this regard should also ensure that compensation for investors remains reasonable, taking into consideration the legitimate regulatory actions of the host State.
23. Furthermore, it would be appropriate to enhance the coherence of the legal regime for international investments. Given the non-existence of multilateral standards on foreign investment and the fragmented, incoherent nature of BITs, imperfections, and inconsistencies arise between these treaties and other international conventions. Consequently, it would be worthwhile to establish a certain harmony to minimize such interference.
24. On the procedural level, it would be desirable to bilateralize arbitration disputes. The proposed solution aims to achieve a balanced outcome by promoting the bilateralization of arbitral disputes, ensuring that both host States and foreign investors have equal opportunities to present their cases and defend their interests before arbitral tribunals. Allowing host States to bring claims against investors under an investment treaty can promote equitable outcomes, improve transparency, and address situations where host States' interests are directly affected by international investments.[46] Although far from being achievable at the moment due to the consensual nature of arbitration, rare traces of this solution can be found in certain investment arbitration treaties. For instance, Article 8 of the BIT concluded on August 25, 1991, between China and Mongolia states:

> (1) Any dispute between an investor of one Contracting State and the other Contracting State in connection with an investment in the territory of the other Contracting State shall as far as possible be settled amicably through negotiations between the parties to the dispute.
>
> (2) If the dispute cannot be settled through negotiations within six months, either party to the dispute shall be entitled to submit the dispute to the competent court of the Contracting State accepting the investment.

25. In addition, it would be plausible to limit investors' access to ICSID tribunals, aiming to enhance fairness. States could consider amending their ratified investment treaties to include dispute settlement clauses that, instead of being

[44] Batifort and Heath (2017), pp. 873–913.

[45] Meškić et al. (2022), pp. 5–7.

[46] Professor Juillard describes the actual procedure as asymmetric, which can lead to disastrous consequences for the States. See Carreau et al. (1995), p. 609.

unconditional, impose limits on their consent to arbitration. Such amendments would effectively rebalance the procedural rights of the parties in international litigation. Reforms should also prioritize transparency in foreign investment proceedings. Facilitating public participation and incorporating the input of affected communities can contribute to ensuring that arbitral awards are made in the broader public interest.

26. Finally, to further enhance the legitimacy of the current system, we may turn to The UNCITRAL Rules on Transparency in Treaty-based Investor-State Arbitration, which systematically apply to the settlement of disputes between investors and States based on treaties signed after April 1, 2014.[47] Consolidated by the United Nations Convention on Transparency in Treaty-Based Investor-State Arbitration, effective from October 18, 2017, these rules aim to improve openness and accessibility in arbitral processes. They achieve this by allowing public access to certain documents and hearings, especially in cases involving investment arbitration. Without any limitations, this set of rules is poised to significantly contribute to the development of a coherent and appropriate legal framework for the fair and equitable resolution of transnational disputes.
27. All of these reforms, encompassing both the substantive and procedural levels, pave the way for a more balanced and protective investment regime. Under these adjustments, each party involved can rightfully claim fair and equitable treatment.

4 Conclusion

28. The ongoing legitimacy crisis within International Investment Law has ignited extensive debates, particularly around issues of transparency, consistency, and perceived biases favoring multinational corporations. However, rather than merely posing challenges, these issues offer a distinct opportunity for substantial reform within the realm of investment treaty arbitration.

Acknowledging the crucial need for transparency, initiatives are currently underway to advocate for the public disclosure of all proceedings. This commitment to openness seeks to demystify the arbitration process, promoting a clearer understanding and strengthening public trust in the integrity of the decisions rendered.

Beyond transparency, ongoing reforms are exploring nuanced strategies to reshape the dynamics of investor-State relations. Proposals include restricting investor access to arbitration without privity, aiming to align the dispute resolution process more closely with the interests and consent of the involved parties. This reform recognizes the necessity for a more balanced power dynamic, steering away from potential biases in favor of multinational corporations.

[47] Bungenberg and Alvarado Garzón (2019), pp. 9–11.

Furthermore, the conversation extends to imposing obligations on foreign investors. This adjustment in the legal landscape seeks to strike a fair equilibrium, recognizing the significant contributions of foreign investments to economic development while holding investors accountable for potential negative impacts, such as environmental or social consequences.

Integrating public interest considerations into the core of the arbitration process represents a crucial advance toward aligning investment law with broader societal goals. This inclusive approach not only adds a layer of accountability but also ensures that the outcomes of arbitration resonate with the values and concerns of the affected communities.

Crucially, these reformative endeavors necessitate the active involvement of various participants, including States and international organizations. Through collaborative efforts, these initiatives aim to redefine the boundaries of International Investment Law, creating a more just, transparent, and accountable framework for resolving disputes between investors and sovereign States. This transformative journey signifies a turning point, where the challenges posed by the legitimacy crisis become the driving force for positive change in the landscape of investment treaty arbitration.

References

Alfaro CE, Lorenti P (2005) Argentina vs. ICSID: unconstitutionality of the BITs and ICSID Jurisdiction - the potential new government defenses against the enforcement of ICSID arbitral - issues that may subject the award to the revision of the judiciary. Trans Disp Manag 3:1–3

Anderson S, Grusky S (2007) Challenging corporate investor rule: how the World Bank's investment court, free trade agreements, and bilateral investment treaties have unleashed a new era of corporate power and what to do about it. Institute for Policy Studies: Food & Water Watch

Audit B, Burdeau G, Dupuy PM, Juillard P, Kahn P, Mayer P (2004) Table ronde: Le système actuel est-il déséquilibré en faveur de l'investisseur privé étranger et au détriment de l'Etat d'accueil? In: Leben C (ed) Le contentieux arbitral transnational relatif à l'investissement - Nouveaux développements. Anthemis, Louvain-la-Neuve, pp 185–202

Balchin C, Chung LKH, Kaushal A, Waibel M (2010) The backlash against investment arbitration: perceptions and reality. Kluwer, Austin

Batifort S, Heath JB (2017) The new debate on the interpretation of MFN clauses in investment treaties: putting the brakes on multilateralization. Am J Int Law 111(4):873–913

Behn D, Fauchald OK, Langford M (2022) The legitimacy of investment arbitration: empirical perspectives. Cambridge University Press, Cambridge

Ben Hamida W (2005) L'arbitrage Etat-investisseur face à un désordre procédural: la concurrence des procédures et les conflits de juridictions. Annuaire Français de Droit International 51:564–602

Ben Hamida W (2008) La prise en compte de l'intérêt général et des impératifs de développement dans le droit des investissements. J Droit Int 4:999–1033

Bernasconi-Osterwalder N (2015) Rethinking investment-related dispute settlement. Invest Treaty News 6(2):6–8

Bernasconi-Osterwalder N, Rosert D (2014) Investment treaty arbitration: opportunities to reform arbitral rules and processes. The International Institute for Sustainable Development

Binder C, Kriebaum U, Reinisch A (2009) International investment law for the 21st century-essays in Honour of Christoph Schreuer. Oxford University Press, Oxford
Brower CN, Schill SW (2008) Is arbitration a threat or a boom to the legitimacy of international investment law? Chic J Int Law 9(2):471–498
Bungenberg M (2012) International investment law. Nomos, Baden-Baden
Bungenberg M, Alvarado Garzón AE (2019) One size fits all? Transparency in investment and commercial arbitration. In: Meškić Z, Kunda I, Popović D, Omerović E (eds) Balkan yearbook of European and international law. Springer, Berlin, pp 1–22
Carreau D, Flory T, Juillard P (1995) Chronique de droit international économique: Coopération Technique Environnement. Annuaire Français de Droit International 41:581–611
Castro de Figueiredo R (2009) Euro Telecom v. Bolivia: the denunciation of the ICSID convention and ICSID arbitration under BITs. Trans Disp Manag 1:1–22
Cazala J (2016) La consécration de la doctrine des Police Powers de l'État dans le contentieux investisseur-État relatif à la lutte antitabac. Les Cahiers de l'arbitrage 4:919–927
Cleis MC (2017) The independence and impartiality of ICSID arbitrators: current case law, alternative approaches, and improvement suggestions. Nijhoff, Brill
Collins D (2016) An introduction to international investment law. Cambridge University Press, Cambridge
Crépet Daigremont C (2007) L'extension jurisprudentielle de la compétence des tribunaux arbitraux du CIRDI. In: Kahn P, Wälde TW (eds) New aspects of international investment law. Martinus Nijhoff Publishers, Leyde, pp 453–516
Dolzer R, Schreuer C (2012) Principles of international investment law. Oxford University Press, Oxford
Fouchard P (1999) L'arbitrage et la mondialisation de l'économie. In: Farjat G (ed) Philosophie du droit et droit économique: Quel dialogue? Mélanges en l'honneur de Gérard Farjat. Frison-Roche, Paris, pp 481–482
Fouret J (2008) Denunciation of the Washington Convention and Non-Contractual Investment Arbitration: "manufacturing consent" to ICSID arbitration? J Int Arbitr 25(1):71–87
Franck S (2005) The legitimacy crisis in investment treaty arbitration: privatizing public international law through inconsistent decisions. Fordham Law Rev 73:1521–1625
Gaillard E (2007) The denunciation of the ICSID convention. NY Law J 237(122):1–3
Gaillard E (2017) Abuse of process in international arbitration. ICSID Rev For Invest Law J 32:17–37
Garibaldi OM (2009) On the denunciation of the ICSID convention, consent to ICSID jurisdiction, and the limits of the contract analogy. In: Binder C, Kriebaum U, Reinisch A (eds) International investment law for the 21st century-essays in Honour of Christoph Schreuer. Oxford University Press, Oxford, pp 251–278
Hepburn J, Kabra R (2017) India's new model investment treaty: fit for purpose? Indian Law Rev 1(2):95–114
ICSID (2022a) Annual Report. ICSID Publications, Washington
ICSID (2022b) The ICSID Caseload – Statistics No. 2
Juillard P (1994) L'évolution des sources du droit des investissements. Collect Courses Hague Acad Int Law 250:18–384
Kahale G (2014) Kahale calls for overhaul of BIT system. Global Arbitration Review
Kentin E (2007) Economic crisis and investment arbitration: the argentine cases. In: Kahn P, Wälde TW (eds) New aspects of international investment law. Martinus Nijhoff Publishers, Leyde, pp 629–667
Kinnear M, Fisher GR et al (2015) Building international investment law: the first 50 years of ICSID. Kluwer Law International
Kodama Y (1999) Dispute settlement under the draft multilateral agreement on investment: the quest for an effective dispute settlement mechanism and its failure. J Int Arbitr 16(2):45–87
Leben C (2003) La théorie du contrat d'Etat et l'évolution du droit international des investissements. Collect Courses Hague Acad Int Law 402:197–386

Leboulanger P, Stern B, Sacerdoti G, Juillard P, Crivallero A (2006) La place du CIRDI dans le contentieux de l'investissement international. In: Leben C (ed) Le contentieux arbitral transnational relatif à l'investissement – Nouveaux développements. Anthemis, Louvain-la-Neuve, pp 345–361

Lowenfeld AF (2002) International arbitration: scapegoat or solution? Am Rev Int Arbitr 13(1):1–7

Mainguy D (2017) L'État partie faible ? J Droit Int 1:7–11

Malintoppi L (2008) Independence, impartiality, and duty of disclosure of arbitrators. In: Muchlinski P, Ortino F, Schreuer C (eds) The Oxford handbook of international investment law. Oxford University Press, Oxford, pp 789–829

Mann H (2003) The right of states to regulate and international investment law: a comment. In: UNCTAD (ed) The development dimension of FDI: policy and rule-making perspectives. United Nations, Geneva, pp 211–224

McKinstry Robin P (1984) The BIT won't bite: the american bilateral investment treaty program. Am Univ Law Rev 33(4):931–958

McLachlan DC, Shore L, Weiniger M (2017) International investment arbitration: substantive principles. Oxford University Press, Oxford

Meškić Z, Albakjaji M, Jevremović N, Omerović E, Adams J (2022) Digitalization and innovation in achieving SDGs – impacts on legislation and practice. IOP Conf Ser Earth Environ Sci 1026(1):1–12

Muchlinski P (2008) Corporate social responsibility. In: Muchlinski P, Ortino F, Schreuer C (eds) The Oxford handbook of international investment law. Oxford University Press, Oxford, pp 637–687

Muchlinski P, Ortino F, Schreuer C (2008) The Oxford handbook of international investment law. Oxford University Press, Oxford

Newcombe AP, Paradell L (2009) Law and practice of investment treaties: standards of treatment. Wolters Kluwer Law & Business, Austin

Nolan MD, Sourgens FG (2007) The interplay between state consent to ICSID and arbitration and denunciation of the ICSID convention: the (possible) venezuela case study. Trans Disp Manag 5:1–52

Nolan MD, Sourgens FG (2010) Limits of consent–arbitration without privity and beyond. In: Fernandez-Bellesteros MA, Arias D (eds) Liber Amicorum for Bernardo Cremades. La Ley, Las Rozas

Paulsson J (1995) Arbitration without privity. ICSID Rev FILJ 10:232–257

Paulsson J (2005) What authority do international arbitrators have over states. In: Van den Berg AJ (ed) New horizons in international commercial arbitration and beyond. Kluwer Law International, La Haye, pp 132–165

Peterson L (2015) Indonesia ramps up termination of BITs. IA Reporter

Pinna A (2008) Réflexions sur l'arbitrage forcé. Gazette du Palais 351:6

Poulsen LNS (2015) Bounded rationality and economic diplomacy: the politics of investment treaties in developing countries. Cambridge University Press, Cambridge

Rao W (2021) Are arbitrators biased in ICSID arbitration? A dynamic perspective. Int Rev Law 66:105980

Redfern A (2005) Investor-state arbitrations: a bridge too far? In: Aksen G (ed) Global reflections on international law, commerce and dispute resolution: liber Amicorum in Honour of Robert Briner. International Chamber of Commerce, Paris, pp 665–675

Reinisch A, Knahr C (2008) International investment law in context. Eleven International Publishing, Utrecht

Rubins N (2006) Les pays exportateurs de capitaux comme défendeurs dans l'arbitrage relatif à l'investissement: l'affaire Loewen c. États-Unis. In: Leben C (ed) Le contentieux arbitral transnational relatif à l'investissement - Nouveaux développements. Louvain-la-Neuve, Anthemis, pp 237–280

Sacerdoti G (1998) Bilateral treaties and multilateral instruments on investment protection. Collect Courses Hague Acad Int Law 269:251–460

Samardžić D, Meškić Z (2017) Pravo Evropske unije II – Povelja EU o osnovnim pravima. Pravni fakultet Univerziteta u Zenici, Zenica
Schill SW (2017) Reforming investor–state dispute settlement: a (comparative and international) constitutional law framework. J Int Econ Law 20(3):649–672
Schreuer C (2010) Denunciation of the ICSID convention and consent to arbitration. In: Balchin C, Chung LKH, Kaushal A, Waibel M (eds) The backlash against investment arbitration: perceptions and reality. Kluwer, Austin, pp 353–368
Schreuer C (2011) The future of investment arbitration. In: Arsanjani MH, Cogan JK, Sloane RD, Wiessner S (eds) Looking at the future-essays on international law in Honor of W. Michael Reisman. Martinus Nijhoff Publishers, Boston, pp 787–803
Schreuer C, Malintoppi L, Reinisch A, Sinclair A (2009) The ICSID convention: a commentary. Cambridge University Press, Cambridge
Schultz T, Dupont C (2015) Investment arbitration: promoting the rule of law or over-empowering investors? A quantitative empirical study. Eur J Int Law 25(4):1147–1168
Shihata IFI (2009) Preface. In: Schreuer C, Malintoppi L, Reinisch A, Sinclair A (eds) The ICSID convention: a commentary. Cambridge University Press, Cambridge
Simmons BA (2014) Bargaining over BITs, arbitrating awards: the regime for protection and promotion of international investment. World Polit 66(1):12–46
Sornarajah M (2003) Right to regulate and safeguards. In: UNCTAD (ed) The development dimension of FDI: policy and rule-making perspectives. United Nations, Geneva, pp 205–210
Sornarajah M (2017) The international law on foreign investment. Cambridge University Press, Cambridge
Subedi S (2008) International investment law: reconciling policy and principle. Hart Publishing, Portland
The International Institute for Sustainable Development (2017) News in brief. Invest Treaty News 8(2):18
Tietje C, Nowrot K, Wackernagel C (2008) Once and forever? The legal effects of a denunciation of ICSID. Institute of Economic Law, Martin Luther University, Halle-Wittenberg
Tzanakopoulos A (2011) Denunciation of the ICSID convention under the general international law of treaties. In: Hoffman R, Tams C (eds) International investment law and general international law: from clinical isolation to systemic integration. Nomos, Baden Baden, pp 75–93
UNCTAD (2010) Denunciation of the ICSID convention and BITs: Impact on investor-state claims. IIA Iss Note 2:1–11
UNCTAD (2016) World investment report - investor nationality: policy challenges. United Nations, New York
UNCTAD (2023) World investment report - investment and the digital economy. United Nations, New York
Waren W (2001) Paying to regulate: a guide to Methanex V. United States and NAFTA investor rights. Environ Law Rep 31:10986
Weiler T (2005) International investment law and arbitration: leading cases from the ICSID, NAFTA, Bilateral treaties and customary international law. Cameron May, London
Werner J (1997) The trade explosion and some likely effects on international arbitration. J Int Arbitr 14:5–16
Williams D (2003) International commercial arbitration and globalization: review and recourse against awards rendered under investment treaties. J World Invest 4(2):251–276
Zakhour GP (2019) Les investissements étrangers: Droit applicable et tribunal compétent. L'Harmattan, Paris
Zakhour GP (2023a) La dialectique de la clause de la nation la plus favorisée en matière d'investissements étrangers: quel impact sur la compétence dans l'arbitrage transnational? Horizons du droit 44:38–52
Zakhour GP (2023b) Vers une compétence arbitrale débridée entre États et investisseurs étrangers? Horizons du droit 44:53–71

The manufacturer's authorised representative in the EU is Springer Nature Customer Service Centre GmbH, Europaplatz 3, 69115 Heidelberg, Germany. If you have any concerns regarding our products, please contact ProductSafety@springernature.com

Printed and bound by CPI Group (UK) Ltd, Croydon, CR0 4YY

28/09/2026

02224070-0014